TECHNICAL ANALYSIS
& BEHAVIOURAL FINANCE
IN FUND MANAGEMENT

the technical *analyst*

**TECHNICAL ANALYSIS & BEHAVIOURAL FINANCE
IN FUND MANAGEMENT**

DISCUSSIONS WITH INVESTMENT MANAGERS AND ANALYSTS

The Technical Analyst Discussion Series

Copyright © 2009 Global Markets Media Ltd, publisher of
The Technical Analyst magazine.

Published by:
Global Markets Media Ltd, Jeffries House, 1-5 Jeffries
Passage, Guildford, GU1 4AP, UK
+44 (0) 1483 573150
www.technicalanalyst.co.uk

A CIP catalogue record for this book is available from the
British Library.

ISBN 978-0-9564003-1-4

The author and publishers will be grateful for any information
that will assist them in keeping future editions up to date.
Although all reasonable care has been taken in the preparation of
this book, neither the publishers nor the author can accept
responsibility for any consequences arising from the use thereof
or from the information contained therein.

Typeset in Times New Roman & Arial
Printed in Great Britain by the MPG Books Group,
Bodmin and King's Lynn
Front and back cover photo: iStockphoto

CONTENTS

Contents

PART 2: BEHAVIOURIAL FINANCE IN FUND MANAGEMENT

INTRODUCTION

The widespread application of technical analysis within the financial markets is now taken for granted as an essential tool in addition to, or substitute for, fundamental research. TA has, to some extent, usually been seen as a trader's tool, best applied to the FX or commodity markets to help make short-term trading decisions. However, technical strategies are just as applicable to the longer-term which has meant that fund and portfolio managers have another technique to use for making investment decisions, and to help with risk management, market timing and position taking.

Behavioural finance is a relatively new area of research that partners well with TA. Not only does BF look to explain much of the emotion and psychology in the markets, it also provides an intuitive explanation for why chart patterns and technical set-ups actually exist in the first place. Moreover, BF makes a convincing case that markets are far from efficient.

This book looks to move beyond the theory to examine how practising investment managers and analysts actually use TA and BF on a day-to-day and week-to-week basis. The range of subjects covered is wide and includes the use of basic technical indicators, relative strength analysis, money and risk management techniques, and uncovering behavioural biases that exist within the market and with individual investors. By interviewing a variety of managers and analysts, we hope the publication will provide readers with a comprehensive, and above all practical, guide to using technical analysis and behavioural finance in the most effective and productive way possible.

We would like to take this opportunity to thank all our contributors for their time, expertise and goodwill in making this book possible.

Matthew Clements
Editor
The Technical Analyst

October 2009

1

PART ONE:
TECHNICAL ANALYSIS
IN FUND MANAGEMENT

Chapter 1

ROB BRAND

HEAD OF DISCRETIONARY PORTFOLIO MANAGEMENT EQUITY

ABN AMRO

Rob Brand joined ABN AMRO in Amsterdam in 2000 working in equity portfolio management before becoming head of Discretionary Portfolio Management Equity. Within the group he is responsible for the equity portfolio managers and the management of model portfolios worldwide for private clients. He is also responsible for the dynamic hedging of equity exposure and co-responsible for the tactical asset allocation of all balanced portfolios.

USING TA FOR TRADE AND INVESTMENT DECISIONS

Can you explain your basic investment style?

We use what we like to call a 'technimentals' approach in our investment strategy. This means basically combining technical analysis and fundamental analysis into one quantitative framework. The stocks in our portfolio are selected on the basis of valuation, earnings quality, technical analysis and analyst recommendations by analysts that have a solid track record. On these four pillars, each stock in the MSCI World gets assigned a score, eventually combined into a final stock score.

Our stock selection is aimed at a longer-term horizon. We use technical analysis and sentiment to hedge our equity exposure using derivatives, and to fine tune our TAA (Tactical Asset Allocation). Our benchmark is the MSCI World Europe tilt, a world benchmark with a 'home bias' in Europe, meaning, we have 60% Europe in our benchmark. Total assets under management are about 1.5 billion euros.

Can you explain how you use TA in making investment decisions?

We express our use of TA as technical analysis for investment management because our proposition is fundamentally different from

5

what is perceived as technical analysis for traders. The main difference is that not only is price, volume, and momentum used, but also the relative movement of a stock or index and the momentum of this relative price development. Secondly, we focus on longer-term charts; this means in practice that for stock selection purposes, we primarily use weekly or monthly charts and price data. Our TA approach consists of three main pillars and one overlay:

Pillar one is the most important and effective: relative strength. This determines whether a stock has the technical strength for being a sector leader. Pillar two consists of the absolute trend of each stock and all analysis related to the quality of trend. Pillar three contains the momentum factor: is there enough momentum to sustain the price trend of an upward trending stock, or is momentum (of price, volume or relative strength) significantly changing?

The overlay, called 'intermarket analysis' is the relative assessment of group rotation taking place in the equity market. This focuses on the effect of these relationships on price behaviour. The overlay puts all individual stock analysis into the perspective of the market. We also use TA in order to tactically hedge our equity exposure. This is done purely on the basis of technicals. We use a framework combination of trend following and countertrend techniques. Trend following techniques consist of the usual suspects like moving averages, and the countertrend techniques consist of a combination of DeMark and sentiment indicators (surveys such as the AAII Bullish Index).

Why did you choose to use TA? What made you convinced it works?

Advances in behavioural finance have led to increased interest in the psychological traits of investors. The emotional pull of the market place as a whole leads to behaviour that is often far from rational. Crowd behaviour fluctuates from periods of pessimism, fear and panic to optimism, confidence and greed. I believe one of the most important factors that affect markets is one that is often overlooked - market psychology.

If we look at the last two bear markets in equities, we have seen fundamental factors fail indiscriminately. During the credit crisis bear market we have seen for many months that stocks are extremely cheap according to the classical valuation metrics, and yet they kept on declining. Technicals and sentiment have proved to be very useful during these types of markets, because of the discipline captured within technical analysis.

6

How does your application of TA differ for short, medium and long-term time scales?

I prefer to use mostly weekly or monthly data. Trends, patterns and reversals tend to work better on these time scales. The application of TA on weekly and monthly data boils down to relative strength analysis (for stock selection, sector allocation and TAA), and trend and momentum analysis. On daily data I find the Tom DeMark techniques very effective. For our timing of entries and exits we use the DeMark Sequential™ countdown technique because it works superbly well. For the very short-term I use candlestick charts to find price reversals in combination with very short-term indicators such as the 2-day RSI (Relative Strength Index).

What is the shortest time scale that relative strength analysis is effective over?

It depends on your investment horizon, but I would say from an investment point of view, you should use weekly relative strength. If you are a stock trader, daily also works fine.

Why do you believe that the TD Sequential™ indicator works so well?

The TD Sequential™ basically measures trend exhaustion and Tom DeMark has managed to find a way to count the days that a trend has existed. The markets have a natural flow and this is captured in his indicators.

What would you do if your candlestick and trend analysis contradicted what the TD Sequential™ was saying? Which would take priority?

Martin Pring says in his book that acting on confirmation is key to being a successful technical analyst. So in this case, I would give the benefit of the doubt to trend analysis. Signals generated by the TD Sequential™ are not that frequent so they are taken seriously when they do. Even so, giving up some of your performance by waiting for confirmation (i.e. trend violation) increases your risk adjusted return.

What do you do if the TD Sequential™ contradicts your relative strength analysis? Which do you attach most importance to?

The TD Sequential™ is more of a timing tool for us, and the relative strength analysis is one of our key decision factors whether we would like to invest in a stock or not. If a stock starts to show relative weakness and is rendering a TD Sequential™ sell signal, then of course, it looks like a strong sell. On the other hand, if a stock is outperforming and not violating any trendlines but is rendering a TD Sequential™ sell, we stick to our guns, maybe lowering the position a bit on the idea that the TD Sequential™ is a short-term tool.

Why do you think that reversals and patterns work better on weekly and monthly data than on shorter-term data?

The main reason is that the shorter-term is polluted by random noise. Over the medium and longer-term, this noise tends to get filtered out.

During the market turbulence in 2008 has TA performed better or worse than usual?

Worse than usual because traditional trend analysis has rendered little result in this steep decline. For instance, if you take a look at the S&P500 on a weekly basis, you can clearly see traditional trough and peak analysis did not work during the steep decline. In a trend reversal year, usually steep declines leave traditional chartists in the dark. On the other hand, if we look at traditional trendline analysis, we can clearly conclude that a violation of the trend and an early response to this has been very profitable (Figure 1).

Also, if we take a look at countertrend methodologies such as the DeMark Sequential™, these have shown their value during the crisis (Figure 2). However, TA has definitely performed better than usual when it comes to relative strength analysis. I use weekly relative strength of sectors versus the world index. This very easy to follow analysis has helped us tremendously during the start of the bear market to spot relative strength and weakness across the benchmark. For instance, if you plot the weekly MSCI World Healthcare sector index and its relative strength versus the MSCI World, you can clearly see the defensive style of Healthcare outperforming significantly (Figure 3). Besides our fundamental analysis, I think this is one of the best techniques to spot winners in the stock universe and especially during bear markets.

Are some asset classes more technically driven than others?

Over the shorter-term it looks like currencies have a special interest for technical traders, so I think this should be one of the most

8

technical driven asset classes of all. Currency pairs show a high degree of autocorrelation in that they are very trending by nature. As a result, trend following techniques tend to work quite well.

In what way does the application of TA differ when using it to pick individual stocks and for analysis of the index?

Index analysis requires a fair amount of market breadth analysis. I find market breadth indicators to be very useful in spotting turning points in equity indices. For instance, I use the Bullish Percent Index developed by Jeremy du Plessis. This can help spot divergences in momentum or turning points in the indices. The Bullish Percent basically counts on a daily basis the number of stocks that form a bullish point-and-figure chart pattern. Also, advance/decline indicators help spot turning points or divergences in equity markets. These tools are obviously not very useful when looking at individual stocks. For individual stocks I use classical momentum and trend analysis.

Are there any market conditions under which TA works better or worse than other times?

I find that during bubble periods momentum indicators can stay overbought for weeks without generating any signal. Sentiment indicators render best value in bubbles as sentiment usually peaks and troughs in extreme territory. These extremes are the most profitable.

However, extremely volatile periods in which market sentiment reaches extreme levels do not offer effective periods for TA, more specifically sentiment analysis. For instance, I use the CBOE Implied volatility index (VIX Index) as a gauge for market sentiment. The VIX Index usually spikes at a market bottom. During the credit crisis sell-off, we saw that this spike did not lead to a significant market bottom; on the contrary, the market fell even further. In my opinion this has to do with panic and volatility clustering; sentiment is really extreme when all correlations are the same and everybody is heading for the exit.

Is there any evidence that fund managers who employ TA do better than those who don't?

Fundamental investors have failed miserably during bubble bursting periods by not applying stop-losses or by negating trend violation rules. Ignoring market signals such as severe relative strength changes of a sector versus the world index can be very dangerous. Even if a fund manager does not believe in TA, he or she can at least use TA as a risk management tool in order to manage the maximum drawdown of the portfolio.

Does TA have anything useful to say about portfolios and diversification?

Research has shown that momentum is a very strong and consistent outperforming factor in stock selection. Also, relative strength has been researched and is found to be a very effective tool. The correlation between a pure momentum strategy and TA (e.g. moving average strategy) is very high. This means you have a high exposure to the momentum factor should you employ TA in your stock selection and portfolio. Using TA therefore can say something about your portfolio (tilt towards momentum and therefore a high chance of outperforming over the longer run).

Diversification is not so obvious; it could be that by employing strict TA rules, you always have an exposure towards certain assets such as those with high momentum. This works fine, except at turning points where you get wiped out. You can compensate for this drawdown by using relative strength to your advantage by employing asset rotation within the asset classes.

INDICATORS AND STRATEGIES

What is your reaction when the charts show a very obvious technical pattern such as a head-and-shoulders or a double top?

I would like to see confirmation in volume but more importantly, a trend violation. For instance, if we are looking at a major head-and-shoulders pattern in an equity index, we would like to see confirmation on several issues. Take the major head-and-shoulders pattern in the Stoxx 600 as an example (Figure 4). The pattern is preceded by a very fierce trend, one of the first requirements for a good and healthy topping pattern. Secondly, momentum (RSI is used here) is showing negative divergence pointing to internal weakness. Thirdly, trend violation and a return to the trend is an extra clue that the market is going to follow this pattern.

How do you indentify when a trend has commenced and may be nearing its end?

I tend to use divergences mostly. For example, weekly charts with simple momentum indicators such as the MACD or RSI have excellent value in spotting turning points. The divergence between weekly indicators and price itself is a very powerful tool next to classical trendline violations. I always use logscale charts in order to assess trendline violations.

Why do you prefer to use logscale charts?

Logscale makes prices more comparable. For example, a move in the S&P500 from 100 to 200 is a 100% move. If the S&P500 were at 900 then it would have to rise to 1800 for a similar percentage increase. Logscale filters out the bias and renders better trend analysis.

What is the best method for measuring price momentum in the market?

The simple Rate of Change (ROC) still works the best. I find the ROC to be the most useful indicator because of its direct link to momentum. The only useful alteration of the simple rate of change is the KST of Martin Pring. It takes into account the different cycles securities undergo (four in total), from short-term to long-term cycles in momentum. Pring advises using different versions in terms of time horizon of the KST. For example, if we look at the daily WTI oil future with a daily and weekly KST, we are looking for an oversold condition in the daily and weekly KST so that we have confirmation on different momentum time frames (Figure 5).

How can TA be used in making sector rotation and asset allocation decisions?

Contrary to popular belief, I think TA is an excellent tool for asset allocation. As mentioned earlier I use the relative strength concept for tactical asset allocation. Different approaches are possible to achieve this. One very simple indicator I follow is the equity/bond ratio plotted on a weekly basis with an exponential moving average.

The rule is simple: underweight equities vs. bonds when the ratio is falling and is below the moving average. TTA can also be done on sub-asset classes such as regional calls, sector calls, etc. by using relative strength. For instance, take emerging markets versus developed markets. A relative strength strategy taking the MSCI Global Emerging Equity Index over the MSCI World Index can render excellent results. Plotting the relative strength and adding a two moving average cross-over system can help decide on sub-asset class selection.

Does TA have a role when shorting the market?

TA can come up with some interesting short signals, e.g. stocks in a downtrend with accelerating momentum or a DeMark TD Sequential™ sell signal.

How does your application of TA differ for different asset classes?

It doesn't really as the principle is the same for all asset classes. Also, point-and-figure charts on the indices are a very powerful tool as a relative strength, and again, applicable on all asset classes. Point-and-figure takes out the time factor in charts and makes the technical condition of different asset classes comparable. For example, if we plot the point-and-figure chart of the S&P500 and the relative strength of the MSCI World Energy Index over MSCI World, we can clearly see differences. The pronounced bear market in the S&P500 has been continuously rendering sell signals and down targets, as opposed to the relative strength of energy versus the world index.

Do you use Fibonacci, Gann or Elliott Wave techniques?

I use Fibonacci retracements and Fibonacci projections. I rarely use Elliott Wave or Gann techniques because of the high level of interpretation involved. I often use Fibonacci projections for the calculation of the reward to risk ratio. The reward to risk expresses the ratio between reward and risk on a potential transaction/portfolio holding. If we do this on all holdings in the portfolio, we can rank all positions by their reward to risk ratio in order to get to a relative conviction assessment.

$$\frac{Reward}{Risk} = \frac{Upside\ potential}{Risk} = \frac{Price\ target - Current\ Price}{Drawdown}$$

The target price can be based upon two techniques within technical analysis: Fibonacci projections and price pattern targets. The

Fibonacci projection technique is used to determine price targets within an existing trend. Common Fibonacci projections are: 61.8%, 100% and 161.8%. If we are in a current trend, pullbacks can be effectively used to step into the stock. Fibonacci projections can be used to set the target for the coming move. The Fibonacci projection is calculated as follows:

Measure the initial movement in price (B-A). Multiply that by the Fibonacci ratios. Add these to the bottom of the correction immediately following the initial movement for potential targets of the current move.

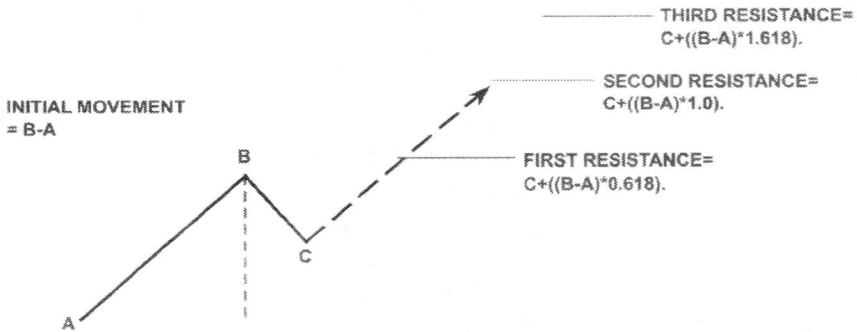

THIRD RESISTANCE= C+((B-A)*1.618).

SECOND RESISTANCE= C+((B-A)*1.0).

INITIAL MOVEMENT = B-A

FIRST RESISTANCE= C+((B-A)*0.618).

Fibonacci projection calculation   Source: Credit Suisse

Recently, the weekly chart of Man Group showed a very important technical break through the level of 1500 (Figure 6). A price target for the next move can be calculated in two ways:

1. The double bottom pattern shows a baseline around 1500. If we take the low to the baseline and add this number to this baseline, we get a target price of 1850. We can see that after a break of a significant pattern it is almost always followed by a pullback.
2. The Fibonacci target can be calculated as: C + (B - A)* 0.618 = 1500 + (1717-1150)* 0.618 = 1850

The 1850 level also coincides with an old high, so in this case, we have extra confirmation that price is bound to stall around this level.

Reward to Risk

Current price: 1625
Target: 1850
Stop-loss: 1500

Reward: 225, 14%
Risk: 125, 8%

Reward to Risk: 1.8

The reward to risk in this scenario is 1.8, assuming the buy signal is generated around 1625, a level on which technically the signal is generated after the pullback.

How do you use moving averages? Which periodicities do you use and do you use them directly to generate trade signals?

The key to using moving averages effectively is to continuously assess the quality of the trend. In this sense, the value of moving averages depends on how trending the market is. On weekly charts a 10-week and 30- or 40-week are the most effective.

If prices reach a major support level do you wait until it has broken through before buying or selling?

I think in investing and trading you always have to have an edge. The edge for the technical investor is to have the odds with you. This means in practice that when a trade is executed, a reward to risk ratio of a minimum of 1.5 has to be maintained. Otherwise, you are not rewarded by the risk you are taking and gambling is the more proper word for your actions. Waiting for confirmation enhances the reward to risk of a trade in the sense that it reduces your return prospects a bit, but it lowers the risk of the trade more.

How do you confirm that a major support/resistance line has been broken?

A simple rule we use is the weekly close rule. In order to have a trend violation in the short-term, a weekly close below the trendline is required. Another rule is the 3-day (or week) close. These rules can prevent you from jumping on the bandwagon too early.

If the market is being driven by emotion, is this entirely reflected in the technicals?

I do not think so. When emotions run high in the market, we can see that support and resistance levels can be pretty useless, so in effect, technicals do not entirely reflect the emotions in the market.

How do you judge if a market is overbought or oversold?

Longer-term momentum indicators have proven to be the most useful, especially during serious bear markets as we have seen recently in 2000 and 2007. A monthly or weekly KST indicator on the main indices does the job pretty well, especially when there are divergences, such as happened during the tops in 2000, 2004 and 2007. An oversold reading with a negative divergence on a longer term chart can be quite effective.

USING TA FOR RISK AND TRADE MANAGEMENT

Can you explain your approach to risk and money management?

Using a stop-loss on the stocks and on the relative strength of stocks versus its sector is actually our main risk management tool. We also look at tracking error versus our benchmark and the decomposition of risk. However, stop-losses on technical levels are by far the most effective risk management tool.

The first and most important technique in our money management plan is the monitoring of our individual stop-losses. Once the stop-loss of every stock has been set, the gap between the current stock price and the stop-loss level will be calculated. This is expressed as a percentage away from stop-loss level. Once the percentage is smaller than 5%, a signal will be given. The stock will then be analyzed as if it were not in the portfolio. If there is no case for maintaining the position, the stock will be sold. The stop-loss is set at the 50-week moving average as this level tends to be the most effective turning point predictor.

If we own a stock for a certain period and the position is profitable, we will tighten the stop-loss. The resulting trailing stop-loss will be set tighter to its current price as we run a profitable position, and will therefore deviate from the standard 50-week moving average level. Losses will be taken if the stock price falls below its stop-loss level given that the technical picture has deteriorated so much. As such, a position in the stock cannot be justified. If we are in a profitable position and the stop-loss is hit, we will assess whether the stock has more technical power left. As the stop is set tighter and tighter, it can be possible that we are stopped out even if the stock has more technical strength left. Therefore, our stop-loss level is not a direct trigger to sell, but more a level of review.

The procedure and rules for the stop-loss level also accounts for target price levels.

Next to these target price levels we will also monitor hurdle levels like:

- Positive and negative price shock of 10% month-to-date
- Positive and negative price shock of 15% month-to-date
- Positive and negative relative price shock of 10% month-to-date
- Positive and negative relative price shock of 15% month-to-date

These price events will immediately trigger a full new technical assessment of the stock. Whenever the target price is met, the full analysis is re-done. We will have to have a strong business case in order to keep the stock. This situation though, is not impossible.

The portfolio chart book is the last but certainly not the least method to maintain a strict money management plan. All the stocks in our portfolio are put together in a chart book that we maintain on a weekly basis, together with our relative strength scan. The chart book contains weekly and daily charts that enable us to monitor price moves visually.

Is TA a part of your risk assessment? For example, do you use support and resistance levels as likely levels to which the market will head?

We use the lowest low and the highest high (40 weeks) as reference lines in weekly charts. Usually, we see the midpoint between these two lines act as a support levels in uptrends. In downtrends this midpoint can act as a strong resistance level.

What impact did the turmoil in 2008 have on your returns? What action have you taken to reduce any losses?

We have been hedging our equity exposure in 2008 and we managed to realize outperformance versus our benchmark. In this sense, 2008 was a very good year for our track record. Unfortunately the absolute return for our clients was still negative. In terms of Morning Star returns, we are in the four star category. We cut our relative losses faster than normal in 2008 just to protect us from having too many blowups.

What are the key performance parameters you look at apart from return?

I look at the maximum excursion, maximum drawdown and Optimum-F measures

What is the maximum drawdown you are prepared to tolerate?

It's generally 15% to 20%, although we would have already been biting our nails for some time. For index trades our maximum drawdown is much lower, around 5% an for individual position.

How do you decide on which position size to take? How much of your capital are you prepared to risk at any one time?

We use a threshold of no more than 5% of the portfolio.

What level of drawdown are you prepared to tolerate?

We almost always look at stocks in relation to their sector index, so the relative return of a stock versus it's sector should not be lower than -15% to -20%. This rule has been proven to protect you from having blow-ups in the portfolio and also it protects against behavioural threats such as loss aversion. For hedging equity indices, the stop-loss is about 5% and trails above the price index.

COMBINING WITH OTHER NON-TA INFORMATION

What sentiment indicators do you look at?

I look at the various well known sentiment indicators such as the put/call ratio, implied volatility, AAII bull/bear ratio, and the new-high versus new-low index. These contrarian indicators have a good track record in spotting extreme market sentiment. For instance, the weekly put/call ratio represents the number of puts traded on the S&P500 versus the number of calls traded. If we see a significant pivot point in the index, and a spike of the put/call ratio, the chances are high that a turning point in the market has been reached.

How can intermarket analysis and cross asset correlations be used effectively when investing in a particular asset class?

I find intermarket analysis to be one of the most fascinating subjects within TA. It is undoubtedly also the most difficult analysis in my view. We can monitor inverse relationships between assets, but can we also predict them? The most effective use of intermarket analysis is the analysis of sector rotation and intermarket relationships. For a better understanding of which stocks have the highest potential to outperform, we not only look at relative strength and the price trend, but also at how different groups of stocks are interrelated in the type of market we are in now. For example, if we are bullish on commodities, we can monitor the CRB to S&P500 ratio. Whenever the trend of this ratio changes, we experience new leadership in material stocks.

The intermarket analysis sector rotation cycle model, based on Sam Stovall's S&P guide to sector rotation, states that different sectors are stronger at different points in the economic cycle. There is a distinct relationship between sectors and the order in which the various sectors should get a boost from the economy. The market cycle precedes the economic cycle because investors try to anticipate economic effects. Monitoring sector relative strength tries to help you see this effect.

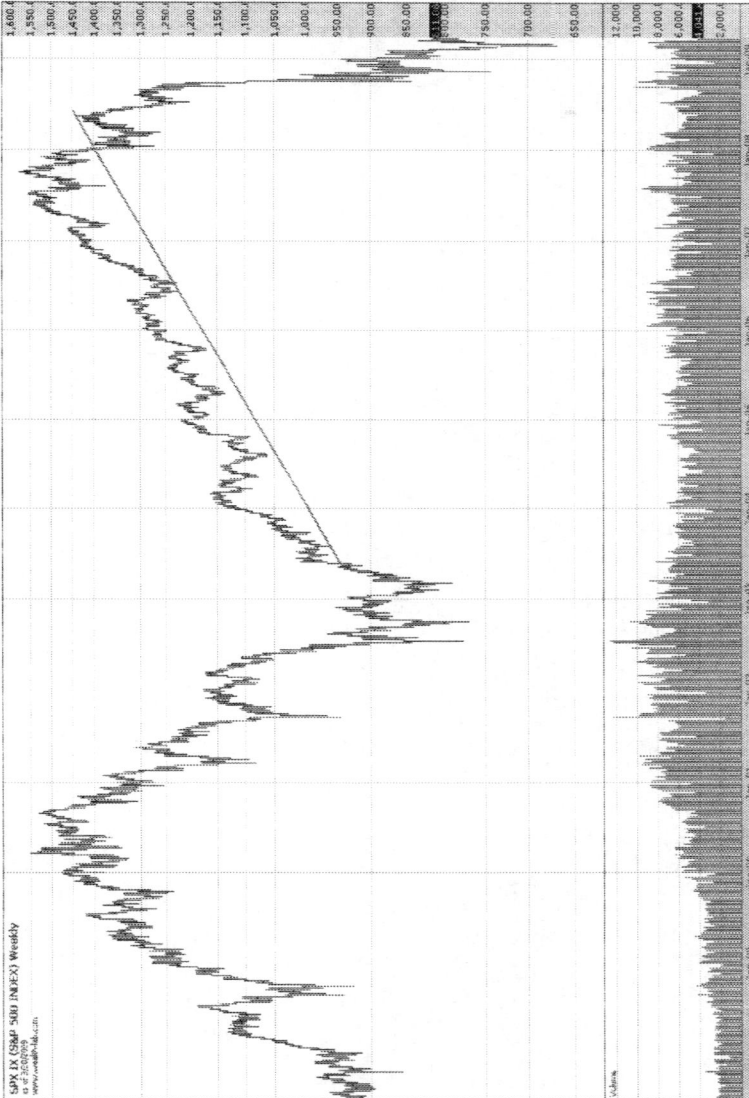

Figure 1 – Trendline analysis for weekly S&P500   source: Bloomberg

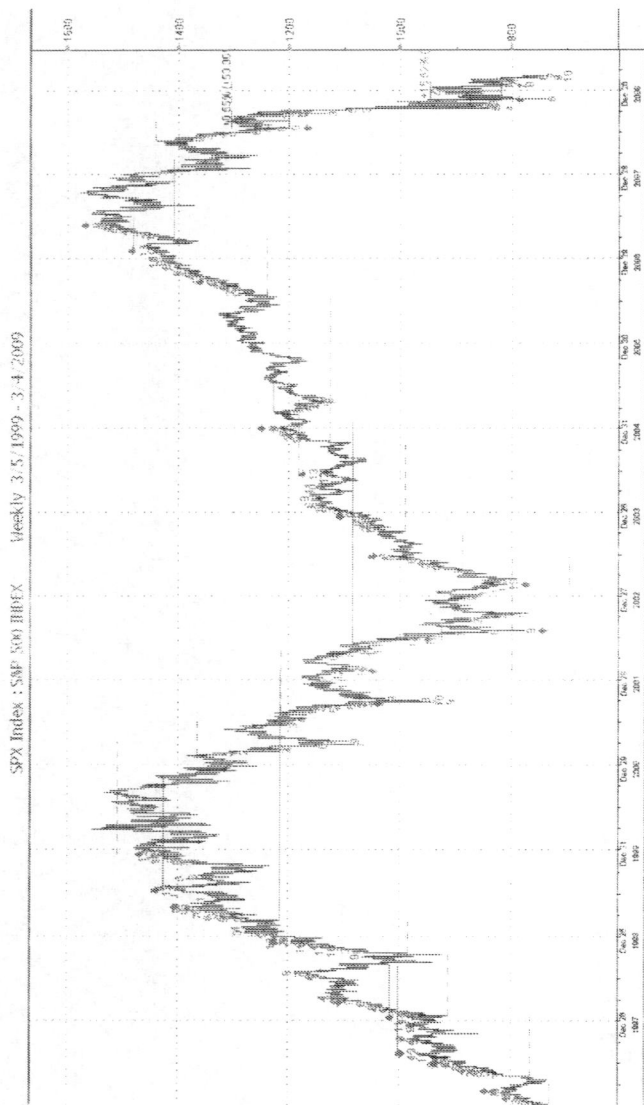

Figure 2 - DeMark Sequential™ on Eurostoxx 50 with arrows depict turning points   source: Bloomberg

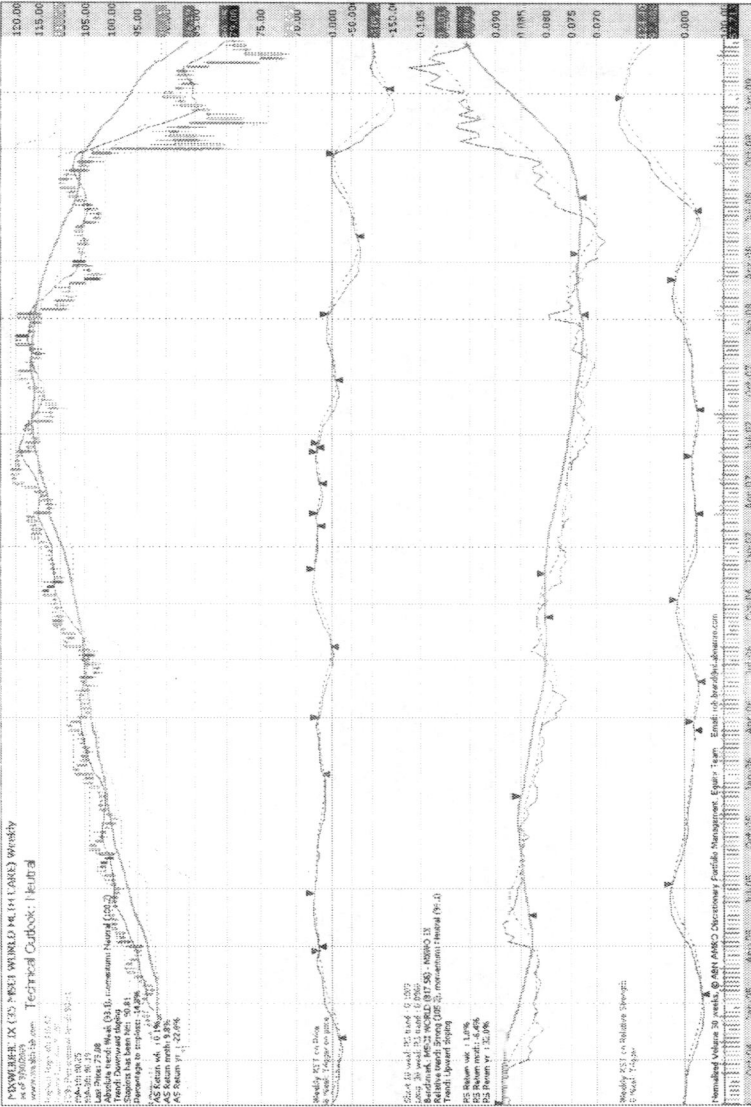

Figure 3 - MSCI World Healthcare index and relative strength versus MSCI World   source: Bloomberg

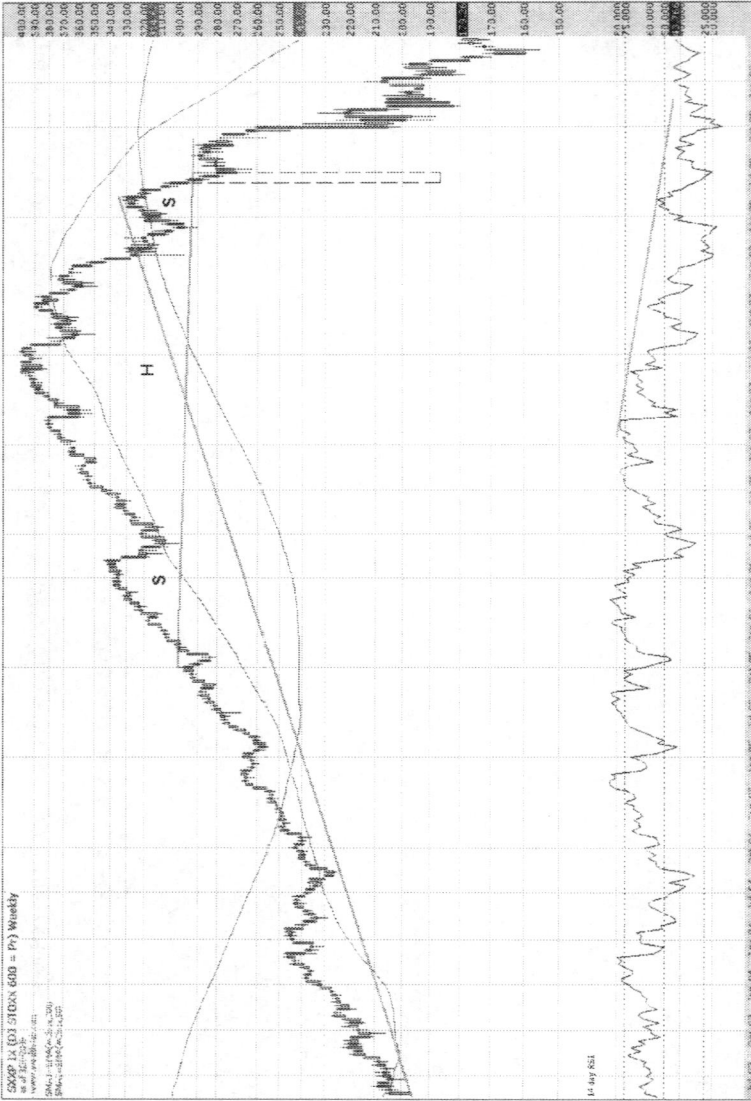

Figure 4 - Weekly Stoxx Index   Source: Bloomberg

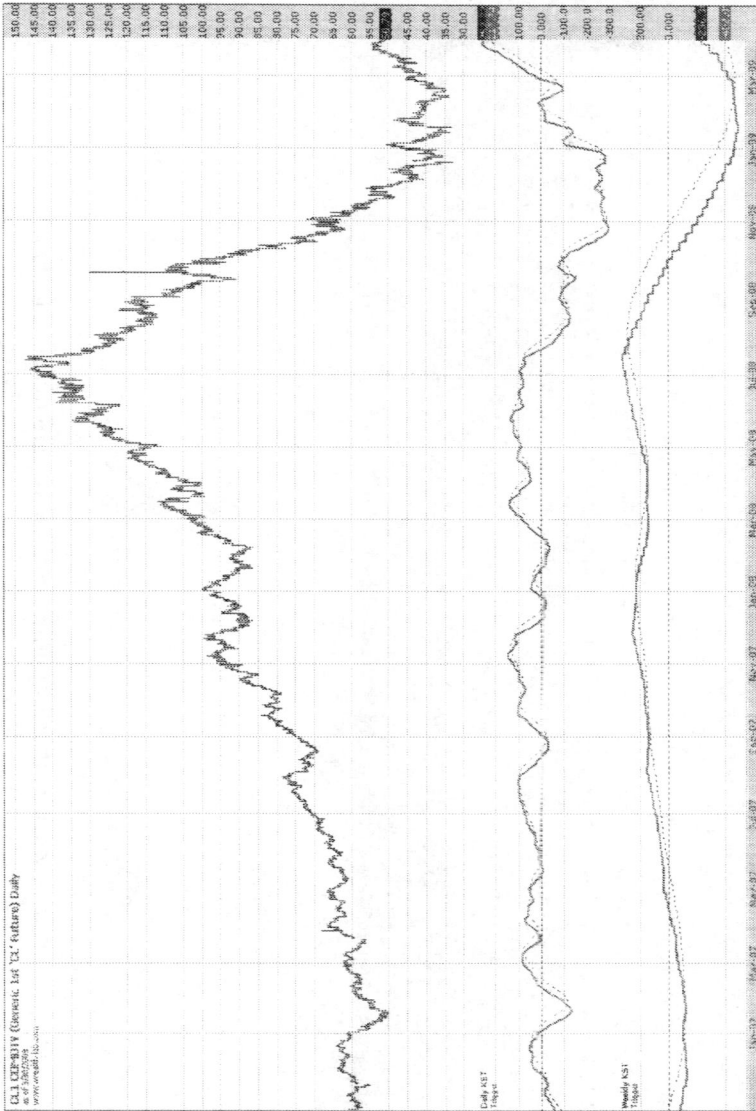

Figure 5 - Daily WTI oil future with daily and weekly KST   source: Bloomberg

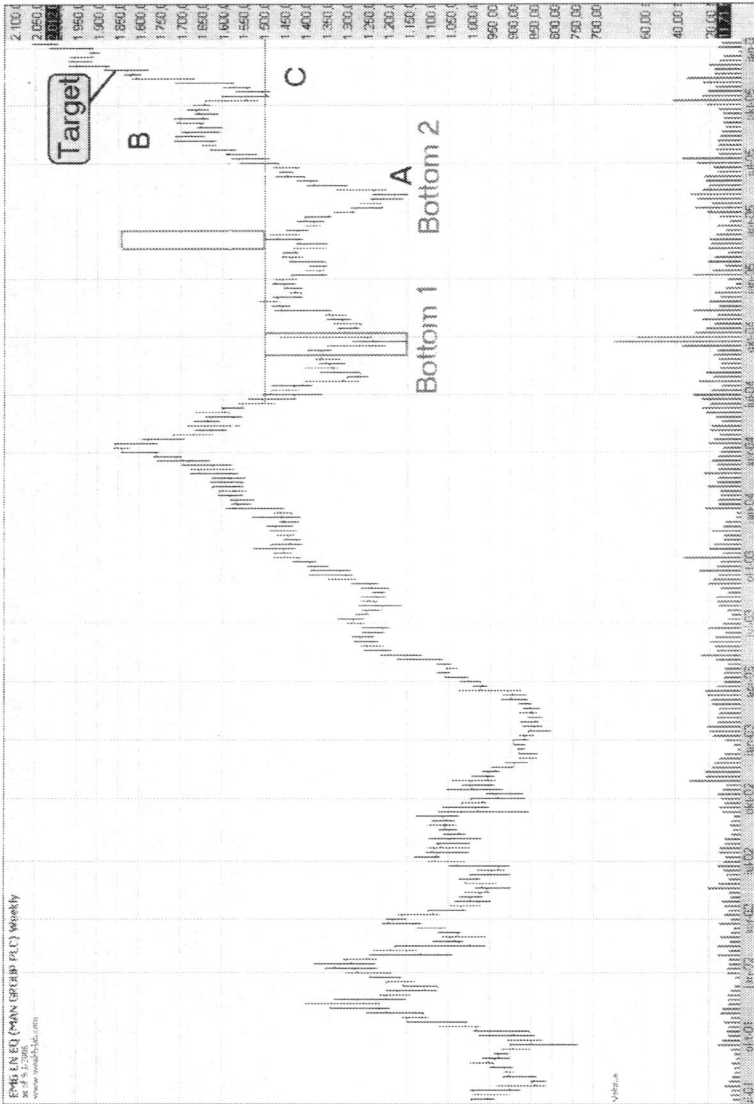

Figure 6 - Man Group weekly chart with target projection and reward to risk calculation   source: Bloomberg

Chapter 2

BUFF DORMEIER

PORTFOLIO MANAGER

WELLS FARGO ADVISORS

Buff Dormeier is a First Vice President - Investments and Private Investment Management (PIM) Portfolio Manager at Wachovia Securities, which is now a part of Wells Fargo. Buff advises and manages portfolios for affluent individual and institutional clients. For his volume indicator (VPCI) development in 2007, Buff was selected by the Market Technicians Association (MTA) to receive the Charles H. Dow Award which recognizes research papers that break new ground or make innovative use of established techniques in the field of technical analysis. He also holds the Chartered Market Technician (CMT) designation from the MTA.

USING TA FOR TRADE AND INVESTMENT DECISIONS

Can you explain your basic investment style?

I am predominately a 'bottom up' manager with three portfolios; the *Winnowed List* (longer-term), *Giddy-Up* (shorter-term), and a suite of *VARSITI* ETF strategies. I also employ a dynamic asset allocation model, FIRM, managed with a market based rotation model.

How do you assimilate the use of TA and fundamentals?

My *Winnowed List* strategy is our long-term growth portfolio with the objective of appreciation over the long haul. Beginning with a universe of approximately 4,000 stocks, the candidates are then fundamentally screened down to only those rated 'buy' by Wachovia Securities and our affiliated research groups. This allows many fundamental perspectives to be examined and narrows our candidates down to approximately 800 fundamentally sound issues.

25

The second and the most important part of the process is the performance driver. This is a proprietary technical screen consisting of two interdependent technical variables - the Volume Price Confirmation Indicator (VPCI) and my proprietary Trend Thrust Indicator (TTI).

TTI is a trend following momentum indicator using inferences from the price volume relationship to discover the momentum of developing trends. When both of these are working together in harmony, it provides the setup I am looking for to enter these positions. In this way, we screen down our remaining candidates to roughly 10 to 30 issues which our analysis perceives to be ripe and poised for a potential move.

INDICATORS AND STRATEGIES

You are well known for your expertise in the area of volume analysis. How do you use volume data in your investment decisions?

Market volume represents a significant contribution to our analysis. Market volume represents the number of shares traded over a given time period. It is a measurement of the participation, enthusiasm, and interest in a given security. Volume can be thought of as the force that drives the market. In physics, force is something that tends to produce acceleration. The same is true of market volume.

Market volume substantiates, energizes, and empowers price. When volume increases, it confirms price direction; when volume decreases, it contradicts price direction. In theory, increases in volume generally precede significant price movements. This basic tenet of technical analysis, that volume precedes price, has been repeated as a mantra since the days of Charles Dow.

How do you identify when a trend has commenced and may be nearing its end?

This is a very good question that leads to my prior research on the relationship between price and volume. I use my indicator to expose the relationship between the prevailing price trend and the volume.

Changes in volume often occur before significant price movements. This is a core foundational belief of TA. This volume analysis potentially equips us to be another step of ahead of the price action. I believe our ground breaking analysis, unravelling the intrinsic relationship between price and volume, is taking this revelation to another level of increasing probability and lowering risk.

If the market is being driven by emotion, is this reflected in the charts?

Absolutely. In such cases, weak minded investors are overcome by fear, and are becoming irrationally fearful until the selling climax reaches a state of maximum homogeneity. At this point, ownership held by weak investors has been purged, leading to capitulation.

How do you use moving averages? If so, which periodicities do you use and do you use them directly to generate trade signals?

Through the use of volume weighted moving averages, we concluded that adding volume to moving averages accomplished three things: responsiveness through quicker signals; reliability through improved accuracy; and reduced risks through lower drawdowns. Ultimately, we should then be able to improve profitability.

How have you optimised your strategies? Is this something you review on a regular basis?

As for optimization, we have not done much of it. With optimization, one can make bad ideas appear good, especially if one neglects the information the indicator is designed to deduct over the time period being studied. Sometimes, technicians are so pragmatic that they forget indicators are designed to uncover information. When using indicators one needs to refer back to the information the indicator is designed to deduce.

What are the key performance parameters you look at?

Gain/Loss Ratio

The *Gain/Loss Ratio* is derived by dividing the absolute percent change of the winning trades by the absolute percent change of the losing trades. For example, if a backtest has an average percentage change of +10% on the winning trades and an average percent change of -2% on the losing trades, the *Gain/Loss Ratio* would be 5 (10 divided by 2). A *Gain/Loss Ratio* of 5 essentially means you are gaining five times as much on your winning trades as you are losing on the losing trades.

Ann Return/Trade

The *Ann Return/Trade* is the average annualized return for all the trades in the backtest. The number is calculated by taking the percent change of the trade, dividing it by the bar length of the trade, then multiplying this by the number of bars in a year.

If a trade returned +10% over 30 bars on a daily time frame, the annualized return for the trade would be about 83.33% (10 divided by 30 equals about 0.3333; 0.3333 times 250 trading days in a year equals 83.33.

If another trade returned +10% over 80 bars on a daily time frame, the annualized return for the trade would be 31.25%. Even though both trades gained 10%, the first one did it in 30 days and the second did it in 80 days.

The *Ann Return/Trade* allows you to compare different strategies to each other when their average time in trades is different. Most would agree a backtest that gains 10% in 30 days is superior to a backtest that gains the same in 80 days. Generally speaking, the higher the backtested *Ann Return/Trade,* the better.

Don't confuse this with the actual annual return for the backtest. The annual return for the backtest would be the return over a year period. The annualized return per trade is a projection number if you made the same trade over and over again for a period of a year.

Return/Trade

The *Return/Trade* shows the average return per trade for each category. If there were two winning trades that returned +10% and +20%, then it will show +15% under the Winners category (15 is the average of 10 and 20).

Time/Trade

The *Time/Trade* shows the average length of the trade (in bars) for each of the trades. If there were two winning trades that were 20 and 30 bars long, then it will show 25 under the Winners category (25 is the average of 20 and 30).

How do you decide on which position size to take? How much of your capital are you prepared to risk at any one time?

I use the following equation:

Maximum loss = investment capital * position size * maximum AVSL drawdown.

For example: Investment Capital = 100k; Position size = 3%; Max AVSL draw down = 10%

$100,000 * .03 * .10 = $300 max loss

Do you use stop-losses?

In all three of our strategies, we use a proprietary risk management tool to target a floor to either limit our losses or preserve our profits. This point is based on a quantitative formula we refer to as Anti-Volume Stop Loss (AVSL). AVSL is a proprietary method incorporating support, volatility and most importantly, the inverse relationship between price and volume. Our positions are continually re-evaluated enabling the possibility of raising the decision point threshold periodically. With Giddy-Up, we seek to raise our maximum loss on a daily and weekly basis. The ETF positions are evaluated weekly.

With the longer term Winnowed List, the decision point is updated monthly. This analytical approach using measurable facts over emotion or gut instincts allows us to maintain an objective approach. Thus objectivity, not emotion, forms our investment decisions.

Inevitably, we will make a decision to prune a losing position only to realize later that we did so at the wrong time. Our AVSL process is designed to minimize these occurrences; however, over time it is clearly unavoidable. Yet we believe selling also creates opportunities to reinvest. As risk adverse managers, we will sell what we feel are under-performers to reinvest in potentially stronger prospects.

What is your view on the use of optimized stop-losses?

We believe it may be a very bad idea. When setting a loss, one should know their maximum loss potential. Habitually, optimizers tend to optimize and keep on optimizing until they have a successful combination. This result is a product characteristic of evolution, not creation. With evolution, tens of thousands of combinations are data-mined until they produce the most successful combination. Indicators are created under a specific set of conditions to uncover information. Random processes simply cannot create intelligent information. With an optimized stop-loss, one simply knows this random combination worked the best in the past. But why should it work in the future? Suppose we invest with this optimized stop-loss and go into a long-term losing streak not experienced in the backtesting, do I keep on losing or re-optimize? I simply do not have enough faith in optimization to make an investment decision from such an illogical position.

USING TA FOR RISK AND TRADE MANAGEMENT

Is TA a part of your risk assessment? Can you explain your approach to risk and money management?

Our risk management discipline attempts to accomplish three important goals: knowing when to sell, controlling emotions, and being aware of opportunity costs. Knowing when to sell is essential because we feel exits, not entries determine the outcome of an investment. In our process, while the security is still being considered for investment, we identify an objective level at which to protect the principal in the case we are wrong.

How do you decide where to place stops?

Keep in mind that the AVSL tailors each security for support, volatility and the price volume relationship. For example, the Giddy-Up portfolio looks for support in the short-term, whereas the ETF portfolio tries to identify intermediate support, and the Winnowed List seeks long-term support. Therefore, the first area of support is contingent upon the goal of the portfolio.

Next is volatility. I believe the more volatile a security, the looser the stop should be. A non-volatile security such as Coca-Cola may move 7% a year, while a volatile security such as Google may move 7% in a day. Should one use 7% for Coca-Cola, it may take a year to be stopped-out while the security underperforms. However, if one used 7% for Google, one could be stopped-out intraday, not allowing the investment an opportunity to develop. The AVSL considers each

Buff Dormeier, Wells Fargo Advisors

individual security's own volatility. Thus a volatile security would be granted more room while a stable security would have a tighter leash.

The last and most important step is adapting the price/volume relationship into this calculation. When a security is in an uptrend and has positive volume characteristics, it is given more room. However, if the security is exhibiting contracting volume characteristics, then the stop is tightened up. In this way, should a negative news event occur to an unhealthy security, the stop will be tighter, thus preserving more of our profit. However, if the negative news event occurs to a security whose price volume relationship is healthy, the stop has been loosened, avoiding the temporary whipsaw of an otherwise strong position. In this way, AVSL lets the market decide when to exit our position.

Can intermarket analysis and cross asset correlations be used effectively when investing in a particular asset class?

Yes. After evaluating the sector rotation 'map' for equities, we then investigate possible intermarket relationships with the bond markets. Using this model, we have found improved alpha while simultaneously reducing standard deviation.

Can you explain how and to what degree you use TA in making investment decisions?

As evident from my portfolios, technical analysis is the predominant driver in determining which issues to invest in and when to invest in them. Also, TA is the sole form of analysis we use to determine when to exit a position. Thus, TA dominates our investment process, and without it, our portfolios would be nothing less than ordinary.

Why did you choose to use TA? What made you convinced it works?

My exposure to technical analysis began early in my career as an investment advisor in 1993. Like most major brokerage firms, we received much of our investment information from an intercom system known as a squawk box. Through this communication system analysts would report on various stock ideas. These stock stories would present a case why a particular company was undervalued, overlooked or discounted to a forthcoming innovation or development. It was the best of these stories which would then be relayed back to the clientele.

31

Unfortunately, few of these ideas came to fruition, at least in a timely manner. Thus, the better of these ideas ended up in the 'long-term holdings' file, while investors waited for the company or industry to come back into favour. I was fortunate to discover early in my career that these stock stories were nothing more than hyped up fairytales told by supposed Walt Street geniuses.

However, one of these analysts was different from the others. His recommendations came without the flashy story. Speaking in terms like support, resistance, trends, patterns, and breakouts, his ideas generally showed profits early and often. In the instances where they did not, he was quick to admit his error, something virtually unheard of from other analysts, thus preserving capital for the next opportunity.

What made this analyst so different from the others? All the other analysts held the title of Chartered Financial Analyst (CFA). However, this fellow's designation was not CFA but Chartered Market Technician (CMT). I was insatiably curious about this technical methodology and began the pursuit of my own CMT designation.

During the recent market turbulence in 2008, has TA performed better or worse than usual?

As a portfolio manager, there is an incredible pressure and expectation to track the market, generally the S&P500. The fear of missing an intermediate move in the index keeps managers invested, often when they should not be. Admittedly, I am not immune to this peer pressure; my relative record of outperforming the S&P500, stressing the word relative, remains strong. However, reflecting back on the information my indicators were giving, I missed opportunities to significantly excel in 2008. It is for this reason I am contemplating launching another ETF fund which will be managed for absolute return, as opposed to the S&P500 benchmark. If there is enough interest in this product, I may launch this portfolio in 2011.

Are some asset classes more technically driven than others?

All markets succumb to the laws of supply and demand. However, noise from changing circumstances (fundamentals) are more evident in equity and corporate fixed income markets than commodities. With equities, I have found that TA indicators often do not work as well with thinly traded issues.

Are there any market conditions under which TA works better or worse than other times?

It is widely perceived that TA works better in bear or sideways markets. However, I believe this to be a misconception. It would be more accurate to say the technician's work is more appreciated in these more difficult markets.

Is there any evidence that fund managers who employ TA do better than those who don't?

If you listen to the pundits, they will tell you that Wall Street portfolio managers are the best and brightest of human capital. The vast majority of them use fundamental analysis as their primary portfolio driver in the selection of securities. Yet, the proof is in the pudding. Depending on which source you cite, 75% to 90% of these professional managers can not beat their S&P500 benchmark. Why? As a technician, I believe the price of a security represents the collective knowledge of the markets. It is difficult for one person, no matter how intelligent, to be smarter than the collective knowledge being priced into the market. Think about it this way. When you buy a stock, from whom do you buy it? Most likely, it's from one of these Wall Street guru's working with a bigger research budget than you have capital. That's generally who is on the other side of your trade. This is not a matter of intelligence but perspective. An acknowledgement of the trend is really just a healthy respect of the embedded collective knowledge of the market.

How easy is it to use TA? Do you think training is required? Are any techniques misused or misunderstood?

Technical analysis is like most other skill sets; a little knowledge without experience could be hazardous to one's wealth. My focus is primarily on the price/volume relationship.

Do you ever need to justify your use of TA to anyone? If so, how do you do it?

Occasionally, I do. In such cases a good question to ask such a sceptic is, "Do you believe in economics?' If the answer is yes, and with all capitalists it is, I then explain that TA is the law of supply and demand working within the exchange markets. For example, when securities change hands on the auction markets, the volume of shares bought always matches the volume sold on executed orders. When the price rises, the upward movement reflects that demand exceeded supply, or that buyers are in control. Likewise, when the price falls it implies supply exceeds demand, or that sellers are in control.

Over time, these trends of supply and demand form accumulation and distribution trends and patterns. Now, what if there was a way to look deep inside these price trends to determine if the current prices were supported by the volume? Well, this is the objective of my analysis, identifying the potential implications of imbalances between price and volume.

Do you often find yourself at odds with your fundamentally-based colleagues?

Drawing out this analogy to the evaluation of markets, a fundamentalist may identify a good valuation point of a stock based upon his analysis of the company. The technician observing the action of the stock may identify the same price level as a potential support level. What is support? Support is an area where buyers (demand) reside. So where does this demand come from? In most cases, it's from the fundamentalist's evaluation of value. In this way, the two perspectives often come to the same conclusions from different methodologies. In cases where it does not, it may not necessarily be the perspective, but a variation in opinions. One is based on the search for intrinsic value, while the other is shaped by extrinsic behaviour.

With more than $900 billion in client assets as of March 31, 2009, Wells Fargo's brokerage businesses have nearly 16,000 full-service financial advisors and 6,000 licensed financial specialists. This vast network of advisors, one of the nation's largest, serves clients through offices in all 50 states, the District of Columbia and in Latin America. Wells Fargo Advisors is the trade name used by three separate registered broker-dealers and non-bank affiliates of Wells Fargo & Company: Wells Fargo Advisors, LLC, Wells Fargo Advisors Financial Network, LLC, and Wells Fargo Investments, LLC (members SIPC). Statistics include First Clearing, LLC, an affiliate broker-dealer of Wells Fargo & Company.

Wells Fargo & Company completed its merger with Wachovia Corporation December 31, 2008. Wells Fargo & Company is a diversified financial services company with $1.3 trillion in assets, providing banking, insurance, investments, mortgage and consumer finance through more than 10,400 stores, over 12,000 ATMs and the internet (wellsfargo.com) across North America and internationally.

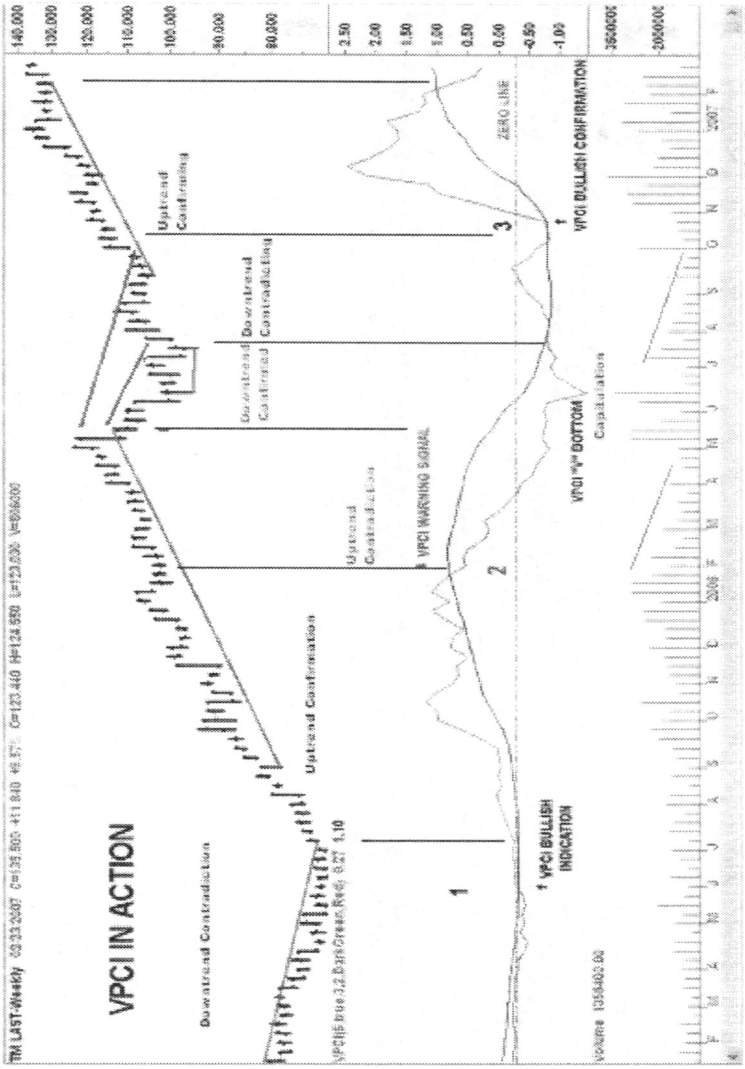

Figure 1 - Understanding trend with the VPCI   Source: Omega Research

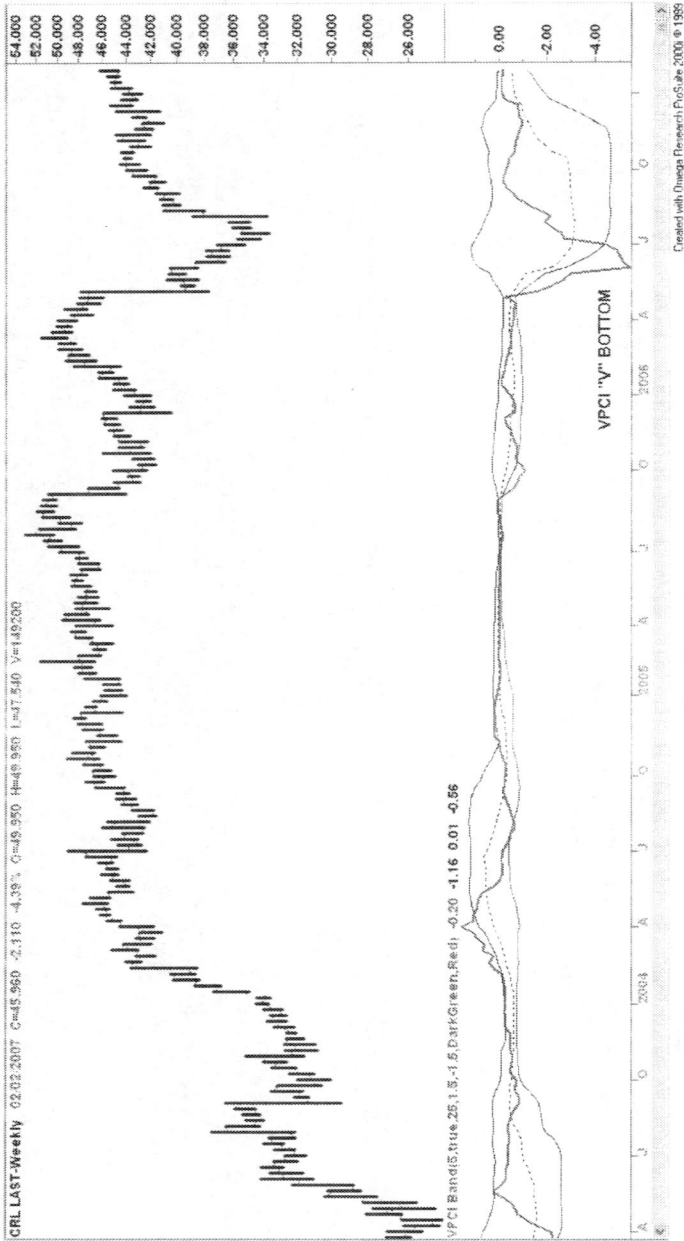

Figure 2 - A VPCI 'V' bottom

Source: Omega Research

Chapter 3

JEFF HOCHMAN

PORTFOLIO STRATEGIST/DIRECTOR TECHNICAL RESEARCH

FIDELITY INVESTMENTS

Jeff Hochman began his career at Chase Manhattan Bank before becoming an equity analyst with Deutsche Bank in Frankfurt. Since 1996, he has worked at Fidelity Investments in London where he provides technical analysis research to the firm's fund and portfolio managers.

USING TA FOR TRADE AND INVESTMENT DECISIONS

Can you explain your basic investment style?

I am a market opportunist, willing to either follow a trend if I believe it is sustainable (usually six weeks plus, to whenever it reverses), or use mean reversion strategies to try and extract alpha from the market. In general, I like to anticipate rather than react, but again this relates to my conviction at the moment.

Can you explain how and to what degree you use TA in making investment decisions?

Fidelity uses TA as a risk management tool to compliment the many fundamentally based decisions our analysts and portfolio managers make on a daily basis. The methodology is therefore used as an objective reality check, irrespective of the fundamentals, to make sure our fundamental assumptions are actually adding value to our portfolios. We employ TA in both our asset allocation decisions, and of course, in the core stock picking.

Why did you choose to use TA? What made you convinced it works?

I first discovered TA in the mid 1980s, just before the market crash, and realized that markets are only semi-efficient and are therefore prone to overshoot what can be a long way from what is termed 'fair value'. I was convinced it worked, at least some of the time, when I saw some colleagues losing lots of money investing on what they thought were sound fundamentals, but others using simple moving averages to help identify and trade with the trend. That led to more exploration and my eventual adoption of TA.

How does your application of TA differ for short, medium and long-term time scales?

Identifying different time scales is very important in framing one's expectations of future returns. It is often that one is wrong in the short-term but less wrong the further out you go. Interestingly, I tend to use fewer indicators the longer the time frame, preferring price action itself to determine the primary market conditions, thereby putting the big picture in perspective. The shorter the time frame the more important it is not be whipsawed by volatility, so I do look at different indicators to confirm the short to medium-term views.

What technical strategies and indicators work best for the short-term (weekly) analysis?

I generally do not trade anything as short as one week unless closing a losing position.

What technical strategies and indicators work best for very long-term (up to 5 years) analysis?

Sometimes very simple things like using quarterly, or at least monthly, data helps keep long-term price action in perspective, as do point-and-figure charts with larger reversal parameters. In addition, simple momentum indicators like the MACD often provide fewer, but longer lasting signals.

What do you thinks are the benefits and drawbacks of using point-and-figure charts?

I use point-and-figure charts especially to chart relative movements. They are great for eliminating unnecessary noise and focusing on the important moves. There really are few drawbacks, and some programs now even allow you to see an x-axis time line as well. They might scare the daylights out of the purists, but they help to put moves into time perspective.

During the market turbulence in 2008 has TA performed better or worse than usual?

2008 was generally a trending environment with most of the trends being down. Due to the incredibly high degree of correlation between many asset classes, if you stayed on the right side of the trends and had the courage to stay with them, then TA worked remarkably well in 2008.

Are some asset classes more technically driven than others?

Almost without exception, the more liquid a market and asset class, the better the principles of TA can be applied to them. The FX markets are very deep and respond extremely well, especially over the short and medium-term, to TA signals. Longer-term, equities and bond markets possibly respond better, as do commodities. But these are very broad generalizations. The truth is that I have yet to come across an asset class which in some way is not TA friendly, i.e. where the basics of supply and demand do not apply.

For the equity markets, does the application of TA differ when using it to pick individual stocks as opposed to analysis of the index?

Many stocks are often more volatile than the underlying index so one must watch out for this excessive volatility and scale bets accordingly, as volatility obviously works in both directions. Moreover, the further down the scale of market capitalization one goes, so often does liquidity; hence the application of TA can become less relevant and reliable when studying a broader index.

For markets generally, are there any conditions under which TA works better or worse than at other times?

In my experience, it is easier to identify and profit from trending environments than sideways, choppy markets that issue many false starts. That is primarily because momentum indicators are often more difficult to interpret in such environments and can give false signals. Oscillators do work better, but then again are open to interpretation. I find little difference in bull or bear markets, however.

What about those fund managers that you have worked with; is there any evidence that those who employ TA do better than those that don't?

From my own experience working with many fund managers over the years, those that systematically understand and observe the markets using TA as a filter tend to be more objective about their holdings and not married to their positions. They are therefore more likely to challenge their convictions, especially if a position is not acting as expected, and are more willing to sell underperforming positions. These fund managers also tend not to be swayed by the emotional pendulum or fall into behavioural traps as much as others.

Do you think TA and quants are closely related?

There are some similarities with TA and quants that use factor analysis to build models, with price momentum being the obvious overlap. TA is in many ways a subset of applied statistics and quants love statistics. Yet, where the believers of TA often adhere to its principles because of its simplicity, quants sometimes loathe it because it is viewed as overly simplistic.

Does this mean that TA is easy to use and apply both in making longer-term fund management decisions and trading over the very short-term?

It is relatively easy for the majority of the public to understand the basic tenets and techniques of TA, yet the successful interpretation of underlying price action, indicators and techniques can take many years and 'market cycles' of experience. In short, some people take to TA more easily than others, but everyone has the basic tools to succeed in employing TA if they chose to and if they have an open mind.

Do you ever need to justify your use of TA to anyone such as a colleague or client? If so, how do you do it?

Yes, especially because I am surrounded by a house of 'bottom up' fundamentalists. I justify its use by stating that active portfolio management, whether stock picking or asset allocation, is a game of probabilities and no one gets it right all the time. In fact, if one has better than a 50% hit rate over a career they are doing much better than the average. So, any technique that can consistently improve that hit rate should be embraced and understood, and TA does a pretty good job of it.

INDICATORS AND STRATEGIES

What is your reaction when the charts show a very obvious technical pattern such as a head-and-shoulders or a double top?

Sometimes patterns appear so obvious that they should never live up to their potential, as anything this obvious would lead to easy profits. If these patterns are reversal in nature, then I monitor them especially if they appear after major trends that could change. Sometimes I anticipate a pattern ending before it is actually completed; other times, if I have a lower conviction, I wait until a certain trigger is given before making a decision.

How do you indentify when a trend has commenced or when it may be nearing its end?

It is usually only with perfect hindsight that we know for sure that a trend has ended. I look for potential divergences in breadth and momentum indicators, as well as any blow-off moves should they occur. This is true for up and downtrends. I will occasionally look at an ADX indicator and also point-and-figure charts for possible reversals.

What do you think is the best indicator to use to measure breadth?

There is no single best indicator for anything in my opinion. At the margin, the Advance/Decline line is a pure way of measuring breadth so I start there, often by taking a moving average. But that's just the beginning of breadth analysis. There are many more indicators and breadth oscillators that I view weekly.

What is the best method for measuring price momentum in the market?

The best momentum measure is the one that you feel most comfortable interpreting and trading with. There are hundreds of different deviations of momentum indicators, but they all share the common denominator of price action. I like those that try to combine the best of an oscillator and momentum into a single indicator. Basic

41

momentum studies such as Rate of Change (ROC) are useful as I will look at it to measure the rate of ascent of prices at different intervals.

How is TA best used to make sector rotation and asset allocation decisions?

The sky's the limit! We employ many different sector rotation models that incorporate various internal breadth readings per sector and show how they have changed week by week. It is then easier, for example, to see which sectors have strong relative strength and which do not. Often if one or more sectors are too far stretched, we do see a period of mean reversion that could last for a few weeks to a few months before the prevailing trend reasserts itself.

TA also plays a very important role in asset allocation decisions, especially in a relative sense comparing different asset classes to determine which should be over/underweight, and by how much. Price momentum is nearly always a factor of good asset allocation models. Deciding which region of the world to invest in is never easy so TA should also be employed to help with currency decisions such as whether to hedge or not. This is especially true for bond markets as a bad currency call can wipe out good underlying performance.

Does technical analysis have a role to play when shorting the market?

Very much so; shorting is always difficult regardless of what anyone says, especially in bull markets. When prices do decline they often tend to do so at a faster rate than when they rally so if you can detect a downtrend that looks like it will last, it is a big benefit. Prices can stay way above fair value for a long time, so it often pays to wait until a significant technical sell signal is evident before actually going short. But one must always be on the lookout for crowded trades when shorting, because being squeezed on the upside can be very painful indeed if you're forced to cover.

How does your application of TA differ for different asset classes?

A well rounded, experienced technical analyst will likely have several favourite indicators, chart patterns, etc. that suits the environment they perceive the market is in at the time. It doesn't matter what market or class that is, as many indicators and trend analysis techniques can be employed equally well on all types of markets. What does matter, however, is the time frame you are trying to capture and the volatility of the asset class. These questions need to be answered up front; then one can use shorter, longer or more/less sensitive indicators to capture that particular trade. Ratio or relative strength is often employed when comparing relative asset classes.

Do you use Fibonacci, Gann or Elliott Wave techniques?

I use Fibonacci often after big moves to help frame possible retracement zones, but generally only for longer time periods; minimum weekly or monthly. The sequence is very good to help frame future target areas. I understand and respect the tenets of Elliott Wave, and indeed the 5 and 3 wave structure does encapsulate many of the larger bull and bear markets and counter trends. But I never employ Elliott Waves or try to make counts on individual stocks as there is way too much uncertainty and subjectivity in establishing starting points and alternatives for my liking. But I'm sure some analysts can do it better than I do. I also understand Gann and find the theory quite unique. However, like Elliott Waves, it is difficult to employ it as an adjunct to more traditional measures of TA, and can be very confusing without a lot of experience.

I look at the 23%, 38%, 50% and 62 % standard retracement levels with long-term charts to get a proper perspective of possible counter moves. They do often tend to coincide with significant support and resistance zones. I do not think there is single reason why some levels are deemed more important, but then again I am not a big wave counter.

Do you use moving averages? If so, which periodicities do you use and do you use them directly to generate trade signals?

I think most every technical analyst employs moving averages in one format or another. For general analysis of most markets, the 40-week (200-day, 9-month) moving average has been adopted to some extent as the 'correct' length to capture what could rightly be the trend of the security in question. For equities, the combination of the 50 and 200-day are pretty good at setting the short and longer time frames, but often I will look at much longer time periods for asset allocation decisions. For equities, it is often worthwhile knowing how many stocks within a certain sector are trading above or below their respective 50 or 200-day moving averages. These statistics can help determine how much impending strength or weakness there is in a specific area, and if it is vulnerable to a bout of mean reversion or not.

It's all about framing your expectations. Moving averages are also at the heart of some basic momentum indicators like MACD.

If prices reach a major support level do you wait until it has broken through before buying or selling?

Generally speaking, major support levels are more likely to be zones on either side that, depending on recent volatility, can be as much as +/-5% or even more from what the eye sees as the exact level. Depending on what time frame you use, prices can often over/undershoot on a monthly basis only to fall back into the range on a shorter-time frame. In short, therefore, I do not employ a pre-described percentage before acting but prefer to use subjective judgment in many cases to determine if the zones are likely to lead to reversals or not.

If the market is being driven by emotion, is this entirely reflected in the charts?

The markets are always driven by emotion; it is the degree or intensity of emotion that dictates how rapidly securities move up or down. In the case of the recent sell-off, it was fairly obvious that an extremely negative sentiment was driving the markets lower. But as always, when the pendulum of emotions swing too far to one side, the ballast corrects itself and eventually swings back towards the center. As long as human beings still actively participate in the markets, this will always be the case.

How do you judge if a market is overbought or oversold?

I tend to employ a wide range of tools, including many of the most common momentum based indicators and oscillators depending on the perceived market environment at the time. Sentiment indicators also play an important role here, as do extreme readings. Markets and securities often mean revert over time. Time frame and perspective are everything though they must be placed in the appropriate context; what is overbought to one eye is possibly neutral to another depending on their respective time frames.

What trading opportunities does price mean reversion offer?

Prices do tend to mean revert over time, but I disagree that there are any consistent rules that can always be exploited. Often for larger cap stocks, prices will mean revert over a simple one-month time frame

How inefficient do you believe markets to be? Are some asset markets more inefficient than others?

Longer-term, I do believe that the equity markets are driven by earnings, but in the intermediate to shorter-term the markets tend to overshoot on both sides of this moving target. Therefore, I characterize the equity markets as being 'semi-efficient', but certainly not random and certainly not entirely predictable either. Our job is to exploit the times when equities deviate away from underlying trends, whether they be long or short-term.

Generally speaking, the larger the market cap the more efficiently the security will be priced as a lot of the publicly disclosed information will have been diced and sliced by the analysts and markets already. The further down the market cap one goes, however, the more likely inefficiencies exist. I believe this philosophy also applies to the largest of the bond, FX, and commodity markets as well, although I am sure shorter-term traders will be able to recognize and extract pricing inefficiencies more often than longer-term players.

If there are more inefficiencies in the small cap market, doesn't this imply that these stocks are more exploitable from a TA perspective?

The problem with small caps is that many are too illiquid and that shows up in volatile trading patterns or stocks that do not trade much. The inefficiencies are more easily exploited at the fundamental level as these stocks are often not heavily followed by the masses.

Do you keep an eye on the academic research that is being done on technical analysis? Are there any themes in TA academic research that interest you?

I am very interested in combining the basic tenets of behavioural finance with technical analysis. Specifically, how people's emotions and decisions translate into the many different and repeatable price patterns we continuously see in markets. This is a bridge that needs to be crossed.

45

Which areas of behavioural finance interest you the most?

I am interested in all of the heuristics and biases associated with cognitive dissonance (confirmation and attribution bias, hindsight bias, and overconfidence) although they might be difficult to always nail down and exploit. By far and away the most prevalent bias at extremes that is exploitable is the herding factor which often leads to capitulation and parabolas at extreme tops and bottoms. If you can recognize those, then one can weigh the odds appropriately and often take a contrary viewpoint and position.

USING TA FOR RISK AND TRADE MANAGEMENT

What are the key performance parameters you look at apart from return?

There are many to help determine how robust any particular strategy is and the statistics must fit the idea behind the strategy. In general, drawdown and the time to reach former NAV highs I see as very important, as are hit ratios and of course volatility readings.

What is the best way to measure volatility?

Standard deviation of returns is a tried and true way of measuring volatility but it really depends on what you are trying to achieve. Measuring the % change of prices over a recent time frame (say 100 days) is acceptable for the big picture, but useless for the short-term.

What level of drawdown are you prepared to tolerate?

I would like to say 10-15%, but this might be too low in extremely volatile markets such as those seen post credit crunch. Sometimes larger drawdowns are tolerable but only if the consistency of returns compensates for the higher volatility.

COMBINING WITH OTHER NON-TA INFORMATION

What sentiment indicators do you look at?

There are so many sentiment indicators that it is very difficult to manage all of them. I tend to group then into different segments. Many common measures such as the put/call ratios, newsletter surveys and other polls can be combined together to smooth out the readings. These indicators are often used as contrary signals, especially if retail investors are involved. Consumer confidence measures often follow the employment cycle so are predictable. Another indicator segment is appetite for risk, which one can better assess by viewing different asset classes like high-yield, CDS spreads, money market spreads, option prices and volatility. Carry trades can also be useful as they are usually only put on as risk appetite increases. And honestly, this is just the beginning. I have a sentiment roadmap that encapsulates all of the human emotions in a full cycle and I subjectively gauge where I think investor sentiment is on the cycle.

Generally speaking, how do you come to a decision when to trade? To what extent is it based on technical and/or fundamental factors?

In my day job I almost strictly use technical factors to remain as objective as possible in order to provide a reality check to the fundamental assumptions of our analysts. In my private investing it is often a combination of the two, especially as I am not at all a short-term trader. For example, when I see a monthly MACD crossover that does not occur very often, say every few years, I pay attention. Same goes for the monthly parabolic and double-top formations that tend to have lasting implications.

How do you assimilate the use of TA and fundamentals?

Where many investors will often screen stocks using just fundamentals first and then look at the chart, I tend to do it the other way around. As I work in a predominantly fundamental house, I am always very aware of the fundamentals, but through experience I try not to be influenced by their thinking from a stock picking perspective. On the asset allocation side, however, I do try to be more sensitive to the fundamentals, but still give the technical interpretation more weight as often the fundamental justifications only come afterwards.

Do you often find yourself at odds with the market and/or your fundamentally based colleagues?

The market by my definition is never wrong as such, so I can't find myself at odds with it. We might not like or agree with its level of valuations, but what you see is what you get, the market cannot be wrong.

Yes, there are of course times when my fundamental colleagues and I have differing views on a stock or sector. Sometimes this can be attributed to the time frame we are basing our decisions on, where price action often moves more rapidly than the fundamentals. However, if our views differ on a very liquid large cap stock, sometimes they will check their assumptions to see why the market does not agree with their view. I always respect the fundamental viewpoint because I make mistakes, and a good fundamental analyst can add tremendous value.

How can intermarket analysis and cross asset correlations be used effectively when investing in a particular asset class?

Intermarket analysis has changed over the years as capital flows now move almost instantaneously around the world and information is digested at lightning speed compared to before. We monitor a wide range of asset classes and correlations to see if they are changing and try to determine if these changes are rational or not. As correlations have increased, it has become more difficult to separate the cause and effect.

What intermarket relationships do you think are the strongest?

There are numerous intermarket relationships that are useful at any given time, but of course, they are often framed by recent market experiences. For example, commodity prices, a falling US dollar, and a strong emerging market performance. Long-term US interest rates and the Japanese stock market is another. The yield curve and inflation expectations are also related. Yet, the cause and effect are often tough to nail down.

What impact has automated trading systems and black box trading had on the charts? What difference has it made to those who still trade discretionarily?

Difficult to say, but in the long run I do not think much as the basic tenets of supply and demand will always rule. Yet in the shorter-term, there has been a general increase in volatility that may be attributable to automated trading systems. This is often noticeable near the end of trading days.

Do you keep an eye on volume levels and if so, how do you use them in your decisions?

I do keep an eye on volumes especially at the stock level, but volume data has become less useful of late as much trading is now done off exchange or in dark pools. I do pay a lot of attention to On Balance Volume (OBV) and its relationship to underlying volume to look for confirmation or divergences. And I believe that reversal patterns like head-and-shoulders should have volume patterns that correspond to the trading direction.

How much importance do you attach to stock market cycles, for example, the January Effect and Sell in May?

I am aware of many of the typical market cycles and believe that many make intuitive sense, but that does not always mean that they will work this season or cycle. So if the seasonal pattern fits with what the technicals say should happen, then I pay more attention. If not, then I tend to ignore them and use my better judgment.

Do you employ any counter-trend strategies? Are there any contrarian indicators that you take notice of?

There are times when I feel fairly certain a longer-term trend has been established, and then after a significant move in either direction, believe it might mean revert towards the trend. Many overbought/oversold indicators can help alert one to this possibility. I do not, however, have any favorite that I always come back to regardless of the situation.

Chapter 4

AVI HOOPER

FUND MANAGER, EMERGING MARKET DEBT

BLACKFRIARS ASSET MANAGEMENT

Avi Hooper is a fund manager at London based investment boutique Blackfriars Asset Management, formerly known as WestLB Mellon Asset Management. His focus is on the development and implementation of technical analysis across all major asset classes. With total assets under management of $2.1billion, the firm's area of specialisation is emerging market equities, fixed income and currencies.

USING TA FOR TRADE AND INVESTMENT DECISIONS

Can you explain your basic investment style?

We look to identify and exploit asset mispricing in equity, bond and currency markets using a combination of fundamental and quantitative analysis.

Can you explain how and to what degree you use TA in making investment decisions?

My style incorporates the use of technical analysis to implement trades and manage risk. Our model generates weekly signals which are then confirmed on a monthly basis.

Why did you choose to use TA? What made you convinced it works?

I found fundamental data to be backward looking and slow to recognize changing price trends. Market dynamics have changed tremendously and only technical indicators have been able to identify this evolution. Ultimately, people drive markets in the short-term and technical analysis is the x-ray for our profession.

How does your application of TA differ for short, medium and long-term time scales?

A multiple time frame approach is a cornerstone of any technical process. Market noise in the short-term may produce false signals within the backdrop of the longer-term trend. The indicators used are the same over any time frame.

What technical strategies and indicators work best for short-term analysis?

The highest probability profits are made in trending markets. I find the use of multiple speed moving averages are ideal for staying with the prevailing trend, while the strength of that trend is best measured by price momentum studies such as the Relative Strength Index (RSI) and Moving Average Convergence Divergence (MACD).

I believe the traditional use of overbought and oversold indications is invalid as bull markets are built on a continued overbought environment and bear markets on an oversold environment. The value of momentum comes from divergence or non-confirmation with price, for example when momentum weakens as prices continue in the prevailing trend, this indicates the trend may be nearing its end.

Trend turning points are the most difficult, but equally important to recognize. Tom DeMark has developed some exceptional tools in this area including the TD Sequential™ and TD Combo™ trend exhaustion indicators.

What technical strategies and indicators work best for very long-term analysis?

As with shorter-term time frames, the trend is your friend. What I have found is that across all asset markets and various time horizons, prices converge and diverge from equilibrium levels. By price equilibrium, I'm referring to support and resistance. For example, the fundamental view may ask what relevance past prices have, given that a company was completely different 10 years ago. From a technical viewpoint, having rejected a level with sellers (resistance), an eventual break higher is extremely impulsive initially, but over time prices return to this level and act as support as buyers have replaced sellers. Many years later these levels act in an identical fashion, as support initially, but then break impulsively and correct back to this level of resistance where sellers have replaced buyers. I call this the price structure.

How do you identify the most important support and resistance levels on a short and long-term basis?

The most important levels are the ones that are tested and rejected the most frequently. Weekly charts reduce market noise and enable a clearer picture of price equilibrium. On weekly charts, I have found the 55 and 200-week moving averages to be useful as support and resistance. It has been fascinating to observe how many markets retraced back to levels that had been resistance levels five or more years ago, and how these levels have since been acting as strong support for the market corrections of the past eight months.

During the recent market turbulence in 2008, has TA performed better or worse than usual?

Markets have trended, mostly to the downside, so TA has performed well. Greater volatility has increased drawdowns but risk management that incorporated the higher levels of volatility have smoothed returns. Strict adherence to price targets and risk levels has been invaluable during these times.

Was the relative outperformance of CTAs during the credit crisis due to their TA based trading approach?

As an observer, rather than expert of the entire CTA community, I would suggest that the systematic application of trend based indicators led to the success of CTA strategies in 2008. However, during the first half of 2009, CTA returns have been sub-par as many markets were range trading during this time.

Are some asset classes more technically driven than others?

I haven't found this to be the case. Although, as my primary role focuses on less liquid emerging market bonds, I recognise that technical indicators can be more useful in highly liquid assets that trade daily.

Is TA used more in the FX markets than for other asset classes? It has been reported that up to 90% of FX traders use TA in some form or another which is probably more than in other markets. Why do you think this is?

I have found TA to add value across all liquid asset classes. I'm not aware of which asset class TA is applied to more than others. If the report is correct, I would suggest that the inability to value currencies fundamentally, the level of daily volume, the multitude of market participants, and the chaotic nature of the FX markets allow for the study of price to help with market direction.

In what way does the application of TA differ when using it to pick individual stocks and for analysis of the index?

If there is any difference it is that volatility is most crucial for managing risk, so stock positions will be sized in conjunction with their inherent level of higher volatility.

Are there any market conditions under which TA works better or worse than other times?

The identification of trend is the most important characteristic of TA. Range bound markets increase the chopping in and out of positions and reduce the probability of success.

Does TA have anything useful to say about portfolios and diversification?

From the perspective of identifying trending markets, countries, sectors, stocks, bonds, commodities, and currencies, TA will construct a diversified and balanced portfolio.

How easy is it to use TA? Do you think training is required? Are any techniques misused or misunderstood?

TA requires hard work and dedication to master. One's knowledge is always developing as markets evolve. The Society of Technical Analysis (STA) offers an intensive course leading to the Certificate in Technical Analysis (CFTe). Having recommended many colleagues and friends to take the course, I found that not everyone will be able to use the technical skills taught. As our minds are created differently, not everyone will relate to the technical techniques of market analysis. The element of art and subjectivity allow for various interpretations of similar charts. The misuse of TA stems from a lack of understanding and laziness when it comes to education.

Do you ever need to justify your use of TA to anyone, e.g. a customer? If so, how do you do it?

The common rebuttal of TA is that it only works because it's self-fulfilling. My reply to that is this; if it works because everyone uses it then why aren't you? The reality is that human beings herd creating trends, the risk of being different is socially intolerable.

INDICATORS AND STRATEGIES

What is your reaction when the charts show a very obvious technical pattern such as a head-and-shoulders or a double top?

'Obvious' technical patterns are more common than you might expect. If these patterns contradict the fundamental view then the position is eliminated.

How do you indentify when a trend has started and when it may be nearing its end?

A trend commencement is identified using a combination of moving average confirmations and price equilibrium breaks. The ending of a trend usually appears with a non-confirmation of momentum against the price, followed by a completion of the Tom DeMark trend exhaustion indicators. On other occasions a price target may be it, leading to a reduction or complete closing of the outstanding position. This may occur before the trend ends, but is a requirement of a complete, disciplined investment process.

What is the best method for measuring price momentum in the market?

My preferred measure for price momentum is the moving average convergence divergence (MACD) indicator. The MACD histogram over weekly and daily charts allows for timely identification of momentum strength.

What are the advantages of using the MACD for measuring momentum over other indicators?

The calculation of the MACD is a second derivative of the trend following variable, the simple moving average. It measures both the strength of the trend (momentum) and trend changes (above and below the zero line). As a measure of momentum (trend strength), it doesn't rely on overbought or oversold extremes. Given the dangers of using momentum oscillators in trending markets, MACD is more versatile in providing leading and lagging characteristics.

How can TA be used in making sector rotation and asset allocation decisions?

Relative strength charts should be created between sectors, sectors versus markets, and other intermarket charts. The same analysis used for single assets can be used for inter-asset relative analysis. The important variables of trend, momentum, trend exhaustion and price structure are employed in the same way.

Does technical analysis have a role when shorting the market?

Market probabilities are symmetrical so when identifying technical signals, rising or falling markets make no difference.

How does your application of TA differ for different asset classes?

Price is the source for analysis. Liquid asset classes make for more fluid analysis. Volatility characteristics are different, but the application of TA remains the same.

Do you use Fibonacci, Gann or Elliott Wave techniques?

I draw Fibonacci retracements for longer-time frames, especially on monthly charts.

What Fibonacci retracements do you use and why?

As a longer-term investor, I like applying Fibonacci retracements and projections on monthly charts. Retracements of 23.6%, 50%, 61.8% and 76.4% are always noted. I believe in a reoccurring pattern in shorter time frames, beginning with impulsive moves that retrace 76.4% before establishing strong trends.

What is the best way to use Fibonacci ratios?

I wouldn't use these ratios or any one indicator in isolation. At a key retracement/projection level on monthly charts, I would be looking at the shorter time frame charts (weekly and daily) for complimentary signals for position, take profit, or entry opportunities.

How do you use moving averages? If so, which periodicities do you use and do you use them directly to generate trade signals?

Yes, I find moving averages incredibly valuable in my technical process. On daily charts, I use the combination of 21, 55 and 200-day simple moving averages, and on weekly charts, the 55 and 200-week.

How do you use moving averages to generate signals?

I use a three-speed approach for moving averages. The spot price relative to these moving averages is inputted into the model. I have found MA crossover strategies to give late signals leading to model slippage. I acknowledge in sideways markets this strategy will increase portfolio turnover, but the early signals provide enough compensation over time.

If prices reach a major support level, do you wait until it has broken through before buying or selling?

Given intraday market noise, risk level breaks are implemented upon daily closes.

How do you determine where to place risk level breaks or stop-losses?

Price equilibrium levels are based on historical price levels where markets have reacted either as support or resistance to the prevailing price direction. The more these levels have been tested and rejected, the more significant the level. These levels, along with multiple time frame moving averages are used as stop-losses and profit targets. The distance of these levels from the spot price are quantified to assess risk versus reward. By observation, higher volatility assets have risk and reward levels further away from spot. A combination of these static price equilibrium levels and more dynamic moving averages are applied in the investment strategy.

How do you judge if a market is overbought or oversold?

Given the importance of participating in trending markets, I don't try to judge overbought or oversold.

How inefficient do you believe markets to be? Are some asset markets more inefficient than others?

Given the significance of human emotion in all asset markets, inefficiencies are readily apparent.

USING TA FOR RISK AND TRADE MANAGEMENT

Can you explain your approach to risk and money management?

Risk management from a technical perspective is implemented with the use of established price equilibrium levels being breached on a closing basis daily. If the technical signal changes prior to risk levels or target levels being reached, appropriate risk management is implemented immediately. For absolute returns, I believe 2% of total assets is a standard position size, although we adapt that size based on volatility.

To what extent do you adjust your position sizes with volatility?

Ideally, my preference is to use the 1-month implied option volatility against the 55 and 200-day simple moving average. I then use the following rules:

If volatility > 55 and 200-day MA, I cut the risk unit to a third

If volatility > 200-day MA but < 55 then use a 50% risk unit and

If volatility < 55 and 200-day MA, use the full risk unit

Risk management (stops and targets) is always used in the same manner regardless of volatility. Different volatility regimes require adjustment to risk unit sizes accordingly. In practice, this strategy isn't always implemented.

Is TA a part of your risk assessment? Do you use support and resistance levels as likely levels to which the market will head?

I have found nothing else better than using TA to drive risk management. I would go further to say that risk management is what drives my use of technical analysis. As discussed, support and resistance levels are the backbone to a disciplined game plan at all levels of the portfolio management process.

Is it possible to create TA-based risk metrics?

The inherent use of price to establish crowd psychology in technical analysis enables TA based risk metrics. If the crowd has changed direction, or become more uncertain (higher volatility), risk levels and unit sizes are amended accordingly.

How have you optimised your strategies? Is this something you review on a regular basis?

I haven't been involved in optimisation. Optimisation is something that sounds like curve fitting which may increase the odds of success but runs the risk of creating a false sense of security. My use of technical strategies is restricted to keeping it as simple as possible without creating over-complications.

Have you attempted to backtest your strategies?

I have been running historical backtests for the last three years on the basic model. The risk of over fitting models creates a healthy scepticism about exact results. I think the usefulness comes more from the timeliness of identifying price evolutions.

What impact did the turmoil in 2008 have on your returns? What action have you taken to reduce any losses?

The turmoil in 2008 had a positive impact on model returns that weren't completely achieved at a portfolio level as risk size was reduced. Overall, given the strong trending markets we witnessed, I found it surprising to see the large negative returns within the absolute return fund universe. I think it highlights that very few managers are using technical based indicators, and most are expensive beta providers rather than alpha producers. Given the performance in 2008 of commodity trading advisors, who are known for trend following behaviour, one should be confident that technical based decisions are valuable.

What are the key performance parameters you look at apart from return?

Adjusting returns for taken risk are important to accurately compare all investment strategies. Depending on your benchmark, the Sharpe or Information ratios are the most useful. A further extension would be the Sortino ratio. Win/Loss ratios are interesting to monitor, but ultimately if risk management procedures are implemented, returns can still be positive even if the number of losing trades is higher than winners.

Can you explain a bit more on how you use the Sharpe and Sortino ratios? What are the relative benefits of either?

Risk adjusting returns is very important. In these formulas the denominator is the standard deviation (Sharpe ratio), or downside deviation (Sortino ratio) of returns over a risk free rate. Higher, positive numbers are better, ideally >1. Simplistically, have rewards been achieved for taking risk? It's too easy to focus on absolute returns in isolation. Using 2008 and 2009 to date, some strategies which lost 50% in 2008, are up 50% in 2009 and all is forgotten. As we know, to recoup the 50% loss last year, we need a return of 100% to get back to breakeven.

Equities, as an asset class, over a 10 year period provided loads of risk but no reward in real terms. Despite the more consistent, lower risk returns of bonds, the asset class struggles to be seen as a sexy asset class to invest.

What annual return do you generally look for in your investing? How do you adjust this for risk?

In an absolute return portfolio, one that is adding risk to achieve excess returns over a risk free rate (cash), excess returns of 400-600 basis points above the cash rate are realistic. Given variations in asset price volatility, position sizes are varied and risk levels are adjusted accordingly. Target prices are at least twice that of risk levels.

If you have a long position open for a particular stock, what hedging strategies do you employ?

Currency risk is the most important element to hedge when implementing equity positions that are not in your portfolio's base currency. However, the importance of implementing only the risk desired is not analysed enough. For example, if a USD based investor goes long a Polish bank, what risks are being taken? The investor is long the Polish Zloty, the Polish equity market, global banking sector risk and then finally the intra-sector risk of that specific security within a sector.

What level of drawdown are you prepared to tolerate?

The level of drawdown corresponds to the volatility of the assets in the portfolio. Portfolios are constructed according to volatility and correlations within the portfolio. Risk levels are at a position level, and position sizes are adopted based on individual volatilities.

Do you use drawdowns for riskmetrics?

This riskmetric is widely used and provided by the prime broker. I have found the win/loss percentage to be more helpful for fund management. From a fund of funds investors viewpoint, I can understand months in drawdown and months to recover as being very useful to assess the robustness and continuity of the managers investment process.

How do measure the degree of risk associated with each trade you make?

The amount of risk is measured by the potential percentage loss if a position is stopped-out multiplied by the position size. A reward to risk ratio is a fundamental decision in position taking.

Which trade exit strategies do you use?

Trade exit strategies are based on pre-established price target levels. A disciplined exit strategy is as important as risk management. When technical signals continue to support the prevailing position and price targets have been hit, incremental profit taking is implemented. I look to exit losing positions following a daily close beyond an established price equilibrium level.

Do you use stop-losses? How do you decide where to place stops?

Stop-losses are a key component to asset management at any level and a disciplined approach to stop-losses should be a key risk management procedure for any investor. My stop-losses are established based on price equilibrium levels where a violation of these levels on a daily close leads to the position being stopped-out. The efficacy of my preferred strategy isn't directly impacted except that volatility swings lead to unacceptable risk adjusted returns. Position sizes are reduced during higher than average periods of volatility.

COMBINING WITH OTHER NON-TA INFORMATION

What sentiment indicators do you look at?

Not enough of them! Investor positioning surveys, put/call ratios, market reaction to events and mainstream media are useful. Overall, I think indications of sentiment are not analysed enough and is something that I'm presently spending more time developing my knowledge of.

How do you judge what market sentiment is at any one time?

When markets react badly to supportive news or react positively to negative news are very interesting signs of market exhaustion of prevailing trends.

How do you assimilate the use of TA and fundamentals?

Fundamental analysis gives you a framework, but the timing of trading decisions and risk management are implemented using TA.

Do you often find yourself at odds with the market and/or your fundamentally-based colleagues?

Yes, very often. Fortunately, the use of TA has been recognised to add value and has become more widely accepted. Nevertheless, the industry remains backward looking in their use of fundamental factors to make short run investment decisions. TA is a market edge that isn't explored enough.

How can intermarket analysis and cross asset correlations be used effectively when investing in a particular asset class?

Charting relative markets and identifying the strength of correlations is helpful. One should err on the side of caution in terms of the weight given to correlations as in the short run they can break down for various periods of time.

Do you keep an eye on volume levels and if so, how do you use them in your decisions?

I think volume is useful and I like to keep an eye on the On Balance Volume (OBV) indicator when it is diverging from the prevailing price. For example, large institutional involvement in a market may not be giving any additional information about impending changes in asset prices.

Chapter 5

KLAUS IKAST AND KIM CRAMER LARSSON

CEOs AND FOUNDERS

FINANCIAL TREND ANALYSIS

Klaus Ikast and Kim Cramer Larsson are both former technical analysts with Danske Bank in Copenhagen. They went on to found Financial Trend Analysis in 2009 where they provide analysis on the financial markets based on technical analysis and behavioural finance. Their focus is on exploiting short-term technical trading strategies for FX markets, fixed income, commodities and stock indices. They also manage a foreign exchange portfolio using a proprietatry trading system called Today's Trading Signals.

USING TA FOR TRADE AND INVESTMENT DECISIONS

Can you explain your basic investment style?

We have developed a portfolio of FX crosses called Today's Trading Signals (TTS), The trading strategies are based exclusively on technical analysis and are short-term with a normal time horizon of 3 to 5 days. Our approach is to take low risk, high return positions with tight stops. We spend approximately 80% of the time working on stop strategies and only 20 % on setting the targets. Since we calculate the risk/reward on a daily basis, we can choose to close down a position even though we haven't met our target. Again it's all about risk and locking in profit. Every morning we review the market and our specific strategy. This means we change the strategy from short to long and vice versa regardless of the previous day's strategy. Even though the original target in the old strategy may not have been met, we can close down a position and wait to re-enter, or reverse the strategy, if the signals have changed.

The return assumes that there is the same nominal exposure in each currency cross every time a new position is taken. Also, the return is non-leveraged; actually there is negative gearing since never is there a position in all the FX crosses at the same time. The average is between 40% and 70% of the crosses.

Can you explain how and to what degree you use TA in your trading decisions?

We only use TA. That being said, when analysing the equities markets we check the Stock Trader's Almanac for seasonal swings to see if it fits with a technical pattern we might have seen in the markets.

Why did you choose to use TA? What made you convinced it works?

We have more than 25 years of experience between us in the markets and have found that it's the most useful trading tool, as fundamental economists are usually too late for the party. Recently, we have seen a 30% rise in the equities markets since the bottom in March 2009, and its taken some five months for economists to say that we might have seen the bottom of the market. Moreover, a lot of the equity analysts still don't want to buy and are downgrading stocks.

How does your application of TA differ for short, medium and long-term time scales?

We use the same techniques and charting styles on any time horizon. We find it much more useful if you use the same set of tools no matter what the time scale. However, we do use a specific tool (Tom DeMark's indicators) slightly differently when looking at intraday charts and longer-term charts. We use both the TD Sequential™ and the TD Combo™; the former for daily and longer-term charts and the TD Combo™ for daily down to minute charts.

Why do you believe that the TD Sequential™ indicator works so well?

The TD Sequential™ measures the degree of fatigue in trends by counting the number of days a trend has been in existence. This is a way of measuring the natural flow that exists in markets. However, in very volatile or emotional markets, the indicator does not work as well.

What technical strategies and indicators work best for long-term analysis?

Tom DeMark's indicators, Dow Theory and candlestick chart formations.

What candlestick patterns do you think are the most reliable?

Morning and Evening Stars, the Doji, Engulfing Patterns, Body Gaps, and Shooting Stars.

During the recent market turbulence in 2008, has TA performed better or worse than usual?

Better. We believe that TA works better the more psychology and turbulence is in, and driving, the market. The way we set our strategies means that the more turbulence in the market, the better it performs. In 2007 our performance was 10.33 %, with 12.43 % in 2008, and so far in 2009 (up until the end of April) we have a performance of 7.13 % non-leveraged. Turbulent markets reflect higher volume, hence more volatility and psychology.

Are some asset classes more technically driven than others?

We think commodities are more technically driven because of more psychology in these assets.

Are there any market conditions under which TA works better or worse than other times?

TA is undoubtedly more effective when the market is trending up or down. When the market is trading sideways a lot of false breakouts can be generated. Then tight stops are crucial.

How easy is it to use TA? Do you think training is required? Are any techniques misused or misunderstood?

The most basic techniques such as trend theory are quite easy to work with since you just have to look for higher highs or lower lows. Also using the basic Tom DeMark studies are straightforward, although it takes a little more learning and experience to use the more advanced indicators and combine the various methods and tools. Once you are more experienced you also learn that most assets have their own life cycle so to speak, such as how far a correction in a certain asset is likely to go.

65

INDICATORS AND STRATEGIES

How do you decide when to enter a trade? What specifically do you look for as an entry signal?

It varies to some extent on market conditions but it's typically the price break of one of the following that triggers a buy or sell signal: an old high or low, pivot points, Fibonacci levels and trendlines.

What is your reaction when the charts show a very obvious technical pattern such as a head-and-shoulders or a double top?

We check other indicators such as RSI, volume and candlestick patterns to see if they show a different picture. Sometimes a pattern can be so obvious that it gets too known in the market so that it actually turns out not to evolve as expected. Then again placing the right stop is crucial. If we are wrong, we react to it which is why we also work with reverse strategies instead of just placing a normal stop-loss.

How do you indentify when a trend has commenced and may be nearing its end?

We look for divergence in indicators such as RSI and volume. We also check for the higher highs/lower lows to see if these have changed.

What is the best way to measure the degree to which a market is trending?

We apply Dow Theory for measuring trends. This means identifying higher highs and higher lows in an uptrend and lower lows and lower highs in a downtrend. Also, Tom DeMark's indicators are very useful again for this. If we are looking to judge when a trend may be coming to an end we look for the latest historic low or peak. We also look for price divergence with the stochastic, volume and RSI.

Does technical analysis have a role when shorting the market?

Yes, we use the same indicators whether the market is bullish or bearish, especially when looking at the FX market.

How does your application of TA differ for different asset classes?

We use the same TA techniques no matter what the asset class, although we do not use volume indicators when examining FX markets since volume information in FX is almost non-existent. Instead we use Bollinger Bands. When it comes to chart analysis, we aim to follow the same rules. I think these are important for anyone looking at charts, no matter what the asset or time scale. Consistency is the thing

How do you use Bollinger Bands?

As everyone knows, the bands are self-adjusting according to the level of volatility in the market. We tend to find that sharp price changes tend to occur after the bands have narrowed more than usual, and volatility is about to change direction and increase.

Are there any cycles in the FX markets?

Not in the way there is in the economy or in the stock market. However, there can be mild forms of seasonality in some currencies, such as the Japanese yen, around the fiscal year end.

Are there any characteristics unique to the FX markets when it comes to trading over the short-term?

Liquidity is normally quite high and the market is open 24 hours from Sunday evening CET till around 11 pm Friday CET.

It has been reported that around 90% of FX traders use TA, more than any other market. Why do you think this is the case?

This is probably because as with the commodity markets, the FX markets are a lot more psychological in nature than other markets. This is partly because there tends to be many more rumours in the FX markets. Also, currencies tend to be more affected by politics, speculation and corporate interests which is difficult to quantify.

Do you use Fibonacci, Gann or Elliott Wave techniques?

We use Fibonacci for support and resistance levels and projections. We also check for Gann days and obvious Elliott Wave patterns. But we do not try to find an Elliott Wave pattern if it's not obvious.

What Fibonacci levels do you use?

We find the 38.2%, 61.8%, 76.4% 138.2% and 200% levels to be most important.

How do you use moving averages? If so, which periodicities do you use and do you use them directly to generate trade signals?

We use the 5, 21, 55 and 200-day moving averages. We do not actually use them that much, although they act as minor support or resistance levels, especially the 200-day. 5, 21 and 55 are Fibonacci numbers and we tend to use these moving average periodicities as we find that Fibonacci numbered moving averages tend to work better than others. We look for crosses between short and long moving averages such as potential Golden Crosses and Death Crosses.

If prices reach a major support level do you wait until it has broken through before buying or selling?

It depends on other indicators such as an old higher high, RSI or Tom DeMark counts. But if it's for one of the major cross in the FX markets, we would normally set a stop-loss perhaps 10 ticks higher/lower than the major resistance/support. But again, it all depends on other indicators as well.

If the market is being driven by emotion, is this entirely reflected in the technicals?

Yes, we believe so. All combined information that all market participants hold is reflected in the prices. That includes any emotions of fear, hope, optimism and panic. Also, since we use human behaviour as a guide, especially in these market conditions, we take these into account. For example, it has been proven that humans feel at least twice as much pain on losing (or the risk of losing) than they do on winning, and this is reflected in the markets.

How do you judge if a market is overbought or oversold?

We do this by looking at volume, RSI and stochastic divergences. Also, we measure the distance to a moving average, or just simple trend analysis can give an indication of overbought or oversold conditions. With the RSI we look to see if there is a low or top using the 40 and 60 levels.

USING TA FOR RISK AND TRADE MANAGEMENT

Can you explain your approach to risk and money management?

Our philosophy is to take low risk, high return positions with tight stops. We change the strategy from short to long and vice-versa or close down a position regardless of the previous period's strategy. That means that even if the original target in the old strategy has not been met, or a level has been broken, we can close down our position and wait to re-enter if we don't believe the signals to be strong enough to justify the position, or the risk/reward is not good enough.

How do you decide where to place stop-losses?

We use Fibonacci levels, TD Sequential™ lines and pivot points. Apart from these indicators, there is a lot of market experience that goes into judging where to place stops. But we also test new stop-loss strategies all the time. We work with a maximum stop of 1.5 %.

Have you attempted to backtest your strategies?

We do backtest some strategies from time to time. But it is our experience that backtesting results can be good but then the strategy doesn't perform as well in real trading. Market sentiment and conditions changes and we think it's important to adapt to them. We also believe that only relatively simple strategies can be successfully backtested.

What are the key performance parameters you look at apart from return?

We generally use the Information Ratio which is a measure of the risk-adjusted return of a financial security (or asset or portfolio). It is defined as the expected active return divided by tracking error. The active return is the difference between the return of the security and the return of a selected benchmark index, and tracking error is the standard deviation of the active return. The ratio is based on monthly data and measured from 1 January 2007. Our ratio is quite high at 5 and reflects our strategy of taking low risk, high return positions in the FX market.

What annual return do you generally look for in your trading? How do you adjust this for risk?

Our goal is to deliver at least 10% annual return, non-leveraged on our FX portfolio. We look for a consistent return without too much fluctuation and a positive return in all asset classes, for example no negative return in any FX cross included in the portfolio.

What level of drawdown are you prepared to tolerate?

In FX, our maximum drawdown is between 1.382% and 1.618 %.

How do measure the degree of risk associated with each trade you make?

We calculate a risk/reward ratio. As a general rule we do not take any new positions if the reward is not at least twice as much as the risk, unless other indicators justify it.

How do you deal with false signals?

We place tight stops. That is the whole philosophy behind our strategies. If we are in any kind of doubt, we close down the position. Anyone can place a target but it's much harder to find the right stop level. Also, when having a position, we work with rolling stops to lock in profits.

How do you deal with volatility? How does very high volatility affect the efficacy of your preferred strategy?

Volatility is our friend. In 2007 when the markets where more quiet, we were working with tighter stop strategies but expanded them in 2008 due to much higher volatility.

Do you keep an eye on volume levels and if so, how do you use them in your decisions?

We use volume to look for divergence and confirmation. In the FX markets we use Bollinger Bands since volume is not reliable.

EURUSD RSI divergence and a completed 13 DeMark Sequential™ Countdown

Chapter 6

JULIUS DE KEMPENAER

QUANTITATIVE STRATEGIST

TALERGROUP

Julius de Kempenaer began his career at Equity & Law, co-running the company's Dutch equity portfolio. He later moved to ROBECO group where he became a full time technical analyst before spending six years at Dutch bank, Kempen & Co. as a technical analyst providing research for institutional clients. Since 2007, he has been a quantitative analyst with Talergroup, an Amsterdam-based asset manager

USING TA FOR TRADE AND INVESTMENT DECISIONS

Can you explain your basic investment style?

I would describe my basic investment style as very simple but disciplined. In our Taler Trend Fund there is no guess-work or subjectivity involved at all.

Can you explain how and to what degree you use TA in making investment decisions?

In the Trend Fund the investment decisions are fully rules based and 100% technically driven. In my consulting work to institutional investors, I rely heavily on the relative strength approach for which I have developed a useful visualization tool. This tool visualizes the relative position of all elements in a universe (be it asset classes, or sectors or individual equities etc) vis-à-vis a benchmark in *one* chart. The interpretation of this chart is a bit more subjective in nature but it gives the investor or trader an instant idea which elements in their portfolio are strong or weak, or where potential opportunities are hidden.

Why did you choose to use TA? What made you convinced it works?

For a very short period I used fundamentals but I found the approach too far away from real market activity. Furthermore, I could not understand why prices were moving all over the place every day of the week while nothing had changed to the underlying fundamentals of a company or a sector. The technical approach made a lot more sense to me and I understood it a lot better.

I think TA is probably as good as, or maybe speaking as a technical analyst, I should say that it is a bit better than fundamental analysis. But quite frankly I see all analytical methods as pretty much equal. They all have some added value somewhere. So it's fair to say that although it works for me, it may not work for somebody else, but that is fine.

How does your application of TA differ for short, medium and long-term time scales?

It does not really differ. I use the same techniques. The only thing that changes is the frequency of the data (monthly, weekly, daily, and hourly, etc).

What technical strategies and indicators work best for the short term (weekly) analysis?

I use the same set of tools for every time-frame: relative strength in combination with a simple price chart, plus MACD and RSI graphs for absolute analysis.

During the recent market turbulence in 2008, has TA performed better or worse than usual?

Much better. We have had huge moves and clear sell signals, with super-down trends all over the place. Even if you did not believe in TA, you could not miss it.

Are some asset classes more technically driven than others?

I don't think any asset class is more or less 'technically driven'. It has more to do with the liquidity of the market at hand. The better the liquidity, the better it can be judged based on technicals. By the way, that does not mean that a relatively illiquid market is totally out of bounds for technicians. I believe that one can 'create' liquidity in a chart by switching to a higher/longer time-frame.

In what way does the application of TA differ when using it to pick individual stocks compared to using it for the analysis of the index?

I don't think there is a real difference. While analyzing indices we have some extras we can look at; sentiment indicators like Advance/Decline lines, market-breadth, etc. Other than that, the same tools can be applied as far as I'm concerned.

Are there any market conditions under which TA works better or worse than other times?

In general I would say that TA is likely to work better in trending markets, as opposed to ranging markets. Having said that, I do know of people who achieve very good results when markets move in a tight range. Overall the big question we all need to answer is whether a market is trending or ranging. Once we know that, the technical analyst will be able to find a profitable set of tools or a trading system to approach that particular market condition. The problem is that we are all very capable of indicating trending and ranging markets on a chart after they have taken place. It's on the right side of the chart when it becomes much more difficult.

Is there any evidence that fund managers who employ TA do better than those who don't?

Not to me but I haven't really done much research into that to make a call. I think there are technically driven funds that are good and bad performers just like there are fundamentally driven funds that are good and bad performers.

Does TA have anything useful to say about portfolios and diversification?

TA can make the call whether to underweight or overweight certain positions or the call to have a position or not have a position, but putting together the portfolio or deciding which instruments to use is a totally different ball-game. I don't think TA is suited to make those calls.

Do you think TA and quants are closely related?

Very much so. Both groups use time-series for their analysis and a lot of things we both do are closely related. Maybe the quants are more number-crunching orientated and technicians are (sometimes) more chart-readers, but at the end of the day both are studying history in order to try to say something about the present or future.

How easy is it to use TA? Do you think training is required? Are any techniques misused or misunderstood?

TA looks easy but it is definitely not. The fact that all the technical analysis tools are so easily and cheaply available to anyone can even be a bit dangerous. People who use them who do not know what they are doing can get into trouble and do real harm to their bank-accounts. I always compare it to a surgeon and a scalpel. In the hands of a surgeon the scalpel can be a life-saving instrument, but please do not ask me to use the scalpel when you're in the operating theatre.

A real problem arises when people start to call themselves 'technical analysts' and offer their services to the public while they have no serious knowledge on the subject. That will hurt TA and give those who are qualified and professionally involved a bad name. Proper training and education (even if only self-study) is definitely needed.

Do you ever need to justify your use of TA to anyone, e.g. a customer? If so, how do you do it?

Most people I work with or for (clients) do know that my background is in technical analysis and most of the time it is the reason why they approach me, so in that case, I do not have to explain myself. If I do have to explain or justify the use of TA I tend to keep it as simple as humanly possible and definitely not go into too much detail.

INDICATORS AND STRATEGIES

What is your reaction when the charts show a very obvious technical pattern such as a head-and-shoulders or a double top?

A very obvious pattern doesn't happen that often so when it does I will gladly make the call and monitor whether it works out as expected.

How do you indentify when a trend has commenced and may be nearing its end?

I use the most basic definition of a trend – higher highs and higher lows for an uptrend and vice versa – and I monitor the charts (on various time-frames) to detect a trend or a change in trend. I maybe add in a simple moving average for justification.

What is the best method for measuring price momentum in the market?

The Momentum indicator and Rate of Change (ROC) are the best methods.

How can TA be used in making sector rotation and asset allocation decisions?

Good question. That's my bread and butter and could be enough to fill a book on its own. The short answer is the use of relative strength. I personally think that that's the only suitable tool in the TA toolbox to help investors make decisions on sector-rotation and asset allocation. The right visualisation of a universe based on relative strength can be of tremendous help for seeing what's going on below the surface. This goes for sector rotation as well as asset allocation or asset class rotation.

Does technical analysis have a role when shorting the market?
Not in any different way I think.

How does your application of TA differ for different asset classes?
I do not vary the application of TA for different asset classes.

Do you use Fibonacci, Gann or Elliott Wave techniques?
Very seldom. I do keep an eye and read work from other analysts, but I'm not using these techniques in my own analysis.

How do you use moving averages? Which periodicities do you use and do you use them directly to generate trade signals?
I use moving averages in all formats. They're an easy to understand tool and they do their job well. Bear in mind that a lot of indicators are

nothing else then derivatives of MAs. In my Taler Trend Fund they are indeed directly involved in triggering trade signals.

If prices reach a major support level do you wait until it has broken through before buying or selling? If so, by how much?

I don't really base trading decisions on the breaking of certain support or resistance levels. I merely use them to justify or confirm an opinion. In the case of completion of a very obvious pattern, I make the call on the breakout (on closing basis) rather than waiting.

If the market is being driven by emotion (such as the post-credit crunch sell-off), is this entirely reflected in the technicals?

Especially then. In such cases the market is 100% technically driven. No other form of investment analysis will come even close to making a reasonable judgement on what's going on. As a matter of fact, I think that TA is nothing else than the analysis of emotions in the market place reflected in the prices of securities. A change of emotions will immediately be picked up by technical analysis as it causes a change in prices. It will never change the fundamental view of a company or a sector.

How do you judge if a market is overbought or oversold?

Mostly by using the RSI.

How inefficient do you believe markets to be? Are some asset markets more inefficient than others?

Efficiency = Liquidity. The deeper the liquidity of a market the less efficient it is and vice versa. Since some asset markets are more liquid than others, they are by definition, more efficient than others.

Can you describe your method for looking at relative strength? How is this an improvement on normal methods?

I have developed a method to visualize relative strength of a whole universe, say a group of sectors or members of an equity index or a group of asset classes, all in one graph. The idea arose while I was doing European equity sales and research for an investment bank. Regularly I ran into situations where I wanted to update a fund manager on my technical sector views and they would tell me that they had no time for the banking sector as that week was insurance week, which meant that they had a whole bunch of road shows lined up. As such, they would speak to all sector analysts covering insurance stocks etc. It did not matter that chemicals were flying and banks were tanking. This sort of tunnel vision made them loose awareness of the big picture which is crucial to the overall performance of their portfolio.

I detected a similar situation with traders and market makers. Some of these guys have to make markets in 15 to 20 individual stocks. As we all know it's pretty much impossible to follow 15 to 20 names all day in real-time and continuously issue bid-offer prices. Of course they can use quote machines to adjust their quotes but what happens in reality is that they closely follow 4 to 5 names in which they have a larger position, and the others in their universe are covered by a machine. Alternatively, they simply put in their bid-offers until they are notified they have been hit or lifted and they are forced into a position they might not even want to have. Enabling them to see the relative positions of all the names in their universe added immensely to their awareness of what was going on in the names they were quoting.

USING TA FOR RISK AND TRADE MANAGEMENT

Can you explain your approach to risk and money management?
Risk management and money management are two hugely important parts of the overall investment process but I do not use TA for these purposes.

How have you optimised your strategies? Is this something you review on a regular basis?
The only time I use optimization techniques is in the research phase of developing new strategies or systems, to get an idea on the results of various combinations of parameter settings. Once a strategy or a system is in place, it will not change as a result of a new optimization run. There is too much risk of curve fitting.

Do you automate your strategies in any way?
As much as possible. Technology is here to serve us and the extra benefit is that it takes out our biggest opponent – ourselves and all of

our views and judgement calls – out of the equation. And sometimes the machines see things or can execute possibilities that we cannot detect or execute fast enough.

Have you attempted to backtest your strategies?

This is a very important part of the research process. It gives you valuable hindsight into what you can expect of your strategies going forward. I would not dare to start trading a new strategy without extensive testing to get comfortable with the behaviour of the strategy in different markets.

What impact did the turmoil in 2008 have on your returns? What action have you taken to reduce any losses?

The funds lost money and the strategies experienced drawdowns that we had never seen before in backtesting situations, volatilities shot through the roof and correlations all jumped to 1. All the good ideas on diversification were put in a fridge for a couple of months. After we recovered from the first blows, in the case of the Trend Fund we continued to execute the strategy as it had been developed, trusting that we had done our homework correctly. The results YTD 2009 suggest that this seems to have been a good call. It was also encouraging to see that the strategy required the Trend Fund to be in a 100% cash position in October and November of 2008.

What are the key performance parameters you look at apart from return? (E.g. drawdown, win ratio etc).

I definitely look at the amount and duration of drawdown.

What annual return do you generally look for in your trading/investing? How do you adjust this for risk?

The fund is absolute return orientated and looks to do better than 10 year bond rates +200 BPS. That metric in itself is not adjusted for risk but we do monitor the Sharp ratio of the fund.

How do you decide on which position size to take? How much of your capital are you prepared to risk at any one time?

That is embedded in the risk and money management process that we apply. For the Trend Fund it is very simple. There are ten buckets/markets and every bucket is 10% of the fund so every position amounts to 10% of the fund when it is initially taken. Of course position size changes together with the change of prices in the markets. For our other fund we use volatility adjusted position sizing.

If you have a long position open for a particular stock what, if any, hedging strategies do you employ?
I do not do any hedging. I like to keep it simple.

What level of drawdown are you prepared to tolerate?
What I was prepared to tolerate based on the backtesting is definitely different to what I experienced in real life. With hindsight, if I have to put a number on it, I think it lies around 15% which is the maximum drawdown of the fund. This is a good 5% higher than the 9%-10% drawdown that we had expected to see based on our test results.

How do measure the degree of risk associated with each trade you make?
The risk management system generates a VaR report but I'm pretty certain that the trading rules will have caused a position to be closed long before the risk limits are reached.

How do you deal with false signals?
I execute them; there is no second guessing. I only know after the fact when I'm forced to do the reverse transaction that it was a false signal. This is not a problem – we know they are there every now and then.

Do you use stop-losses? How do you decide where to place stops?
The exit rule is the stop-loss. The strategy is rule based so no judgmental decision has to be made on where to put the stops.

What is your view on the use of optimised stop-losses?
It is the same as my view on optimised trading rules. There is a great danger of curve fitting, so I do not use it.

How do you deal with volatility? How does very high volatility affect the efficacy of your preferred strategy?

As I use a trend following strategy, very sudden changes in trend tend to have a negative impact on the results. Nicely rounding tops and bottoms are best for these kinds of system, but spiking volatility does not usually coincide with these patterns.

COMBINING WITH OTHER NON-TA INFORMATION

What sentiment indicators do you look at?

None in particular, although I keep an eye on Advance/Decline lines, put/call ratios, and investor sentiment surveys.

Generally speaking, how do you come to a decision when to trade? To what extent is it based on technical and/or fundamental factors?

For the Trend Fund it's laid down in the trading rules; no subjective decision is necessary. For our other fund, the Focus Fund, the adjustment of positions is based on an extensive investment process. Once the decision has been taken, we use TA to some extent to time the adjustment but the time window cannot be too long as the investment process for the fund is leading.

How can intermarket analysis and cross asset correlations be used effectively when investing in a particular asset class?

One can use intermarket analysis to determine where to be invested or overweight and where not to be invested or underweight, and use cross asset correlations in money and risk management

What impact has automated trading systems and black box trading had on the charts? What difference has it made to those who still trade discretionarily?

Events happen quicker and things that used to take weeks to pan out now do so in days or hours but I don't think it has really impacted the charts as such. I don't think for example one could point out on a chart of one of the major indices the moment when automated trading systems and black box trading really started to take off.

Do you keep an eye on volume levels and if so, how do you use them in your decisions?

Less and less I have to say. I think volume figures are getting less and less reliable with the growth of alternative trading platforms and dark pools of liquidity used by institutional investors.

How much importance do you attach to stock market cycles and statistics? For example, the January Effect and Sell in May. Do you actually trade on them?

I sometimes look at them, take notice but do not trade on them.

Chapter 7

BARCLAY LEIB

PRINCIPAL AND FOUNDER

SAND SPRING ADVISORS

Barclay Leib founded Sand Spring Advisors in 1999, a financial advisory firm based in New Jersey that offers trading analysis and fractal commentary to hedge funds. He began his career at J.P. Morgan where he ran commodity and FX derivatives trading. In 1987 he became head of proprietary trading and arbitrage within PaineWebber's Fixed Income Department. He later worked for J. Aron Goldman Sachs where he was a senior member of their global currency and commodity option trading team. Barclay moved into strategy and hedge fund sales work between 1993 and 1998 working first as a vice president in FX options trading at Barclays and then later at Societe Generale.

USING TA FOR TRADE AND INVESTMENT DECISIONS

Can you explain your basic investment style?

I have a strong belief that markets move with clearly defined fractal rhythms. Elements of so much importance in the physical world of geometry - concepts such as *pi* (3.141) and *phi* (the so-called Golden Ratio of .618 and 1.618) – are also of similar importance in the more abstract world of markets. My approach focuses on a hidden order, perhaps geometric or fractal in nature, hiding behind the chaos of daily market trading.

Phi ratios inherent in Fibonacci retracement bands may be stretched to anticipate 'complete' market rhythms, where multiples of pi and phi are important in anticipating cyclical market turns. All the little jiggles of a given market must eventually 'fit' a geometrically defined pattern of some sort before they reverse in trend.

Not every chart pattern yields obvious analysis, so the trick is to search for those where a clear missing high or low may be seen on a fractal basis, and to focus on those select situations. I like to be patient for a clear chart pattern where I feel I have a discernable edge

83

with my fractal methods and feel no compulsion to become involved in marginal situations. I like to wait for low hanging fruit, only attacking when a set-up looks obvious, but then generally retreating early when my fractal edge may disappear or becomes less unidirectional in its implications.

The second part of my approach is to be aware of important cyclical turn dates where a shift in overall market or sector sentiment is to be anticipated. The combination of cycle and fractal analysis is like having a market roadmap, and knowing where you are in terms of general risk-reward of a given trend.

Can you explain how and to what degree you use TA in making investment decisions?

At the end of the day, I know that the world must reflect fundamentals and they will rule in the long-term. It is thus nice to trade with the fundamentals at your back. You don't want to sell cheap stocks, nor do you want to get caught long playing in some overhyped go-go situation that suddenly falls from grace. To this extent, I start my approach to the financial world with a value bias. I then add into this equation a dose of sector thematics and macro thinking to define the areas where I might expect to find opportunities.

But at the end of this initial fundamental and macro thematic filtering process, I want to be comfortable with a given chart pattern before I trade it. I want to see certain attributes in that pattern implying a real edge. This takes us back to Fibonacci.

I like to use the following Fibonacci settings which are arithmetic and geometric functions of each other: .618, .382, 0.50, and 0.23 (= 0.382 x 0.618), 0.764 (= 1 - 0.236), 0.0901 (= 0.382 x 0.236), 0.9099 (= 1 - 0.0901). With these ratios in hand, one is finally ready to examine a chart pattern. In doing so, it is important to start with as much data as possible by using a weekly or even a monthly chart. Get the big picture straight first, and then drill down to shorter time intervals. If the asset being examined has been in a major uptrend, one must locate the last significant major low and pull Fibonacci bands up from that point to a recent major high. If an asset has been in a major down move, one needs to go back to the last major high and pull the bands down to the last major low.

I then look to see if the bands fit the intervening price action that took place between the high and the low that I have chosen, with each (or at least most) minor highs and lows along the way touching an intervening Fibonacci band. If they do, then I am likely looking at a 'complete rhythm', and one can likely expect a trend reversal to transpire into a subsequent trading range. However, if the bands do not fit the pre-existing price action, then the existing trend is likely not yet over, and one must stretch the bands to a price level where the bands will fit the price action. Once this is done on a weekly basis, I then drill down and repeat this process on a daily chart, and then on a 60-minute or even a 5-minute chart. The goal is to find similar price levels where each chart is happy completing its fractal movement.

Can you give an example of how you might trade a fractal rhythm?

Let me go back to a late 2007 example of a chart to more specifically illustrate this. Using the approach above, one might have seen a long-term Fibonacci target on a weekly chart of the stock Nvidia (NVDA) popping out as a complete rhythm at around $39.50-$40.00, as I did when it touched $39.67 in mid-October 2007. Figure 1 shows how well that level fit earlier highs in terms of the bands touching. Several lows also hit, but fitting highs is always more important to me than fitting lows.

To confirm this level, the next step is to move to a shorter time interval, perhaps a more recent low and a daily chart basis, to see if the fractal rhythm of NVDA to $39.67 a share was also satisfied on that basis. Figure 2 is a repeat of the weekly chart, but with new Fibonacci bands drawn between the more minor July 2006 low in NVDA and the $39.67 level where the weekly chart appears complete.

Figure 3 shows these same lines zoomed in on a daily basis, with yet another set of Fibonacci lines drawn between the March 2007 low and the $39.67 high. On both we see the rhythm looks complete again, and the daily bands pick out many of the same Fibonacci lines as the more major weekly chart. The double hit at the minor $25.70 high in December 2006 is particularly pleasing. I refer to such an occurrence as a 'double vibration' fractal hit.

As a next step, on the daily chart, we will start to pull some Fibonacci bands lower from the $39.67 high to try to fit the price action since that time. Using the beginning part of the NVDA decline, we obtained a harmonic vibration fit at $22.57 which was my actual initial target exit price on the short sale of NVDA that I executed.

I then moved to one last step and pulled bands down again to ask the question: "If NVDA were to break $22.57, what would be the next obvious harmonic vibration stopping point?" To do this, I stretch some bands to the next level were the recent minor high-low price action would be captured between the lines and where we may already have a cluster of other Fibonacci bands. The obvious target was between $18.30-$18.90.

By using Fibonacci bands I thus developed three useful opinions over time:

October 19th 2007: NVDA was likely to experience a trend reversal between $39.50 and $40. The actual $39.67 high was a great 'natural attractor' level to take profits on longs and reverse to being short.

October 19th 2007 through mid-January 2008: NVDA was in clear downtrend mode to an initial target of $22.57. I took initial profits there.

Mid-January 2008 onward: NVDA moved to being in a range with a $29 top and a possible new 'missing low' target down at $18.30-$18.90. Which side of this range would be touched first was less clear at the time. My approach at this juncture was to generally look for other more compelling chart patterns in other equities where a clearer fractal pattern could be found, or at least until my $18.30-$18.90 NVDA support zone was reached for a countertrend long trade. It is an approach of consistently hitting singles, and occasionally missing doubles and triples.

In this instance, NVDA did subsequently reach a closing weekly low in late March 2008 at $18.52 (exactly in its expected fractal support zone), and then promptly rallied to $25.32 again. At this juncture, more data had accumulated on the chart and on a weekly basis one could start discerning that NVDA had an extrapolated 'missing low' (using stretched bands) all the way down at $3.90 somewhere in the future. It was time to start trading from the short side again in the mid-$20's range.

NVDA subsequently fell as low as $5.75 and bounced once again to around $10.85. In my mind, a $3.90 'missing low' eventually still beckons. As more data emerges, the nature of that data often provides additional information about the future. The astute technician moves forward one step at a time. An initial vision that NVDA would fall to $22.57 eventually gets expanded to the potential for NVDA to reach $3.90. But a good trader ends up trading NVDA both short and long in between leaning against known fractal support and resistance when these levels are first touched for the inevitable short-term technical reversals.

86

How does all of this tie in to your work with pi cycles?

While Fibonacci ratios may rule the amplitude of market moves, I have come to believe over time that another magic mathematical constant, pi, is a more dominant force when looking for rhythms in markets across time.

The circumference of a circle can be measured by the equation $2\pi r$ (r equalling the circle's radius). If this equation measures a full circle or cycle in the physical world, maybe $2\pi r$ might hold significance in the financial world. To this I apply the Base 10 system of 10, 100, and 1000, using $2\pi 1000 = 6282$ days, or 17.2 years.

The August 1982 equity market low was exactly 17.2 years in front of the first quarter 2000 equity market high. This was a boom period. But 17.2 years prior to August 1982 was late May 1965, which for a long while, was the all-time high in the DJIA in real terms before Johnson-era inflation set in. 1965-1982 as a whole was a period of stagnating markets, war, inflation, and political scandal. But go back another 17.2 years from May 1965 and you come to March 1948. 1948-1965 ended up being, of course, post-War boom years. However, the 17.2-year period prior to this encompassed the difficult 1931-1948 depression era and WWII years. Do you see the pattern?

The immediate implication is that the boom high left in early 2000 ushered in 17.2 years of general market stagnation, unpopular presidents, and war that will stretch to 2017. In other words, we're just more than half done in a general period of pain. As an investor you need to approach this type of environment very differently than boom periods. During boom 17.2-year cycles, you basically want to buy and hold. During the current type of market cycle, you need to be a good market timer and trader to make much money.

There are likely several different overlapping pi cycles. The one I describe above is just one. Martin Armstrong also focused on a high-to-high pi cycle of just pi x 1000 (3141 days or 8.6 years). Using this cycle, he correctly forecast that July 20 1998 would be a significant high in global equity markets. That date marked the exact high point before the LTCM and Russian ruble crisis of 1998 transpired. Exactly 3141 days prior to this day was December 13, 1989, which was within spitting distance of the all-time high of the Nikkei in Japan and just in front of the nasty 1990-1991 period of S&L and banking distress in the U.S.

Why did you originally choose to use TA? What made you convinced it works?

I started my career at JP Morgan in 1980, and after a few days having watched how flow traders reacted to fundamental news and customer order flow, I decided that there had to be a better way to trade and invest. I basically thought their flow information was too anecdotal and partial to be that important, and I saw the impact of news as often being most perverse and hard to interpret. I was fortuitous enough to then stumble across a copy of Edwards and Magee's classic text, *'Technical Analysis of Stock Trends'*, and concluded that using technical analysis was the way that I wanted to trade and invest.

When I knew TA really worked hit in August of 1982 when I found a reverse head-and-shoulders bottom in gold around the $330 level. Everything was perfect in the pattern including diminished volume on the second inverted shoulder. With an inverted head down at $300, and a neckline at $360, the minimum target was $420. Five days later, Fed Chairman Paul Volcker started cutting interest rates, and gold exploded to the upside. I sold my gold at $420 the following week.

Gold subsequently moved as high as $510, and using a variety of technical tools, I caught portions of that move. Then I started watching the Bullish Consensus figures zoom above 90% bullish for gold, and also looking at negative divergence on certain momentum oscillators, I expected the run was over and we'd likely retrace. Gold fell dramatically in the early spring of 1983. It was a wonderful and powerful first experience using TA.

While over time, I came to appreciate a variety of tools, it was the ability of Fibonacci bands – properly used and often 'stretched' to price levels that would fit pre-existing highs and lows in a chart pattern – that led me to believe in an inherent fractal rhythm to financial markets. Over a 29 year period, using these bands on a combined weekly, daily, hourly, and five-minute chart basis, I have simply seen them locate zones of important resistance and reversal far too often, and far too easily, for it to have been random happenstance.

As a general approach, one needs to watch for self-reinforcing technical signals that may happen one after another (as opposed to concomitantly); i.e. the RSI becomes overbought at or near a Fibonacci fractal target, momentum oscillators show divergence and sentiment numbers become too extreme. On top of this volume patterns may change, trendlines break and perhaps lastly, a moving average crossover occurs. In such an example, it is the combined weight of the technical evidence that cumulatively foretells a trend shift.

How does your application of TA differ for short, medium and long-term time scales?

The shorter the time scale, the more random a market becomes. Thus applying technical analysis to a 1-minute chart is inherently more dangerous than applying it to a 5-minute chart; the 5-minute chart is more prone to spurious noise compared to the 60-minute chart which in turn is less reliable than a daily chart, etc. But each does have a fractal rhythm, and when they all point to a similar level in the market they are very powerful. Most good Fibonacci technicians start with the big picture monthly and weekly rhythms and then work downward in time.

During the recent market turbulence in 2008 has TA performed better or worse than usual?

I thought TA worked very well across the early part of 2008. The decline into late March 2008 (Bear Stearns day) found a low near a minor pi cycle date window, and the bounce into early May 2008 was an obvious rally to be sold. The reversal in energy and commodity stocks in July 2008 was also pretty well ear-marked technically and cyclically, even though many hedge fund managers got caught by it.

Are some asset classes more technically driven than others?

People tend to apply TA more regularly to the world of commodities and currencies, maybe because the fundamentals of these markets are often harder to get your hands around. That said, some of the analysis involving soft and energy commodities gets complicated because of data adjustments for contract roll-overs.

Applying TA to a futures contract (where the active front-month contract keeps changing every few months) is never quite as clean as it is to a stock that has been trading for 20 years. Thus, I would argue that the strength of one's convictions can likely be higher applying TA to a good old fashioned equity than to a futures contract.

*In what way does the application of TA differ when using it to pick
individual stocks as opposed to analysis of the index?*

There is obviously more noise around a single stock than an index of
stocks. You will get more jump moves related to earnings releases
and occasional takeover events that may or may not always be easy to
anticipate using traditional TA. In addition, you will get sudden
technical short-covering squeezes when the borrow for a given stock
evaporates. Individual stocks thus tend to be inherently more volatile
than equity indices, so overall, added caution must always be taken
using TA for positioning in a single equity compared to positioning in
an equity index.

*Does TA have anything useful to say about portfolios and
diversification?*

Properly applied, TA should allow an adroit hedge fund manager to
rotate the position sizing of his portfolio components to continually
overweight the best risk-reward opportunities, while harvesting
positions which are at (or fast approaching) technical support. This
process should in the end improve not only absolute returns, but also
the risk-adjusted path of those returns.

Do you think TA and quants are closely related?

No. The quant is far more dangerous than the technician partly
because his approach naturally requires high leverage and continuous
exposure and trading in the market. A good technician only steps into
the market when the risk-reward of a market situation at hand is
deemed to be on his side. Otherwise stated, as a weapon of choice,
the quant yields a shotgun but the technician may be viewed as using a
more precise stiletto.

*How easy is it to use TA? Do you think training is required? Are any
techniques misused or misunderstood?*

Using TA adroitly is akin to learning chess or backgammon. The goal
in all instances is to reach sound conclusions that have a higher
probability of success than failure, and one definitely becomes better
at this with both time and experience.

As previously discussed, there are different branches of TA; some
straight quantitative techniques, and other more artistic and pattern-
oriented approaches. It is important to choose a repertoire of tools

that fits one's own proclivities and mental temperament. The bottom line to trading success is to get to know what your own psyche tends to be good at, and to pick technical tools that fit that psyche.

INDICATORS AND STRATEGIES

What is your reaction when the charts show a very obvious technical pattern such as a head-and-shoulders or a double top?

Circa 1980-1985, I would have believed the pattern and traded the obvious implications of it. Circa 2005-2009, I have become more attentive to the fact that everyone now has charting software and obvious patterns sometimes need one last gut-wrenching mis-directional move before they work.

To handle this possibility, I might commit half of my ultimate desired position size to an obvious situation, but keep the other half in reserve for the potential stop-out affair of weak hands. Being short a triple top in sterling in 1991 comes to mind here. The British pound was up at $1.97 and felt very top heavy both fundamentally and technically. But alas, there had to be one last stop-out session where the pound traded up to $2.015. It was only after this final mis-directional move that the pound then collapsed. Some weak-handed person had been stopped, and only after such an event was the market free to go down.

What is the best method for measuring price momentum in the market?

An oscillator built around the 5-day and 35-day moving averages is a nice tool. Divergence versus price on a 13-day RSI indicator is another basic indicator.

How can TA be used in making sector rotation and asset allocation decisions?

As discussed above, TA can be vital in this regard. Not overstaying one's welcome in a given sector is always a tough timing decision to make, but TA may easily provide an objective tool to shift sector exposures. It is also a key tool to use in the setting of equity stops. Gross investedness and beta bias may also be adjusted to be more aggressive when a technical setup is clear, while conversely prompting less exposure when the charts temporarily turn muddy.

Does technical analysis have a role when shorting the market?

Technical analysis is crucial, especially to shorting. Shorting by itself is one of the hardest parts of portfolio management. But if TA can reveal entry times and prices that have a non-random special edge for establishing a short position, the overall angst and risk of selling short can be substantially reduced. When a given equity becomes technically oversold, it may then be time to harvest this position and rotate exposure into another less washed-out situation.

How do you use moving averages? If so, which periodicities do you use and do you use them directly to generate trade signals?

I like to watch a short-term 5-day moving average and its relationship to a more intermediate term 30-day or 40-day moving average. I also always want to know where the 100-day and 200-day moving averages reside. On 'first touch' of the 200-day moving average, there is almost always a short-term reaction reversal in the opposite direction of the trend. It is good for a fast trade, even if the 200-day may eventually be broken and thereby suggest a more major trend change.

If prices reach a major support level do you wait until it has broken through before buying or selling?

I love to trade the first touch of a major support or resistance zone. I don't wait for anything because I know that against such a level there will almost always be some sort of short-term bounce/reversal. This is the type of high probability short-term outcome that I like. But after a given level has been knocked against for a while, I become less comfortable positioning against the pre-existing trend. Support and resistance levels don't last forever.

If the market is being driven by emotion, is this entirely reflected in the technicals?

In general terms, I would say yes. TA arguably works best in a period of market stress. The nice part of stressful markets is that they tend to move quickly, and thereby yield much instant gratification for an astute trader. Think of a ping-pong ball moving quickly and clearly between clearly defined walls. The problem with bull markets is that they tend to be slower moving with less clear momentum. In bull

92

markets, imagine more a small tugboat chugging against the wind and the waves.

How do you judge if a market is overbought or oversold?

I always have an eye on the Bullish Consensus measure and other mechanical sentiment indicators (put/call ratio, RSIs, oscillators) and try to spot divergences. I also look for volume spikes and abatements. But my key indicator revolves around stretched Fibonacci bands which highlight key price levels to expect resistance.

How inefficient do you believe markets to be? Are some asset markets more inefficient than others?

I will go out on a limb here and say that I believe markets have become less and less efficient over time. The slow demise of the NYSE Specialist system to negligible importance today means markets are more thin and volatile than they used to be. Fair price levels are constantly getting overshot.

Do you keep an eye on the academic research that is being done on technical analysis? Are there any themes in TA academic research that interest you?

I believe that it is just a matter of time before someone wins the Nobel Prize in Economics for adroitly explaining the fractal manner in which financial markets truly behave. At present, there are at most a handful of possible candidates. These include geo-physics UCLA Professor Didier Sornette who in 2003 applied super-parabolic sine wave rhythms to financial markets in his text *'Why Stock Markets Crash'*. Edgar Peters who has penned some highly mathematical tomes on chaos theory as applied to fractal market analysis, and more recently Benoit Mandelbrot in his text *'The (Mis) Behaviour of Markets'*.

The list likely may also include Yale-educated Robert Prechter, who after being regarded largely as a non-academic Elliott Wave newsletter writer, has in recent years made a substantive push to become more academic in the defence of his methodologies and approach. Prechter has actually branded a whole new name for his studies, *'Socionomics'*. Maybe that buzzword will eventually catch on and Prechter will get credit for it.

USING TA FOR RISK AND TRADE MANAGEMENT

Can you explain your approach to risk and money management?

I like to be as lightly invested as possible as much as possible, but then step up to the plate with a directional view or a relative value view between securities, commodities and currencies. I do this when the technical outlook looks most compelling, for example, going into an expected pi cycle date. When I am actively trading, I like to end up with a portfolio averaging 5-15 positions, with each position sized in the 3%-10% of portfolio region.

If I start losing money, then I reduce the number of positions and the sizing of the positions. I re-examine the positions on a daily basis and question whether what I thought I saw yesterday in a chart pattern still appears valid today, or whether some intervening piece of price action has made my original view more or less probable.

I try to stay reasonably unemotional about my positions, and occasionally book out positions too soon, sometimes out of boredom when I have not achieved some modicum of instant gratification. I like to invest in the direction of a clear long-term trend, but then hardly ever have the patience to actually ride that entire trend. Instead, I will be in and out of a given asset at singular moments of the trend that appear to offer the easiest set-ups for trading success. I hardly ever overstay my welcome in a market, but more regularly do sometimes enter a position too early and/or also exit positions too early.

When an anticipated pi cycle turn date is at hand, particularly a major one, and other TA techniques confirm a potential major shift in a given market, it is an exciting moment. It is a time when I tend to increase my bet size somewhat from normal levels and play the turn. But once a market has turned by 10%-15%, you have to be more careful. The relevance of that pi cycle turn may last for 1-2 years, but it says less about what may happen over the coming few days or even weeks. In addition, you have to be attentive to having misinterpreted a market turn in the wrong sector, as I initially did in February 2007. The pi cycle date that hit February 24, 2007 basically worked, but it ended up being a more important turn in the credit markets than in equity markets. You could have still lost a great deal of money if you had stubbornly remained short stocks between March and October 2007. Stocks didn't really start to turn down until 8.6-months later in November 2007.

On an overall basis, having some technical basis for a stop is in my mind highly superior to using some arbitrary distance away from original cost.

What annual return do you generally look for in your trading? How do you adjust this for risk?

25%-30% returns per annum are certainly possible given my active trading approach. I trade with a prop trader's mind, and simply never let my P&L fall consecutively over more than a day or two without taking some sort of defensive action, including just making a simple retreat.

How do you decide on which position size to take? How much of your capital are you prepared to risk at any one time?

I take 3%-10% positions weighted by strength of my starting conviction, the distance to stop, and the natural volatility of the asset. The greater the volatility of a given stock, the smaller I will generally trade it in terms of position size. The goal is to never let any given position clip your portfolio as a whole for more than 1%, with a pre-disposition to start cutting positions in half when they may have cost the portfolio between 25-50 basis points.

What level of drawndown are you prepared to tolerate?

Approximately -10%.

How do you deal with false signals?

If I don't get immediate satisfaction on a position, I generally blow it out and move on to another situation. I don't have as much patience as I'd like.

How do you decide where to place stop-losses?

Stops are an integral part of my approach, and technical levels such as the 200-day moving average, prior minor highs/lows, and trendlines are levels beyond which a stop will typically be placed.

How do you deal with volatility? How does very high volatility affect the efficacy of your preferred strategy?

The more volatile a market, the better I tend to do. Fractal targets appear, get reached, and positions get quickly harvested and rotated. Slow moving markets give one too much time to think and agonize over an exposure.

COMBINING WITH OTHER NON-TA INFORMATION

What sentiment indicators do you look at?

Market Vane's Bullish Consensus statistics have always been a primary tool that I look at to gauge sentiment, followed by TRIN, put/call ratios, volume, advance-decline ratios, RSIs, and moving average oscillators in order to judge internal market momentum along with sentiment.

Generally speaking, how do you come to a decision when to trade? To what extent is it based on technical and/or fundamental factors?

In an ideal world, you enter a position only when both the fundamentals and technicals line up. If the fundamentals are there but the technicals aren't then you wait. If the fundamentals aren't necessarily supportive of the technical view I might still trade a very small token position, but I also would have a very tight stop-loss on it.

Do you often find yourself at odds with the market and/or your fundamentally-based colleagues?

I am something of a contrarian at heart, so yes I do find myself at times reacting to the market's excessive swings with some incredulousness. These excessive swings are of course the source of much trading opportunity, but sometimes I can be a tad early and it takes a while to break a pre-existing trend. Differentiating when you may simply have been early and when you are simply wrong is perhaps the hardest part of TA. It requires great psychological skill to make the mindset shift when evaluating these two possible paths.

What impact has automated trading systems and black box trading had on the charts?

The equity trading day typically can be broken down into three sections: Towards the opening, you tend to have a fair amount of retail order flow. Toward the end of the day, you may have more institutional or professional order flow. In between, you increasingly have a great deal of algorithmic trading. Institutional clients will set up electronic programs to participate in the trading of a stock as a percentage of its traded volume or the passage of time, or a combination of these two factors. This middle part of the day is somewhat unnatural in my mind as it does not tend to exhibit the same type of human-induced rhythm as you may see at the opening or towards the close. You can literally watch the slow ripple of VWAP, TWAP, and Percent Participation orders gently driving a stock in a steady fashion in the direction of least resistance. It is something just to be aware of.

There are other instances where intermediate term trend followers (i.e. Commodity Trading Advisors) may all flip their exposures in a given asset because of a momentum change or moving average crossover type of event. These are more important types of days to try to recognize as they tend to be non-reversing breakout affairs, at least for that one day. Occasionally, when the players in a given market are too large relative to available liquidity, these moves can be quite large and dramatic. CTAs tripping into a given market in undue size get front-run by the investment banks and the combination can result in outsized moves well beyond any fundamental news of a given trading day. To a certain extent, these breakout days represent a clustering of changing market emotions as channelled by black boxes. They are worth trying to spot.

Do you keep an eye on volume, and if so, how do you use it?

I try to use volume in a common sense 'Edwards & Magee' type manner. For example, a second shoulder of a head-and-shoulder top should ideally be marked by low volume. If it's not, then maybe the pattern is something other than a second shoulder. Upside breakouts should transpire on high volume. RSI divergence across three subsequent thrusts should see diminishing volume on the last rally attempt. The apex of a pennant should exhibit very low volume just before the pattern resolves itself into a higher volume breakout.

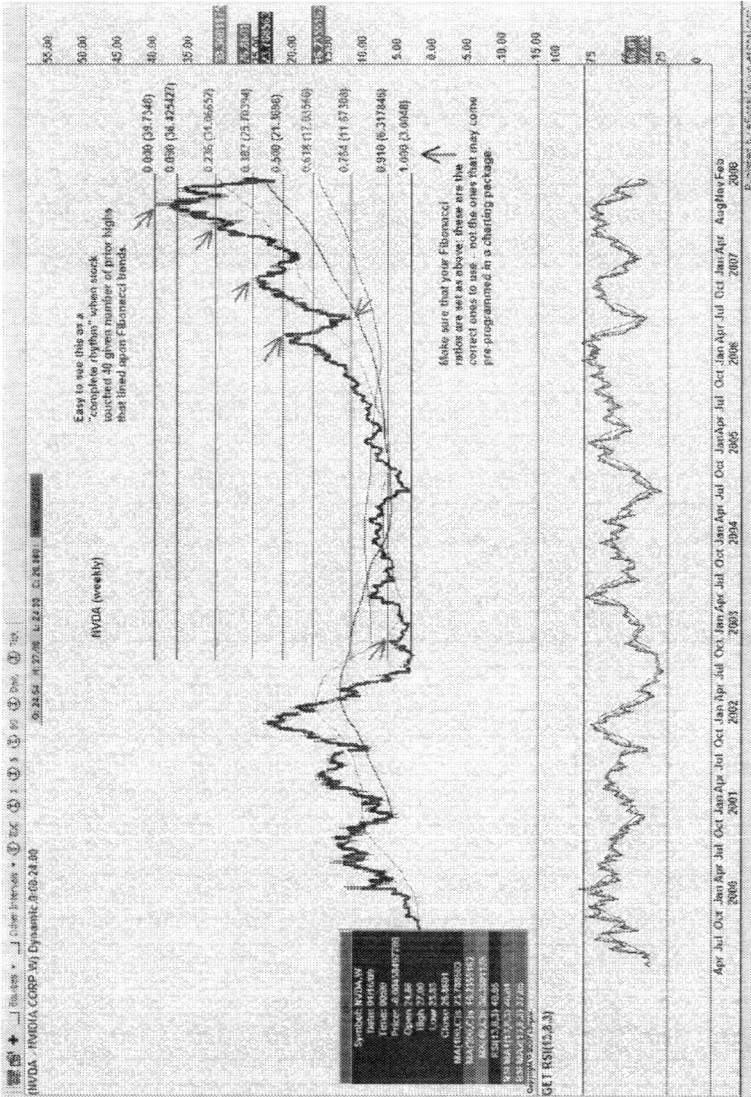

Figure 1 - Weekly chart for NVDA showing long-term Fibonacci target   Source: eSignal

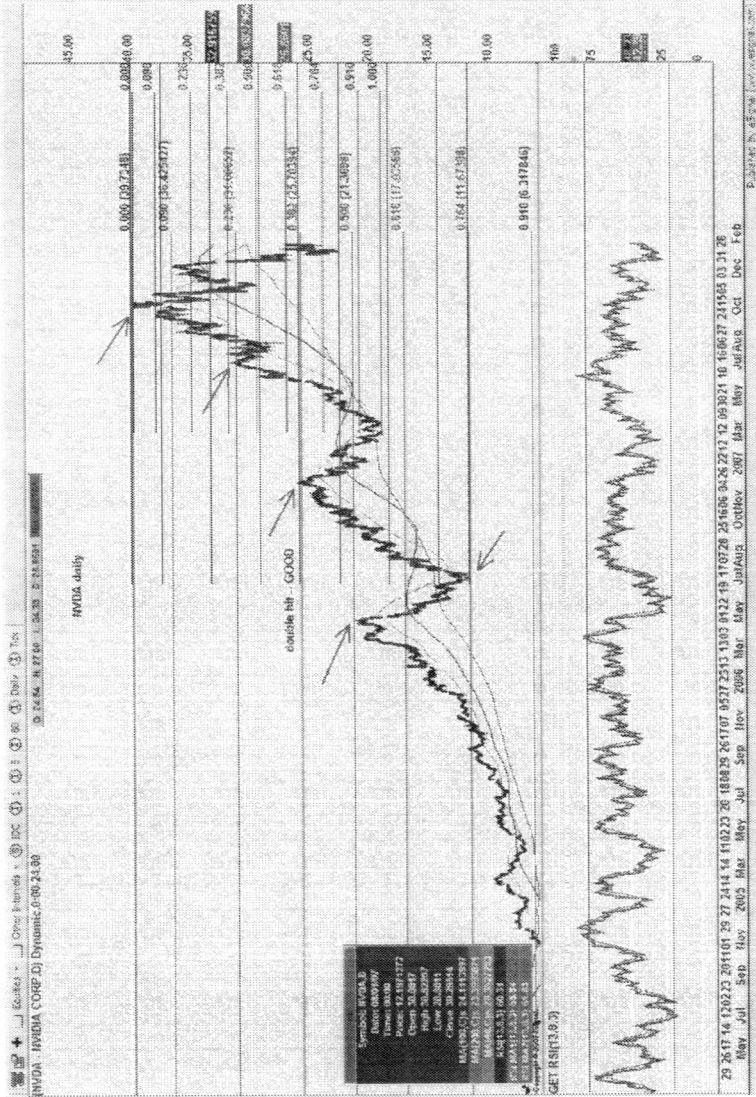

Figure 2 - Weekly chart for NVDA showing new Fibonacci bands   Source: eSignal

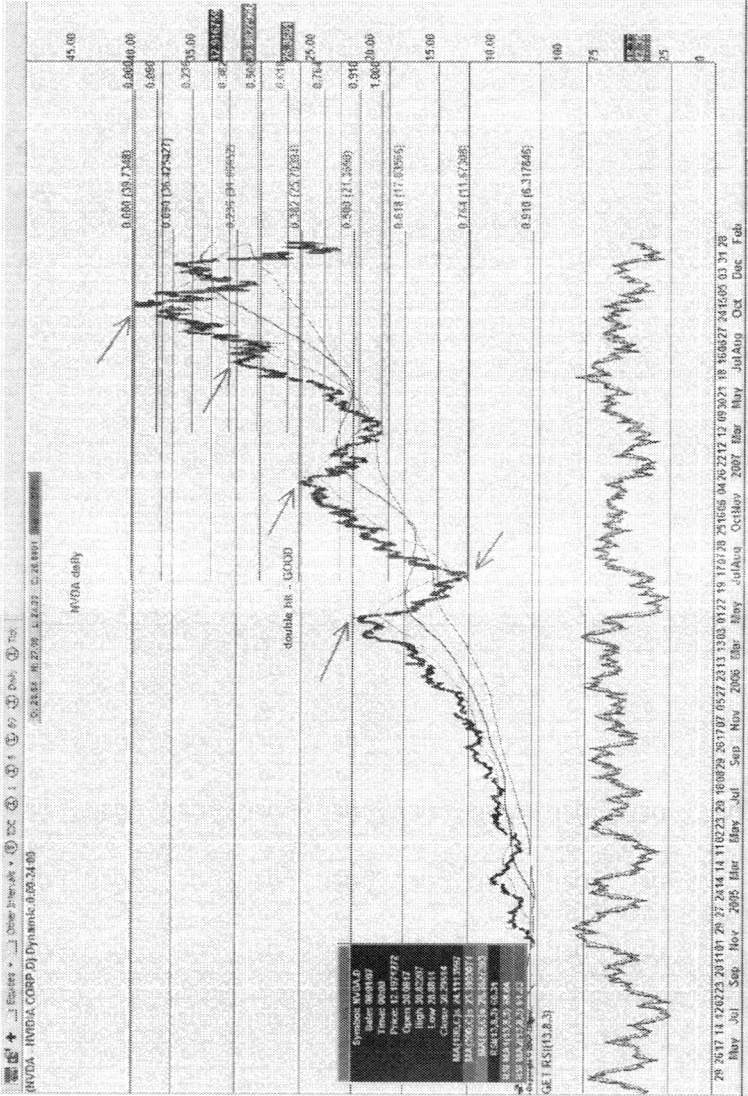

Figure 3 - Daily chart for NVDA showing new Fibonacci lines   Source: eSignal

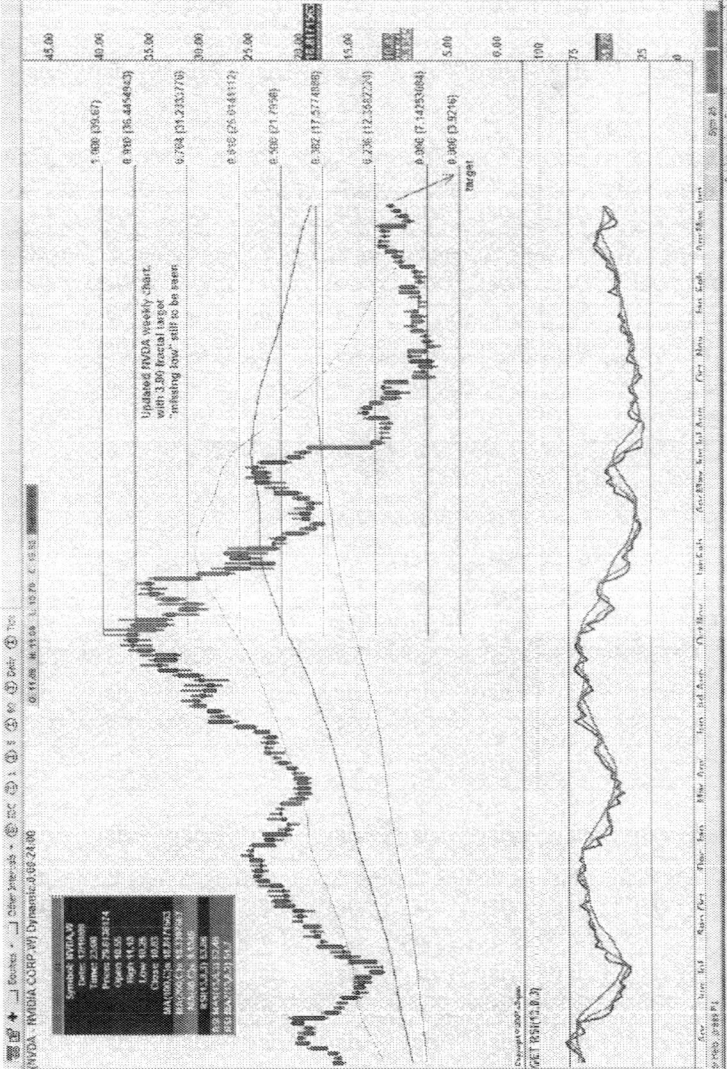

Figure 4 - Weekly chart for NVDA showing fractal target   Source: eSignal

101

Chapter 8

ANTONIO MANZINI

EXECUTIVE DIRECTOR, INVESTMENT SOLUTIONS EMEA

UBS GLOBAL ASSET MANAGEMENT

Antonio Manzini is senior project manager at UBS Asset Management in Zurich where he focuses on providing quantitative investment solutions to EMEA region clients. Antonio started as a senior economist at the Swiss Bank Corporation in the early 1990s, before going on to work in investment analysis at SBC Brinson and UBS Brinson. He joined UBS Asset management in 2000 when he was also Chief Investment Officer of UBS Alternative Investments in Italy.

USING TA FOR TRADE AND INVESTMENT DECISIONS

Can you explain your basic investment style?

In my department we search for early signs indicating the future direction, or trend, of the market, in this case the S&P 500. Contrary to the standard methodology employed by technical analysts, the approach followed here, which is purely rule based, does not attempt to uncover useful information from past prices. Rather, it looks for supporting evidence elsewhere, in this case, from the volatility index (VIX).

How do you use the VIX index as a guide to market sentiment?

The VIX is a widely followed index. It is calculated by the Chicago Board Options Exchange (CBOE) by blending the implied volatility of a wide range of S&P500 index options, both calls and puts. The VIX index provides, at any point in time, an estimation of the expected volatility of S&P500 returns over the next 30 days. Several studies have documented the accuracy of this estimation: the VIX offers a reasonable forecast of the future realized volatility. Also, it moves inversely to the S&P500 and this relationship is stronger when the S&P500 declines. That's the reason why the index is also known as the 'fear gauge'. Indeed, from the beginning of 1992 to the beginning of 2009, the correlation between the weekly returns of the VIX and S&P500 was equal to -0.43 for an increase in the S&P500, and -0.58 for declines in the stock index.

Few studies deal with the possible relationship between implied volatility and future stock returns. This is a challenging topic, while VIX *per se* is not intended to forecast market directions. Indeed, a high level of the VIX simply indicates that investors are particularly uncertain about near-term expected returns. Yet, market participants, and in particular traders, share the belief that swings in implied volatility yield good clues to the future direction of the market. An increase in the implied volatility value is associated with fear in the market, whereas a decline indicates complacency. As a measure of fear and complacency, implied volatility is often used as a contrarian indicator: prolonged and/or extremely high VIX readings indicate a high degree of anxiety – or even panic – and are regarded as a bullish indicator. Prolonged and/or extremely low readings indicate a high degree of complacency, and are generally regarded as a bearish indicator.

Can you explain how and to what degree you use TA in making investment decisions?
TA is indirectly used in making investment decisions. Indeed, if we believe that history has a tendency to repeat itself, then the relative level reached by the VIX provides useful information on future S&P500 returns.

Concretely, the implementation of the trading strategy necessitates, as a prerequisite, a workable definition of high and low VIX readings. As a matter of fact, the lion's share of the strategy hinges on the development of a quantitative procedure transforming the daily implied volatility into a signal indicating whether it is opportune to open a buy-and-hold long position. More precisely, the current VIX level is set against the levels it reached during the previous two years, which are divided into 20 equally spaced percentiles. If the current VIX level fits into one of the top percentiles, then the VIX is regarded as high and, consequently the return expected from opening a long position on the S&P500 is correspondingly high. The reverse holds true: VIX levels corresponding to bottom percentiles point to an overbought stock market.

How does your application of TA differ for short, medium and long-term time scales?

Because of its rule based nature, the investment methodology may be readily applied to various investment horizons. Actually, it can be assessed historically on which horizon predictions were most accurate. To this end, from the beginning of 1992 to the beginning of 2009, I associate the VIX level of each trading day with the forward return achieved by opening a long position on the S&P500 over a period of 5, 15 and 60 trading days. I then compute the average return for each reading of the VIX. For instance, over a 5 trading day investment horizon, the average forward return stands at -0.13% when the VIX falls into the lowest percentile (this occurred in 536 days out 4500), while it is equal to 2.09% when it falls into the highest percentile (in 50 days). The average forward returns for the intermediate VIX readings are contained within these two boundaries. The same exercise can be undertaken for the forward returns over 15 and 60 days. The results confirm the pattern that was found for the five days calculations.

The traders' belief seems to be proven accurate by the data: if we stay away from the market when volatility is low, then we avoid low (even negative) returns. On the other hand, we could reap appealing returns if we open a long position when volatility is high. The question about over which time horizon the strategy performs better may be answered in different ways. I opted for determining to what extent the average return can be raised if I stay out of the market whenever the VIX readings are low. The benchmark is provided by the return achieved when I am invested all the time in the stock market. It turns out that, for investment periods of 5 and 15 days, the highest increase in the average return can be obtained if we refrain from investing whenever the VIX falls into the lowest 30% of cases. For the longest investment period considered (60 trading days), the best result can be achieved by heeding the VIX signal whenever it falls into the lowest 70% of cases. Over the 5 days investment horizon, the average return increases by 31%, over 15 days by 13%, and over 60 days by 6%. Hence, the strategy is successful over short periods. Beyond 60 days, the signal of the VIX blurs: I take this as a clear indication that the efficiency of this strategy fades beyond the three month horizon.

During the recent market turbulence in 2008, has TA performed better or worse than usual?

The trading strategy didn't perform very well during the recent market turbulence. However, it should be pointed out that as an indicator of fear, VIX sent an unambiguous signal. Indeed, when the readings of the VIX were particularly high, the associated forward returns have been correspondingly high. The best result in turbulent market conditions (that is, June 2007) were achieved over the 5 days investment period.

Does TA have anything useful to say about portfolios and diversification?

If TA has anything to say about portfolios and diversification, then it is relevant in making tactical asset allocation decisions. These investment decisions require a judgement to be made about which asset class the portfolio manager wants to over or underweight. One possibility of making such judgment consists in performing a fundamental analysis of the different asset classes in order to predict their future relative returns. This is not an easy task though, in particular due to problems in identifying the model that produces the optimal predictions and in collecting the relevant information. Is the difficulty of reading an optimal decision a sufficient reason to give up any hope of making a good decision? Not if the portfolio manager can rely on a heuristic that is a fast and frugal decision-making strategy that allows him or her to make decisions without having to gather an extensive amount of information. From this perspective, TA is a heuristic, whose potential in asset allocation decisions is largely still to be explored.

Do you think TA and quants are closely related?

Yes, they are. I consider them as complementary tools, more than substitutes. Interestingly, even the most distinctive activity within TA, namely chart reading, has recently received some attention from the 'quants'. Indeed, in a paper published in the The Journal Of Finance in August 2000 *(Foundations of Technical Analysis: Computational Algorithms, Statistical Inference, and Empirical Implementation)* Andrew W. Lo, Harry Mamaysky, and Jiang Wang develop a systematic and scientific approach to identify regularities in the time series of prices by extracting nonlinear patterns from noisy data.

In other words, the authors' aim is to separate significant price movements that contribute to the formation of specific patterns from random fluctuations which should be ignored. The authors conclude that the indicators they derive provide incremental information and may have some practical value.

Do you classify VIX analysis as a form of technical analysis?

Yes, like standard TA, VIX analysis seeks to detect signals from repetition of old patterns.

Can you explain in more detail the procedure by which you transform the VIX reading into a trading signal?

The idea behind the transformation of the VIX reading into a trading signal is relatively straightforward. A 'high' reading of the VIX signals that it is opportune to open a buy-and-hold long position, whereas a 'low' reading suggests staying out of the market. But what is a high and what is a low level? A quantitative procedure that performs this transformation is needed. The one I adopted here ranks firstly all the VIX readings of the previous two years from the lowest to the highest. This list contains a little more than 500 values. These values are then classified into 20 equally spaced percentiles. Finally, a figure is given to the current VIX level according to its relative position in the list (1 if it is at the 5th percentile, 2 at the 10th percentile, etc.). If its value falls below the nil percentile, the current VIX receives a 0 value, and if it's above the 100th percentile the VIX reading receives a value of 21.

This transformation allows the switch from a qualitative description of the VIX level to a quantitative one that ranks the current level according to its recent history. If the VIX is high, it will be ranked at, say, 15 and above, whereas a very high VIX lies at around 20. When the VIX is at 21, it means that the current level is higher than the maximum value reached in the previous two years.

The final step consists of defining the trading signal that is setting the rank above which a long position will be entered into. This is an empirical issue. Let's consider the following picture: relating the VIX rank to the following 5-day return from opening a long position on the S&P500. Figure 1 has the rank on the horizontal axis and the return on the vertical one. For instance, from the beginning of 1992 to the close of the first quarter of 2009, there were 142 occurrences where the VIX fell into the 7th rank. The average return realized on the following 5 days over these 142 occurrences was equal to 0.47%.

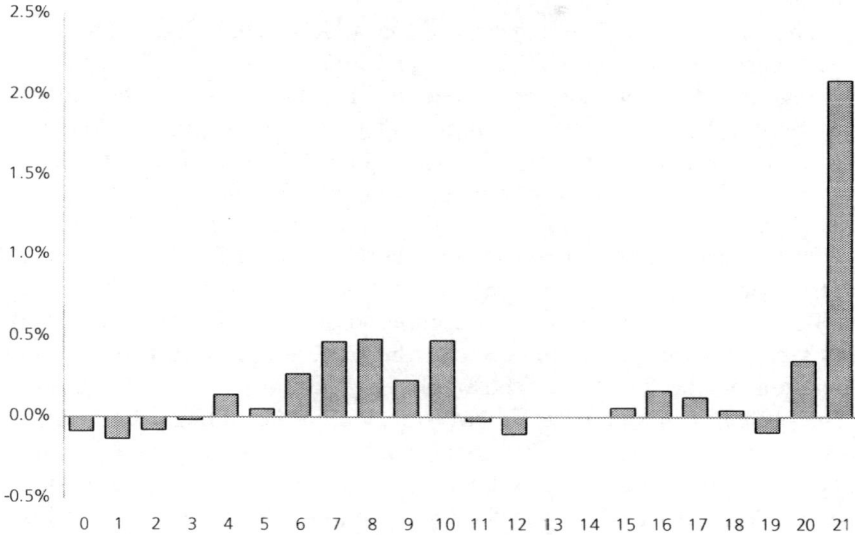

Figure 1

The picture reveals a pattern. To the lower ranks are associated negative average returns, whereas opening a 5-day long position when the VIX rank was equal to 21 (the maximum) would have returned on average 2.1%, visibly the highest return. This explains the VIX popularity: high levels of implied volatility seem definitely to indicate a stock market bottom. Noteworthy is the fact that there is no clear pattern between rank 10 and rank 15.

To further illustrate the results, I define the trading signal as the VIX falling into the 6th rank or higher. This means that whenever the VIX falls into the 6th class or higher, then a long position on the S&P500 is opened. Below this mark, money is not invested in the S&P500 and returns the Libor rate.

Do you have any historical data on how reliable the VIX is in forecasting market movements?

There are different possibilities to assess the reliability of the VIX in forecasting market movements. Ideally, every time we receive a signal from the VIX we would like to transform it into the right investment decision; either open a long position on the S&P500 or invest in a risk free instrument.

The simplest way of measuring the VIX's reliability consists in counting the number of times the signal resulted in the right investment decision, as opposed to the number of times the signal misfired. To recap, the signal for opening a long position on the S&P500 occurs whenever VIX is ranked 6th or higher. Figure 2 summarizes the results from the beginning of 1992 until the end of the first quarter of 2009. Over this period, there have been 4501 trading days, or possibilities, to make an investment decision based on the VIX reading. The graph is constructed as follows: For each of the 4501 investment occurrences, I compute both the 5 day return of the VIX-based investment strategy and the same length return of a long position on the S&P500. These returns define a point on the graph. The perfect VIX signal would have resulted in the strategy returning a small positive amount (Libor) when the market was falling (corresponding to a point on the shaded line), whereas a rising market would have resulted in the strategy yielding the same return (this occurs for points on the 45° green line). If all the points lie on both branches of the green line, then the hit ratio would be equal to 100%. Over the period considered, the hit ratio was equal to 54.4%, which is more than enough to add value to the strategy portfolio over the long-only portfolio.

There is a drawback to this measure: all investment decisions are treated equally. In reality, it could very well be the case that I make many 'small' wrong decisions, but I hit a few large positive decisions. Hence, the financial consequences of each decision should be taken into account. Since investment decisions are made on the basis of the VIX ranking, it is natural to compute the average return associated with each rank. The picture above illustrates this relationship over the 5-day investment horizon, whereas Table 1 shows, in addition, the values for the 15-day and 60-day horizons. The pattern at the shorter horizons (5 and 15 days) is similar and confirms the impression that lower returns are associated with lower ranks, while the highest return can be achieved when the VIX rank is equal to 21. At the 60-day horizon the quality of the signal weakens.

How reliable is the VIX in anticipating market turning points?

The VIX offers a high degree of reliability in anticipating market turning points, in particular, market bottoms. This can be verified by exploiting a characteristic of market bottoms. If it's indeed a bottom, the return from a long position in the stock market opened at the bottom and held immediately thereafter is positive, whereas the return of a position opened immediately before and sold at the bottom is negative. Hence, if the latter return is deducted from the former, then the result is a positive amount. For instance, on the 20th of November 2008 the VIX level was ranked in category 21 (the maximum) and the S&P 500 reached a bottom at 1206. The return realized by opening a long position that day, and holding it for 5 trading days, would have been equal to 18%, whereas closing a long position opened 5 days before would have resulted in a loss of 17.4%. The difference between the two is equal to around 35%; a clear indication of a bottom. By systematically calculating the difference between the forward return and the backward return in all occurrences when the VIX was ranked in category 21, we find strong positive data consistently above the results associated with other VIX ranks. Figure 3 illustrates the relationship between the VIX category 21 and the S&P 500 since the end of 1999. The vertical line indicates that the VIX was ranked in category 21.

Figure 4 shows the correlation between the VIX and the S&P 500. I filtered the daily data by applying a 50-day moving average to both series. With short-term volatility filtered out, it is visible that the two series are negatively correlated (-0.63 over the whole period, -0.73 over the last 10 years).

You mention the correlation with returns being -0.43 and -0.58; How tradable are these figures? Is it possible to develop a trading strategy based almost exclusively on the VIX index?

It is difficult to develop a trading strategy with just current values of both VIX and S&P 500. Indeed, I often receive the signal when I don't have materially the possibility to trade on it. That's the reason why I developed the framework linking the current VIX level with the future S&P500 return.

The VIX is often quoted in the press as a fear gauge and a measure of market sentiment. Do you think the value and usefulness of the VIX is accurately represented?

Probably but this should be verified on sentiment data. Apparently the relationship between the put/call ratio and the VIX is not that strong.

rank	# occurrences	5	15	60
0	62	-0.09%	0.15%	1.58%
1	511	-0.13%	-0.08%	0.78%
2	295	-0.08%	0.08%	0.48%
3	219	-0.02%	0.08%	0.26%
4	231	0.13%	0.22%	0.61%
5	179	0.05%	0.26%	1.15%
6	170	0.26%	0.49%	1.35%
7	142	0.47%	0.79%	1.96%
8	137	0.48%	0.88%	1.89%
9	133	0.23%	0.96%	2.26%
10	137	0.47%	0.52%	1.19%
11	140	-0.02%	-0.15%	1.13%
12	138	-0.10%	0.34%	-1.32%
13	164	0.00%	0.11%	-0.52%
14	171	0.00%	0.20%	-0.35%
15	169	0.06%	0.89%	1.83%
16	205	0.16%	0.84%	2.39%
17	220	0.12%	0.14%	1.86%
18	263	0.04%	-0.37%	1.15%
19	292	-0.09%	0.43%	1.83%
20	473	0.35%	0.66%	3.54%
21	50	2.09%	2.49%	4.52%

Table 1

To what extent do you quantify the value of the VIX? For example, can you make an accurate interpretation of what a reading of 30 (for example) actually means or is it all relative?

It is essentially a relative play. This means that if today's reading of the VIX is 30 and the values immediately before were similarly high, then 30 is not a 'high' reading. However, if VIX scored between 10 and 20, then 30 is a high reading.

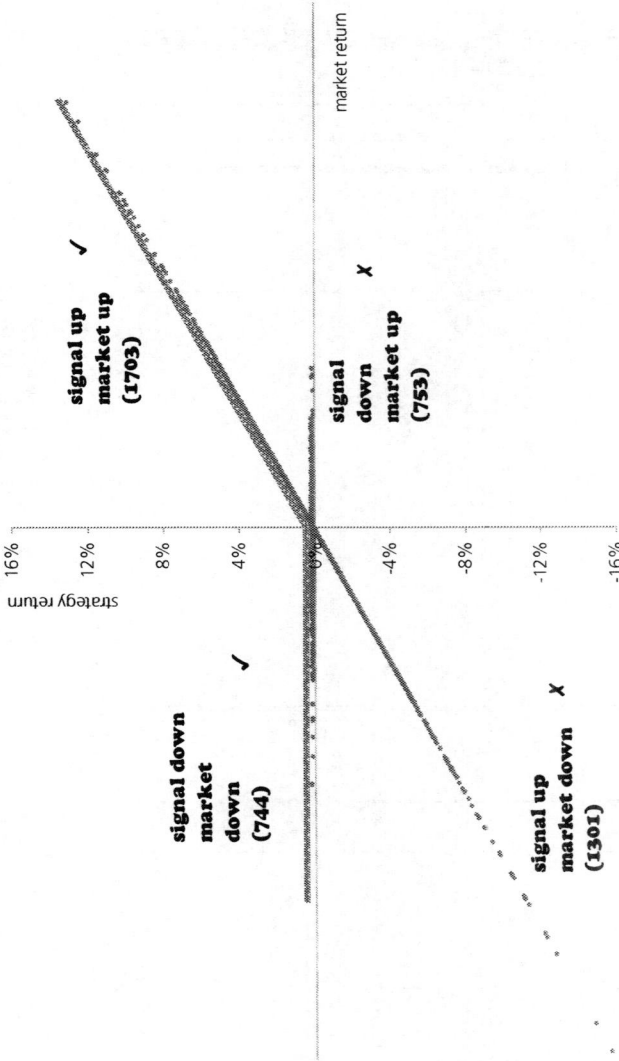

Figure 2   Measuring VIX reliability 1992-2009

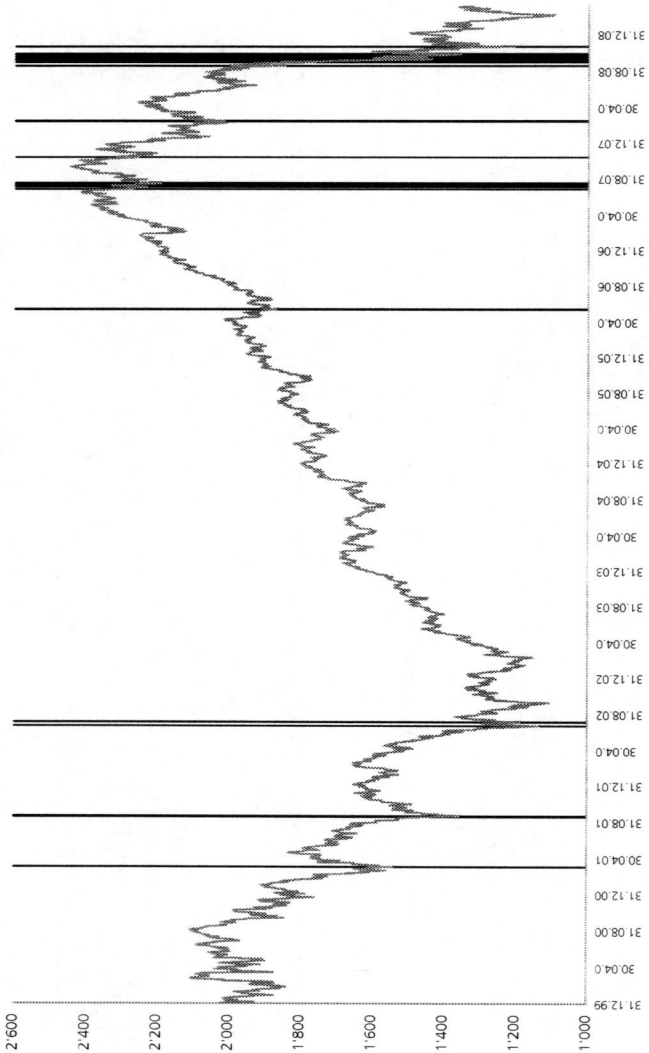

Figure 3   VIX category 21 and the S&P500

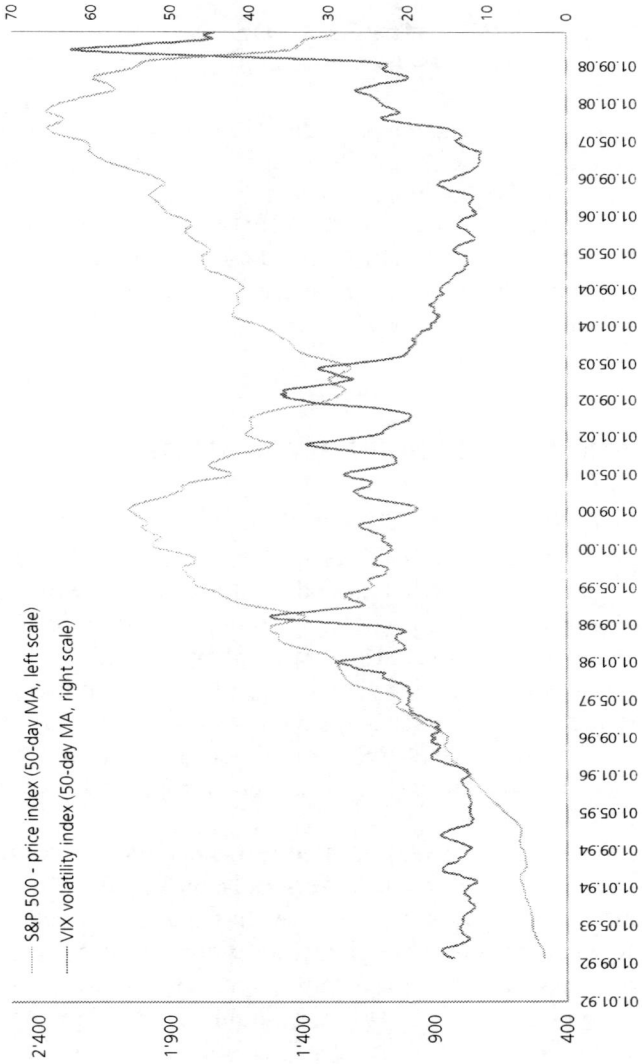

Figure 4   Correlation between VIX and the S&P500

Chapter 9

CHARLES MORRIS

HEAD OF ABSOLUTE RETURN STRATEGY

HSBC GLOBAL ASSET MANAGEMENT

Charles Morris is a director of HSBC Global Asset Management and is head of the Absolute Return Strategy team with total assets under management of US$2 billion, invested in global equities, bonds and commodities. He also manages the HSBC Global Trend fund which is the core equity strategy for Absolute. Working in a team of four, his clients are mostly high net worth individuals. Prior to joining HSBC in 1998, Charles was an officer in the British Army's Grenadier Guards.

USING TA FOR TRADE AND INVESTMENT DECISIONS

Can you explain your basic investment style?

I am a trend follower focusing on relative strength (RS). RS is also known as 'price relative' but should not be confused with RSI. In its simplest form, RS is determined by dividing a historic price series by its reference index series. The result shows whether the asset is stronger or weaker than its peer group. The most important driver being the fact that the asset I am buying is stronger than the others around it, and this is what RS is all about. That means the primary driver is stock selection and not market timing, which often causes confusion in TA circles.

RS increases the odds that the trends that we follow will be strong. Some might say that trend followers only move after the event and buy things that have already gone up; this has some truth but in so doing, the odds of success are significantly improved. Stocks that lead the market, identified by RS, can continue to rise for much longer that you might typically expect. In my opinion, trend following with the support of RS works approximately 70% of the time. During the other 30%, you'd be better off tracking the index or sitting on the sidelines. This also enforces the idea that RS needs a rigorous stop-loss discipline as long-term trends do eventually end. Although I do not sell short, I would suggest that RS should only be used as a long only strategy and is unsuitable for short selling. I will expand on that a bit later but essentially, RS is a medium to long-term strategy and short selling is inherently short-term.

So you are a great believer in momentum strategies?

Numerous studies have proven the momentum effect whereby stocks that have already outperformed the market continue to do so which is RS in its simplest form. The most notable work in recent times was carried out by Dr Paul Marsh from the London Business School. He backtested various stock markets back to 1900 and concluded that momentum was one of the greatest sources of excess return. Some describe that opportunity as 'alpha', but I would describe it as 'beta'. I say that since alpha is supposed to be an uncorrelated source of excess return and the momentum effect is highly correlated to the market, it is almost certainly beta. That means it rises and falls harder and faster than the market, but is a great way to make money. The volatility may be high but the returns can be even higher. All in all, it is a better bet than applying leverage to the index, so it is therefore effective.

Can you give an example where relative strength has worked well?

As an example, Microsoft was a truly great investment, rising 624 fold over 12 years from 1987 to 1999 at a compound rate of 43%. This stock had spectacular RS and to buy the dips would have been a very profitable strategy. Buying and holding Microsoft would have been even better due to the extraordinary compounding effect, but that is easy to say in hindsight. Of course few people did, as most fundamental investors would have sold out far too soon as the stock was forever outrageously expensive. It is only now that the company is no longer a growth stock that it has finally become cheap, but that is no reason to buy it. The reason that Microsoft no longer has RS is because Windows is a mature business model that has faced great competition since 2000. My approach is to identify the greatest names in the business using RS and trade them using conventional TA techniques.

The reality is that buying low and selling high is a dangerous strategy when the underlying stock is questionable, but it is a great strategy if the stock is sound. The fact that a stock has been able to beat the market is a sign of its success and that it has the potential to do more. It is wrong to assume that a stock that has already risen has reached its top; we only need to remind ourselves of Microsoft's 624 fold rise to illustrate that point.

Can you explain how you use TA in making investment decisions?

The quick answer is that TA lies at the heart of my investment approach. The more detailed answer explains why and centres upon the three factors that I consider to be worthwhile in evaluating an investment: quality, value and trend.

Quality tells us how robust an asset is. The price of bonds may rise or fall but since the government owns the printing press, they are guaranteed to deliver what they said they would. Corporate bonds are less certain as the company can go bust, so they are lower quality than government bonds and pay higher yields as a result. The same is true in the stock market and it follows that the consumer staples, food retailers and pharmaceuticals tend to be higher quality companies than the mining, technology or industrial sectors, as they have much better earnings visibility and stability. High quality companies are better placed to shake off the economic cycle, whereas lower quality companies are at its mercy. Note that I haven't stated which one will make more money, but which one is more stable.

How do you assess the viability of a stock?

Quality can be assessed by fundamental factors or on a qualitative basis by researching the asset. However, I think the market does a good job of this and delivers a reliable result more quickly and efficiently by using technical factors such as volatility and correlation. Periodically the market is wrong and a seemingly low risk security can disappoint, but more often than not the market turns out to be a pretty good judge of how things are. Understanding asset quality is important as it can be used as a style overlay which can be adjusted according to market conditions. You may have heard the phrase 'GIGO' which stands for 'garbage in, garbage out'.

If you apply a technical strategy (breakouts, DeMark, oscillators etc...) to low quality stocks, don't be surprised when you get a GIGO result when the market turns against you. Low quality stocks love bull markets but hate bear markets and a trading strategy requires high portfolio turnover. For a high quality strategy, the opposite is true and whilst the portfolio will lag the bull market, it will almost certainly beat the bear and thus play the role of the tortoise who always wins in the end. Sometimes, you want to own low quality assets as they make

116

much more money when the going's good, but this should be a tactical factor and not a permanent investment style. For me, the leading factor in determining asset quality is price volatility, so that is technical; however I also look at balance sheet strength such as the Altman Z score and ROCE which are fundamental.

Does technical analysis have anything to say about stock valuation?

Valuation is impossible to read on the charts and should be left to fundamental analysis. Something that has fallen in price may not be cheap and something that has risen may not be expensive, but it is a common failing to confuse the two. As the saying goes, don't look for support at the bottom of the page as it isn't there. Holders of Marconi, Worldcom and Northern Rock learnt that lesson only too well. Cheap stocks don't necessarily perform well, but expensive assets do have a tendency to unwind at breakneck speed when the music stops, particularly if their quality is low, so ignore valuation at your peril.

Don't forget that high quality assets are often expensive as you are paying for a 'stability premium' and you also receive dividends. It is important to combine quality and value factors as you can give up ground on one, provided you make it up on the other. Basically avoid stocks that are both expensive and low quality as they are destructive. In determining value, I would stick to fundamental analysis. I don't think this needs to be overly complex and dividend yield, price to sales, price to earnings and price to cash flow are all useful metrics.

Trend is determined using technical analysis by assessing price and volume over different time horizons. There is an army of indicators to accompany this analysis which tends to seek out either trend or reversion strategies. Other technical factors can be helpful such as sentiment or market positioning. Quite obviously, trend is determined by TA. So the answer to your question weights asset quality at 30% (mainly technical but some fundamental), valuation at 20%, and trend at 50%. In other words TA is the most important factor.

Why did you choose to use TA? What made you convinced it works?

Let us examine a company that makes widgets which are very profitable and the order book is healthy. Do the shares go up or down? The one dimensional answer would be 'up' as the company is making money. But perhaps the market already knows that so has already priced the shares high enough to reflect the merits of the situation. Then the company reports its results and they make a lot of money, perhaps even more than the market expects, so you might think the shares should rise further. But, what you may not know is that the story has already been heavily marketed by the company's broker, so the story fails to attract new money despite the great earnings. Moreover, the whole sector is doing well and some of the competitors are doing even better. This might cause some traders to sell their holdings, causing the price to fall despite the higher profits. Add to this the behaviour of short sellers, the state of the overall market, the currency, interest rates and government policies and you soon realise that market prices digest an enormous amount of information.

Technical analysis studies the prices that digest all of this information through supply and demand, resulting in price equilibrium. When the balance is tipped, a trend occurs either north or south. It will always be the case that the secular trends continue for longer than you would normally expect as it takes a long time to shift popular thought. Stockbrokers often say 'buy the rumour, sell on fact', and this illustrates that as soon as the information is known, equilibrium is reached, and thus the trend is complete. We should remember to read the market as it is a leading indicator and drags the real world in its wake.

How does your application of TA differ for short, medium and long-term time scales?

Long-term trends (months) tend to be sustainable and it is an expensive habit to bet against them. Short-term trends (days) are fickle and tend to revert to their mean. In other words, bet against the short-term and go with the long-term. The medium-term (weeks) flirts with both trend and reversion making it not only the most challenging horizon over which to invest, but also the most profitable when you get it right. It is no surprise that the short-term is dominated by traders, the medium-term by hedge funds, and the long-term by the dividend collectors. My preferred areas are medium to long-term.

What technical strategies and indicators work best for the short-term analysis?

I do not trade much over the short-term but in principle I would try to act against the market. Some trend followers buy breakouts but the problem with this is that you are buying a heavily overbought stock which is statistically likely to revert.

118

However, there is one exception. Distressed stocks do not have trends as they are stocks that have fallen by 90% or so, yet are still liquid and capitalized above one billion dollars. This is important as the really bombed out ones will fall to zero and liquidity will evaporate, so I believe the floor in market cap is an important control measure. Also large companies with low market caps are more likely to recover than smaller ones, so I think size helps. These stocks can perform exceptionally well in a short space of time as they have the ability to multiply in price very quickly indeed, and so this universe is interesting although volatile. If you buy and hold all of them, you are destined to lose money as they can be deeply troubled companies.

However, on a case by case basis, trading short-term momentum is profitable. I would use short-term breakouts, DeMark weekly and monthly reversal signals, and perhaps even insider buying* as they wouldn't do that if it was going bust, (insiders are company officers such as directors and should not be confused with the illegal practice of trading on inside information). The volatility is high so position sizing should be reduced to reflect that, but it is an interesting area of the market. Sadly, the idea flow all comes at once, typically after a large market fall. However, there are special situations that occur during bull markets. For me, this is a side line and not my core strategy.

Over the medium-term, I use price relative moving averages and split them into five groups known as the 'quintiles'. Originally, I used to buy into the upper quintile of my screening universe. However, I have learnt a great deal in recent years and this strategy, whilst statistically successful, is very volatile. Now I blend the short, medium and long-term time horizons, aiming to identify the best long-term names and then buy the dips without chasing the market. To help me do that I use indicators such as moving averages, DMI, RSI, Bollinger Bands and DeMark.

What technical strategies and indicators work best for very long-term analysis?

In the long-term, I think trend and price relative are the most important factors. They enable you to identify the bull and bear markets and the leadership within them. In the 00s, that has meant the focus should stay on emerging markets and resources, avoiding the financials. In the 90s, the markets favoured technology stocks but disliked emerging markets and commodities. Understanding the secular trend stops you wasting time on the small stuff. Only a trader with a crystal ball and perfect foresight could have made money trading emerging markets and commodities in the 90s, whereas an average Joe could have cleaned up trading tech stocks over the same period. Why fight the tape?

During the recent market turbulence in 2008, has TA performed better or worse than usual?

That depends on how you judge it as technical styles vary far and wide. I did poorly last year (2008) as my portfolio lost 15%, although this wasn't bad for a long only portfolio. Not many of my competitors did much better, but one managed to make money as they hid in Japanese yen and bonds whilst sterling and the market fell.

Do you think CTAs (managed futures) did better in 2008 because of their greater use of technical strategies?

Some CTA funds (commodity trading advisors which follow trends in futures markets) did well, primarily because they can invest on a directional basis, both long and short in different asset classes. Their strategy is overwhelmingly technical and did well when it really mattered, and the underlying futures contracts that they trade remained liquid. That turned out to be a hugely important factor as many assets could not be sold at any price. The TA behind a successful CTA is not rocket science, but risk management is the factor that separates the men from the boys.

Trend following equity funds did poorly, even many of those that were able to sell short. The market leadership did well up until July 2008 and then collapsed along with commodities and emerging markets. 2008 was a bloodbath and we reduced risk in late 2007 and early 2008 thinking we were relatively defensively positioned, but the Lehman Brothers event dragged everything down with it. It has changed my attitude towards liquidity forever. That doesn't mean illiquid assets are out, just that I will assume that they are all correlated regardless of which asset class they are, and so will reduce the position size to reflect their higher risks.

Are some asset classes more technically driven than others?

I am not sure about dividing TA's usefulness along asset class lines as much as liquidity. Less liquid assets have low trading volumes meaning their price equilibrium is less valid than for liquid securities.

120

Once liquidity is established, TA works in currencies, bonds, equities and commodities. The lower liquidity tiers require a very different form of TA than the liquid universe. In other words, small caps, corporate bonds and peripheral commodities (e.g. emissions, butter and lead) can be analysed in different ways. There is less competition and so simpler stuff is more likely to work. So feel free to buy breakouts and watch the volume patterns.

In what way does the application of TA differ when using it to pick individual stocks as opposed to analysis of the index?

The index is diversified and therefore has much lower volatility than individual stocks. It tends to move like a supertanker whilst the stocks are the speedboats. Indices trend for longer periods of time whilst the underlying securities rotate in and out of favour. The index is driven by the cumulative flow of money into and out of equities, whereas individual stocks can be good or bad according to their merits.

The indices that best capture the prevailing leadership are good examples of this as the underlying stocks are seriously volatile, whereas the index tends to be fairly orderly. Tech stocks in the 90s and emerging markets in the 00s are good examples. To say that the index is boring or average misrepresents the situation as an investor's objective is to achieve healthy risk adjusted returns. That means healthy returns with lower volatility.

The market leadership is driven by huge capital inflows as the global funds can take years to get up to weight. By owning the index in the leadership, you surf this bow wave fairly effortlessly and achieve a good Sharpe ratio. By diversifying the various leading themes simultaneously, you can have a very profitable strategy during bull markets. The point of trading the individual stocks is so that you beat that effective, simple and profitable strategy. I aim to own the leading ETFs, alongside focusing on individual stocks. Since volatility is an important factor for me, I find the combination of the two works well as I can own ETFs in the more volatile leadership themes, and own the greatest cherry picks within developed markets in the Trend Fund.

How do you measure price volatility?

I measure volatility using two techniques: the first is the volatility of price and the second is the volatility of the RS. The simplest way is by using bandwidth from Bollinger Bands; I calculate it in Excel by using the standard deviation function over a data range of percentage change data. For weekly data, multiply the result by 52 (weeks in a year) which gives you the variance. To get volatility, just square root the result. For monthly data, multiply by 12 instead of 52, and so on. Price volatility can be useful for trading set ups such as volatility breakouts and so forth, but for my techniques, the key is the measurement of asset quality for which I use the RS volatility and not price.

What do you think are the drawbacks of using Bollinger Bands?

Bollinger bands (BBs) show trend, volatility and deviation. I do this same task digitally in my models on a currency adjusted basis for both price and RS. BBs are charts and so are laborious to view for many securities, so I prefer to do the same thing via a quant process. Like everything, they are not the Holy Grail, just a useful tool. Volatility breakouts can work well if the prior trading range is mature and the BBs are tight (low bandwidth), but I tend to think these signals work better at the macro level and not so well for individual stocks. Sure, there will be some great examples, but the statistical hit rate may be surprisingly disappointing.

Also don't forget that the signals all come at once, and when supported by a macro move (i.e. index breakout), will work much better than if they are not. In a nutshell, when the bands are wide and the price is beyond an outer band, use them to forecast a reversion to the mean against the trend. When they are tight, go with the trend. Many securities can live inside BBs and give no signals at all and so the comparison of different time horizons can help. Like everything, they need support from other technical methods.

Is a volatile stock usually a poor quality as you see it?

A stock with high RS volatility is poor quality in my opinion. That doesn't mean that it isn't an exceptional potential investment. High price volatility signifies that it has had a large directional move and doesn't measure quality per se. RS volatility is useful for defining your investable universe but you get what you wish for. Low RS volatility stocks are unlikely to excite, but there again they won't destroy you either and they can be considered a long-term investment. High RS volatility stocks can make you very rich or very poor so you have to trade them well and have good money management skills.

I am agnostic as to which you should trade; I just want to emphasize this incredibly important factor which will dictate your success or failure. Low RS volatility stocks can be bought on the dip relatively aggressively, whereas high RS volatility stocks really need more trend confirmation as buying the dip can be painful. High RS volatility stocks are more likely to be effective in short-term momentum strategies.

Are there any market conditions under which TA works better or worse than other times?

TA works best in bull markets because the trends are stronger for longer. Bear markets are fast and furious with frightening levels of volatility. To win during bull markets requires hard work and patience; let the market do the rest. To win during bear markets requires first class risk management. The trading style should be shorter-term and the asset quality should be high. Ideally, the best thing to do in bear markets is to shut down your book and hold government bonds until the Coppock indicator signals the green light. The difficulty is that not all bear markets are savage. If they were, we would routinely sell everything when the index dropped below its 200-day moving average. Unfortunately many are relatively mild corrections and separating the bad ones from the gentle ones is tricky.

Is there any evidence that fund managers who employ TA do better than those who don't?

It is impossible to prove which works as it is not the TA that is good or bad but the operator. I would say most investors look at charts but with varying degrees of success and the answers can, at times, be very subjective. TA is a very useful tool but does not provide all the answers.

Does TA have anything useful to say about portfolios and diversification?

Yes it certainly does. Technical factors such as trend, correlation, volatility and oscillator readings can be cumulatively added on a weighted basis across the portfolio and shown as risk factors. For example, diversification levels may be too low if the correlation between the holdings is high (beta) resulting in 'diworsifiction' as opposed to diversification; or a portfolio may have too many stocks that are overbought at the same time on a particular time horizon, meaning it would be very sensitive to market shocks.

Do you think TA and quants are closely related?

That depends on what is being quantified. My approach is based upon a quantitative process driven by technical factors where the sole input is price. I can't speak for all, but most quants would tend to have a multi factor model looking at earnings momentum, valuation, balance sheet strength and price momentum. Where they often fall over is that the behaviour of short-term price and earnings momentum are remarkably similar. I would argue that by following the short-term price action, you'll do better than by following analysts' forecasts as price is quicker off the mark in reflecting change. The standard quant momentum component is often simplistic and focuses on the medium-term horizon. As I said earlier, the medium-term is the most dangerous as it flips around at great speed from hugely deviated positions. Thus quants, or the bad ones a least, end up owning the overbought momentum stocks that are very crowded at the top of the market.

Remember that by embracing long-term RS, the top quintile represents just 20% of the market. So you have already cut your work load by 80% on this simple screen. Thereafter, keep the screens light and just eliminate factors that you don't like such as too overbought, too crowded, too volatile, illiquid, low quality, expensive, and so on. You'll soon have a manageable list from which the technicals can do the rest. Screening for good stocks is an easily crowded concept as the positive factors are so obvious. My model covers 2500 global stocks and my watch lists are cut down to around 200 names, but this varies according to market conditions. To cut it further would be detrimental as we are in the business of improving the odds, not looking for the Holy Grail.

How easy is it to use TA? Do you think training is required? Are any techniques misused or misunderstood?

TA is an art and the outcome is subjective. There are numerous disciplines and you will never stop learning. My advice is to find something that you can relate to and the best way to do that is by reading good books and talking to experienced people. The classics by Murphy, Pring and Weinstein are a must too, but don't mistake TA with trading. TA is all about forecasting whereas trading is entry, exit, position sizing and money management. It takes practice and hard work to understand any technique and I would advise against overconfidence.

INDICATORS AND STRATEGIES

What is your reaction when the charts show a very obvious technical pattern such as a head-and-shoulders or a double top?

I do not rate these sorts of patterns. I once saw a study that showed head-and-shoulders tops to have a 50% success rate. I am not saying they aren't valid but there are better techniques out there that will deliver better results. We have to study a pattern for what it is. Head-and-shoulders tops are simply trends that failed to make new highs as the last move is a lower high. Does that mean collapse is impending? Of course not; it means falls on some occasions and consolidation on others, hence the 50:50 outcome.

How do you identify when a trend has commenced and may be nearing its end?

The common technique that is written about in some technical texts is the 'range breakout'. It sounds good as you hope that you are buying at the beginning of a huge move. However, in reality, what you are really doing is buying a security that is heavily overbought at the start. That means that in order to be a successful trade it has to generate additional returns to compensate for the initial overbought position. Text book case studies flatter this method, but statistically, the hit rate will be disappointing unless the market is especially strong. I mentioned earlier that the exception is distressed stocks which have been serial underperformers. They can rally very quickly, which is why I'd urge caution shorting them without good risk management.

It may sound obvious but trends do not begin at the breakout, but instead at the lowest price point just before they reverse. By the time a trend has confirmed itself, a portion of it has already taken place and you mustn't forget that. Being in at the low sounds ideal, but your time is better spent seeking higher probability and stronger stocks than focusing on the lowest price. That is something best done by value investors who know a great deal about the company they are buying and are happy to add to their position as the price drops. The DMI (directional movement indicator) can be effective as it is more subtle and identifies breakouts as they are happening, as opposed to after they have happened. Generally speaking, I would bet that systematically buying new price trend signals is much less effective that one might think. I do go along with some breakouts as from time to time you have to, but I prefer to go against the short-term trend and go with the established long-term trend.

The end of the trend is the most difficult thing to spot until afterwards. Lows are generally deemed to be easier to spot than highs. Most recently I have become a fan of DeMark indicators. I wish I had discovered them long ago as I think they are really effective and objective in identifying exhaustion. Of course, DeMark would have gotten you out of Microsoft about ten years early! It is the winners that generate your returns and running them is vital. I suggest that when you suspect a top, you reduce your position rather than sell it as that also helps to reduce trading costs.

What is the best method for measuring price momentum in the market?

I use RS over different time frames. I also currency adjust it resulting in what I call CAPR (pronounced "Cap R"). That means a Mexican stock is converted into dollars and then divided by the world index measured in dollars. The currency is the same on the numerator and denominator and therefore eliminated, resulting in a ratio. I think the longer-term measures over many months are really effective in identifying the universe of tradable stocks. I also calculate CAPR on a weekly and daily basis so I can measure the trend strength, volatility and so on. All of these factors help me to build my screens. As a general rule, RS works best on a medium to long-term basis and price is more effective in the short- term.

How can TA be used in making sector rotation and asset allocation decisions?

In managing the asset allocation for my fund, I often look at the ratio between equities and bonds, equities and commodities, gold and silver and so on. I look at these relationships over different time periods and form a view. All in all, there are over a thousand of these ratios set up on my Bloomberg and I am forever creating new ones. As I write, the last two I have set up are US long futures measured in euros and commodities relative to emerging market equities.

Does TA have a role when shorting the market?

I do not sell short but have considered this question on numerous occasions as it is so often asked. The whole point of what I do is to identify trends. Good companies compound in value as the price rises, so there can be an unlimited profit. Bad long trades have limited losses as they can only fall by 100%. Short sellers work in reverse and have limited profits and unlimited losses which is potentially devastating. Short sellers are better off knowing that the targets are facing a material change that is not reflected in the price. Technical analysis can then be used to help manage the risk and identify suitable candidates, but I would advise against shorting the weakest as measured by RS. Sometimes it will work well, especially during the depths of a bear market, but that doesn't happen very often. During bull markets, oversold stocks tend to rally, and I do not believe the hit rate will be good enough to make it a useful screen. I am talking about medium to long-term RS, not some data series of a few days or weeks. What I would say is that long-term RS bear candidates that are heavily overbought, are more likely to deliver on the short side in bull markets. These stocks are the same names that other TA traders are buying as they have just broken out above a medium-term resistance level. The poor long-term RS suggests that their follow through is unlikely to be sustainable. So technicians can be at opposite sides of the same trade. Remember, I said that distressed stocks can be a buy on the breakout? Well to clarify, it is when those rallies are mature that there is an interesting opportunity to go short. Distressed RS stocks are full of excitement in both directions which is why hedge funds focus on them so much.

How does your application of TA differ for different asset classes?

As previously mentioned, I buy strong RS stocks against the trend in the equity fund. However, when trading ETFs for my fund, short-term momentum works well as indices are less likely to pull back so violently due to their diversification. I like to own the global leadership assuming factors such as liquidity, volatility and fundamental factors stack up.

How do you use moving averages? If so, which periodicities do you use and do you use them directly to generate trade signals?

I use 25-week, 35-week and 50-week simple moving averages. I don't think that tweaking with those time horizons will make much difference. I first heard these periods at a presentation given by Rick Bensignor who at the time was the technical strategist at Morgan Stanley. They work well in my opinion but I also like the idea of volatility adjusted moving averages but have never managed to bring them into my process.

How do you use moving averages?

I use all sorts of moving averages. The time horizon is the key to what you are trying to discover. For example, to ascertain long-term bull markets, I use 40-month simple moving averages. For macro trend confirmation, I use 30, 40, 50, 60 and 70-week moving averages in a ten year chart for indices. For the daily charts, I am currently using 22 and 26-days as we are in a high volatility environment. If the market cools down, I will increase them.

How do you judge if a market is overbought or oversold?

Bollinger Bands can be effective and they convinced me to sell Asia in late October 2007, right on the high. They also gave a strong signal on agricultural commodities in early 2008 which also turned out to be spot on. I tend to use weekly and monthly bands to capture the big picture; the daily readings are just noise. Long-term volatility breakouts are worth keeping an eye on, the best example of which is the S&P500 in early 1995; a spectacular signal.

Do you keep an eye on volume levels, and if so, how do you use them in your decisions?

I take the view that the huge flows in ETFs and OTC business has changed the nature of the market from how it was in the history books, so I don't see the value in volume studies. In small caps where these forces are less apparent, I think traditional signals such as breakout on volume may even work.

Do you employ any counter-trend strategies?

I mentioned Tom DeMark's indicators earlier. I went to one of his talks and he is unquestionably a genius who has done some pioneering and brilliant work. He has worked alongside some of the greatest hedge funds in the world and they clearly value his indicators, as do Bloomberg who distribute his system. I am only a DeMark beginner but his indicators have been extremely helpful in plotting where a trend is in terms of its maturity and risk. You can also get different readings over different time horizons which help to gauge the bigger picture. Above all, trading counter to the trend is psychologically difficult and having an indicator that guides you through the process, and can advise on conviction and risk, is a huge leap forward for me. Tom would say it is an indicator and not a system, so use it as a tool alongside your existing process.

As for contrarian indicators, well the obvious ones such as the front cover of the tabloids will always be timeless tools. However, I follow Ned Davis's sentiment indicators, the Commitment of Traders report, AAII data and the general market noise.

Chapter 10

RASHPAL SOHAN

ASSET ALLOCATION ANALYST

RATHBONE BROTHERS

&

ROBIN GRIFFITHS

TECHNICAL ANALYST

CAZENOVE CAPITAL MANAGEMENT

Rashpal Sohan graduated from the London School of Economics with a first class degree in Actuarial Science. He joined Rathbone Brothers in 2005 as an asset allocation analyst working with Robin Griffiths, the head of asset allocation. He specialises in the use of quantitative techniques in the analysis of global markets, with particular emphasis on building models for system trading and investment purposes.

Robin Griffiths joined Cazenove Capital Management in early 2008, prior to which he was head of asset allocation and technical research at private wealth management company Rathbone Brothers, in London. Robin was previously with HSBC Investment Bank and is one of the global financial markets' best known and most respected technical analysts.

USING TA FOR TRADE AND INVESTMENT DECISIONS

Can you explain your basic investment style?
The basis of our system centres on the fact that markets move in trends. These trends appear more frequently and last for longer than the laws of chance allow. This idea withstands all backtesting on different universes and in differing time periods.

The second step in our reasoning is based on probabilities rather than certainties. When the rate of rise or fall of the trends is measured and arranged in descending order, there is a significant probability that the strongest trends will persist; the chances of them suddenly reversing are low. By always buying only the strongest rising trends, or shorting the strongest downtrends, the risk to reward ratio of this strategy computes favourably in the long run.

We prefer to use regression analysis to identify trends. In this respect, we visualize the trend as a line down the middle of a data set, with deviations above and below it. Any deviation bigger than three standard deviations is inherently likely to be a breakout into a new trend rather than a continuing old trend. In this way we can use accepted statistical techniques to judge an overbought or oversold condition. In practice, using the rate of rise of moving averages works as well as regression analysis.

The next part of our system is to know when to do a regression, and in this regard we relate to the cycles that appear in economic activity. In particular we use a version of the model published by Joseph Schumpeter. In this there are very long-term trends we call *secular trends*. They tend to rise or fall for periods of 16 to 24 years, so that a complete cycle can be as short as 30 years, or as long as 50. Around these there are bull and bear phases. The next shorter cycle is a ten year rhythm named the *Juglar wave*. This has a strong probability of giving a recession in the early part of each decade and a stock market low between the 00 and 02 years.

Then there is a four year cycle, originally known as the *Kitchin wave*, but now called the *US Presidential Election Cycle*. The four and the ten year cycle only fit together every twenty years. Finally there is an annual seasonal deviation we relate to, which is not part of the Schumpeter model, but powerful nonetheless. This gives a tendency to fall in May, have a summer rally, and then drop again sharply in October. We can show that only being in the market from late October to May makes about as much profit as being invested full time, but has the advantage of halving the risk.

The final part of our system is a money management discipline using a *reverse martingale*. The idea is to always place bets, or trades with a small unit of money. This is kept at a fixed percentage of risk to the portfolio. For example a dealing unit could be 1% of the current value of the fund. If the fund is performing well then this will be a growing sum of money, but a fixed proportion of the fund. Once a holding goes up in price we can add to it. We pyramid upwards. If it goes down, we will sell it.

In this way if we start a new holding and are wrong, we will cut a small loss quickly. By the time we have a large holding it will, by definition, already be in profit. In this way the risk to reward ratio is such that we have a high probability of making money over time, even allowing for some mistakes. The mistakes should be less frequent than the winners, and the profits should be larger than the losses.

It only remains to decide when and where to activate a stop-loss order. Our system makes this proportional to the volatility of the underlying stock price movement. We measure how volatile the stock or index usually is with what we call the *volatility signature*. We then make sure that our stop-loss is just looser than these normal swings in price. In other words we tolerate normal, but not excessive volatility.

Can you explain how and to what degree you use TA in making investment decisions?

At the heart, our work has always been driven by a fundamental analysis of the forces at work in the market (stock market valuation, demographics, economic cycles, etc), which we then interweave with a technical analysis of what is actually happening, to build a clearer picture.

As trend followers, we use simple trend following techniques (no more sophisticated than moving average crossovers, comparing individual markets with respect to their long-term averages and regression analysis), used in conjunction with the economic and business cycles. To measure the long-term trend of the market, in the context of one business cycle, we tend to use the 200-day moving average as a default. This is not some sophisticated backtested number, but the convention used by most technical analysts. With weekly data, this is equivalent to the 40-week moving average, and when using monthly data, the 9-month moving average.

We find relative strength (not to be confused with RSI, the relative strength index) to be a very useful tool for identifying those stocks, sectors, markets and asset classes that are performing the strongest at each stage of the business cycle. When helping to pick individual stocks and sectors, we compute the trend rate of rise of relative strength with respect to the market (or some predefined benchmark) over a defined period, and rank these in descending order of merit. When used in conjunction with the absolute trend rate of rise, this we find to be a very effective method for identifying the strongest rising issues at any point in time. We use the same method to identify those assets most preferred at each stage of the business cycle, using key relative strength comparisons. In particular, we track the commodity/bond ratio, as a gauge for inflation/disinflation (deflation), the stock/commodity ratio and the stock/bond ratio.

In addition to our core methodology, we emphasise the use of a dynamic asset allocation approach – investing in commodities, bonds, cash and equities – aided by simple market timing techniques. In this way, we can take advantage of those stocks, sectors, markets and assets that are most advantaged at every stage of the business cycle, with the aim of producing favourable risk adjusted returns over the long-term.

The data shows that in all markets, there is frequently an orderly rotation of assets around an economic cycle – cash, to bonds, to equities and finally commodities. Starting with the period of maximum risk, cash is king; this is never a long-term investment but a parking place till the odds improve on an asset with a better reward. Bonds then take up the running; eventually bonds will have risen and seem less valuable in comparison to equities. Equities then become the dominant asset class with considerable growth being achievable in this phase, but it is of course accompanied by more risk.

Finally commodities rise, and ultimately risks seem high and values hard to find, making cash king again. It is the realisation of this process that provides a framework to tactically allocate assets at every stage around an economic cycle, and improve the risk-reward characteristics of our investment strategy.

The market timing techniques that we use for this purpose are no more involved than the trend following techniques already mentioned, along with intermarket analysis of the different asset classes by way of the key relative strength ratios mentioned. To gauge the internal strength of the market, we look at stock market breadth (the percentage of stocks rising above their respective long-term trends versus those falling).

We use global market breadth (the percentage of advancing versus declining markets) for timing the business cycle and gathering evidence in support of increasing or reducing exposure to equities. The idea here is that if the market is rising, supported above its primary trend, and breadth is additionally rising, then we have greater conviction in the bull market enduring. Conversely, when the market is falling below the long-term moving average, which in turn is trending lower, and this happens to be confirmed by deteriorating breadth, then the high probability bet is that the primary trend remains bearish. In a bull market, when breadth does not confirm the direction of the primary trend, we remain cautious by reducing our equity exposure, believing this to be a sign that the trend is maturing (as the market is being supported by fewer rising issues). Global market breadth, calculated as the number of rising markets vs. the number declining, serves as another useful breadth indicator in determining the primary direction of the global macro tide.

Lastly, when picking stocks and individual markets to populate the equity portion of a diversified portfolio, we use a simple trend ranking algorithm. This aims to identify the strongest trending stocks and markets on both an absolute and relative strength criteria (with respect to the market or a predefined benchmark). We remain aware of other technical indicators such as volume and sentiment but they do not form the core of our methodology.

Why did you choose to use TA? What made you convinced it works?

While our method is driven by a fundamental appreciation of the forces at work in the market, TA is the tool which we use to clearly map out what is happening at every juncture; primarily where we are positioned in the business cycle, at any given point in time. In this sense, TA fits in symbiotically with our fundamental process.

The technical methods that we use are very simple, but highly effective in as much as they compliment our investment process. In particular, we place a lot of emphasis on those techniques and methods that can be rigorously backtested and demonstrate a high probability of working. In this respect, we rate technical trend following techniques very highly.

To give an example, we have backtested the simple use of a 200-day moving average by buying the market when the price crosses above the 200-day moving average and selling when it dips below it on a number of markets and market environments, and found this to be a very effective market timing strategy. An investor utilizing this strategy, invested from 1951-2006 and switching between the S&P500 and US 90-day commercial paper made good money, far superior to passively investing in the market, principally because it kept him out of the market when it was falling, thereby lowering risk. $10,000 invested in the S&P500 from 1951 to 2006 using this strategy compounds to roughly $2,100,000; in comparison, a buy-and-hold strategy would have amassed $710,000 (ignoring dividends and commission costs)

What's particularly impressive about this strategy is how it performed over the period 1966-1982, a time during which the market went sideways for sixteen years. Over this period, the market managed 2.50% per annum, from Jan 1966 to Dec 1982, whereas the 200-day market timing strategy yielded 8.65% p.a. with significantly less risk.

Anyone curious as to how this strategy has performed in recent times (2008-2009) will be content to learn that it has beaten buy-and-hold hands down. An investor adhering to the above strategy would have produced returns as good as, or better than, the market, but with the added benefit of significantly lower risk. Risk is defined here as the maximum drawdown or volatility of investment (standard deviation).

How does your application of TA differ for short, medium and long-term time scales?

In the context of the economic cycles that we relate to, we define medium-term as one business cycle of roughly 4 years duration (one Kitchin cycle); long-term we define using secular trends (16-20 years), and short-term as anything less than one business cycle.

We use trend following techniques across all time scales, but for the short/medium-term we concentrate on using a dynamic asset allocation approach incorporating market timing techniques. In this context, we encourage investors to invest in equities, commodities, bonds and cash, timed using simple trend following techniques and intermarket relationships to determine the optimal asset class during each stage of the business cycle and weighted accordingly.

In the short-term we use the same process but tactically alter our weighting to participate in the medium/long-term trends across all asset classes over the business cycle. Additionally, we monitor technical measures such as stock market breadth to determine the internal strength of the market, and in the medium-term to determine the strength of the primary trend and how much risk we should take accordingly.

In the very long-term we identify that the market moves in secular trends, driven by various fundamental factors traceable using simple technical relationships. One such relationship is the strong inverse correlation between financial assets (equities and bonds) and physical assets (commodities) since the beginning of the twentieth century. This relationship appears to be deep rooted in investor psychology and supported by strong supply-demand fundamentals. The Dow/gold ratio and the stocks/commodity ratio demonstrate this.

The idea is to incorporate these secular trends into our dynamic asset allocation approach by overweighting those markets and asset classes with a secular uptrend bias, and underweight those assets with a secular downtrend bias. Since 2000, the Dow/gold ratio has turned in favour of a secular uptrend bias in commodities and a secular downtrend bias in US equities (Dow). This means that relative to commodities, US equities are in a secular bear market which is unlikely to end anytime soon.

History shows investors frequently accumulate gold as a store of value after losing faith in financial assets as a passive investment. This leads to gold outperforming equities over these periods.

What technical and indicators work best for short-term (weekly) analysis?

As long-term investors we do not place a lot of emphasis on very short-term moves, finding it difficult to clearly separate volatility from trend on this basis. Instead, we prefer to use the short-term to tactically position ourselves to participate in longer-term trends by way of dynamic asset allocation assisted by market timing. In this case, we use the same trend following techniques as we do for the long-term.

During the recent market turbulence in 2008 has TA performed better or worse than usual?

TA emphasizes the need for a disciplined exit strategy to take investors out of the market early enough to prevent large losses. In this respect, TA lived up to its capital protection and risk reduction role.

Markets move in secular trends driven by various fundamental factors that can be measured using simple technical relationships. Evidently, we believe that western global equities have been mired in a secular bear market since 2000. The last time we saw a secular bear market in western equities was over the period 1966-1982. Secular bear markets are notorious for producing large volatility and prodigious losses, as witnessed by the Dow's 2008 performance. Investors who blindly adhere to a buy-and-hold approach will find investing a Sisyphean task as any gains acquired in the previous bull-market cycle (2003-2007) tend to be eroded by the succeeding bear market cycle (2008).

During secular bear market periods, even very simple technical methods can help investors achieve better risk adjusted returns than buy-and-hold investing. One of the market timing techniques that we prefer, the 200-day moving average crossover, would have got investors out of the market (or more specifically significantly underweight equities) early enough to prevent large losses in line with global equity markets. In this respect, TA has performed as expected, based on our investment techniques.

Are some asset classes more technically driven than others?

TA is applicable to a number of asset classes, but undoubtedly performs best on liquid markets. For this reason, research shows that TA works best on FX markets, where there is unmatched liquidity. Thinly traded stocks and futures can be easily manipulated by institutional buyers, market makers, commercials, etc. rendering TA ineffective.

For this very reason we restrict our investment universe to the most liquid entities: developed and advanced emerging equity markets, commodities and bonds. Additionally, when dealing in individual stocks, we find that our stock grading system works best on large market capitalized stocks as opposed to small cap stocks where top management often have access to privy information not yet discounted in the share price.

Are there any market conditions under which TA works better or worse than other times?

This depends very much on the timeframes and methods you use. Some people use TA for scalping, others for swing trading and others for investing. Based on our methodology, we find it is especially potent during secular bear markets where we can add significant value by timing the business cycle with the aim of divesting before the business cycle moves into a recessionary phase.

Since we rely on trend identification for market timing purposes, but trends remain prone to whipsaw, we need volatility to be small in proportion to the trend strength for our methods to be effective. For this reason, when the VIX index (a commonly used gauge of the market's expectation of 30-day volatility, constructed using the implied volatilities of a wide range of S&P500 index options) shot up to 90 last year from a low of 20, our trend following techniques were rendered less effective (one way of countering this problem is reducing exposure to risk assets, and also the dealing size).

Is there any evidence that fund managers who employ TA do better than those who don't?

This is no doubt the topic of a virulent debate. There have been a number of studies conducted without any conclusive evidence either way. But the fact of the matter remains that the large number of successful fund managers who testify to using technical methods speaks for itself. Even Anthony Bolton – arguably UK's most feted professional investor and former manager of the Fidelity Special Situations fund – admits to having found a use for TA in his investment approach.

Does TA have anything useful to say about portfolio diversification?

In our view, the key ideology behind portfolio diversification lies in the domain of work put forward by Harry Markowitz, the father of modern portfolio theory. However, TA nonetheless provides a large number of tools and methods that can be used in the management of portfolios, and to assist in diversification. Our investment approach is centered on maintaining a diversified portfolio, with the weightings in each asset class dynamically altered using trend following market timing techniques. A diversified portfolio accords greater room for error if we get our market timing wrong. It also allows us to tactically adjust our allocation on the basis of greater evidence at each stage of the business cycle.

Particular technical relationships such as the Dow/gold relationship signal the secular trends that exist across key asset classes. Investors can incorporate the information gleaned from this by overweighting those asset classes in secular uptrends and underweighting those in secular downtrends. Simple intermarket analysis by way of key relative strength ratios, allow investors to tactically alter portfolios with the aim of selecting assets, stocks and sectors most advantaged at each stage of the business cycle.

Do you think TA and quants are closely related?

A recent study ("Perpetual Motion" by Susan Trammell, published in the January-February 2007 CFA Magazine) points to a clear overlap in a number of techniques shared by both disciplines (momentum, trends, reversals, indicators based on similar statistical concepts, etc), but there are also a large number of differences to warrant caution in brandishing quantitative analysts as technical analysts, or vice versa. In particular, quantitative analysts place a greater emphasis on numerical techniques and a scientific rigour. Those technical analysts who conform to a more objective approach, in trying to quantify the effectiveness of their methods, will definitely share more in common with conventional quants than the broad class of technical analysts.

How easy is it to use TA? Do you think training is required? Are any techniques misused or misunderstood?

New students to the technical discipline are cautioned against falling into the trap of using too many methods and indicators (or constantly switching between the same) in pursuit of the elusive 'holy grail'. Part of a good education involves understanding the methods and tools best suited for analysing each asset class, in a particular environment and over a specific timeframe. Additionally, with some techniques more subjective than others (e.g. Elliott Wave) and others requiring more diligence in their utilization e.g. DeMark Studies, students need to find those that fit in their comfort zone.

INDICATORS AND STRATEGIES

What is the best method for measuring price momentum in the market?

There is a large number of price momentum indicators, each a slight variation on the other, generically aimed at measuring the velocity of price moves, e.g. *Rate of Change, Price Momentum Oscillator* developed by Carl Swenlin, *Know Sure Thing* by Martin Pring, *MACD* by Gerald Appel, *Stochastic* by George Lane, *PercentR* by Larry Williams, *CCI* indicator by Donald Lambert… and the list goes on. We would be hard pressed to identify any one indicator as better than the rest considering that each has its own merits and demerits.

Does technical analysis have a role when shorting the market?

Technical analysis defines a number of highly effective tools and techniques that can be used to identify high-probability shorts in the market, over various time frames and across a variety of asset classes. Some of these methods tend to be based on trend following techniques, others are contrarian (RSI, percentage deviation from trend, DeMark studies, etc), while yet others involve an analysis of The Commodity Futures Trading Commission's Commitment of Traders report, amongst a plethora of other techniques. TA also provides a number of tools and methods which can be used to control risk when adopting shorts in the market, e.g. volatility adjusted position sizes and stop-loss levels.

However, as investors, with a long-term horizon, we prefer not to defy the primary trend and go short stocks, markets or other asset classes, during a primary bull market, instead of choosing to underweight or overweight an asset class as we deem fit, based on the technical methods we outline. (Short-term traders and scalpers will undoubtedly find much more use for many of these tools and methods for shorting purposes). During a bear market, we prefer to overweight risk-free assets including government bonds and cash, in lieu of shorting the market, and underweight risk assets such as commodities and equities.

Do you use Fibonacci, Gann or Elliott Wave techniques?

Gann and Elliott Wave are valid technical tools, and we remain aware of key levels dictated by the approach, but they do not form the basis of our system. Fibonacci provides invaluable support and resistance levels on stock market indices which we note, but again, this does not form the core of our system.

If the market is being driven by emotion, is this entirely reflected in the technicals?

One of the key benefits of TA is that it provides investors with a quick and very effective method of mapping out what is happening in the markets at any juncture in time. To this end, if the market is being driven by emotion, this is entirely reflected in the technicals. In this case, we get an exponential rise or fall in the market; the former often goes by the name of a 'bubble' and the latter a 'crash'. The characteristic signature of a bubble is a deviation that extends drastically from the long-term trends; we saw this with the NASDAQ bubble in 1999/2000.

The academic discipline of behavioural finance has long pointed out that stock market bubbles and crashes are the collective action of irrational investors driven by emotion, conforming to herd behaviour.

When plotted against each other, bubbles and crashes map out uncannily similar patterns.

How do you judge if a market is overbought or oversold?

We do take notice of conventional measures such as RSI and stochastics, but find a very simple measure of the deviation of the markets current price to its long-term trend (200- day or 40-week moving average), a very useful indicator of the same. In this case, we frame the current level of deviation in the context of the historical norm, using one and two standard deviations, to determine exactly how oversold or overbought the market is.

In addition, to this we also monitor technical indicators such as market breadth and sentiment indicators such as the put/call ratio. The idea is the more indicators that are in agreement, the more reason we have to believe that the market is overbought or oversold – since no single indicator is always right.

How inefficient do you believe markets to be? Are some asset markets more inefficient than others?

Warren Buffet has described his views on the Efficient Market Hypothesis (EMH) by pithily stating that he "would be a bum on the street with a tin cup if the stock market were efficient."

If the markets were indeed efficient, as the EMH claims, then stock price movements should conform to a random walk and follow a normal distribution pattern. The net effect would mean market prices cannot be reliably exploited to make an abnormal profit (especially when taking into account transaction costs). In reality, stock price movements do not follow a random walk, but instead more closely resemble what is known as a *leptokurtic distribution.*

If you were to plot the frequency distribution of the market's daily returns on a graph, you would end up with the probability of gaining or losing a certain amount on any day. If the markets were indeed normally distributed then the majority of the time you would gain or lose very little; occasionally you would gain or lose a lot, but very infrequently, you would win or lose a fortune. The reality is that the markets win or lose you a fortune much more frequently than the normal distribution allows for.

To prove this, we have plotted the Dow daily returns over the last 80 years on a graph, ending up with a distribution with a much more pronounced peak and much fatter tails than the classical normal distribution allows for. The fatter tails translate into the fact that there is a higher probability of making a very large loss or gain than the probabilities dictated by the normal distribution. This shape, is none other than the leptokurtic distribution, we mentioned earlier ('lepto' meaning 'slim' in Greek, refers to the central part of the distribution).

To give you a feel for how different these probabilities are from theory, Benoît Mandelbrot, the mathematician who invented fractal theory, calculated that if the Dow followed a normal distribution, it should have moved by more than 3.4% on 58 days between 1916 and 2003; in fact it did so 1,001 times. It should have moved by more than 4.5% on six days; it did so on 366. It should have moved by more than 7% only once in every 300,000 years; in the 20th century it did so 48 times.

Another big flaw of the EMH theory is that it assumes that investors are rational, always acting in their own-self interests. The emerging discipline of behavioural finance has challenged this theory, arguing that markets are not rational, but instead are driven by investors exhibiting bouts of fear and greed; the sell off in the markets in October 2008 was definitely testimony to the latter. Andrew Lo, the prominent MIT Professor, has presented a contending theory that aims to reconcile some of the flaws of the standard EMH model to try and incorporate behavioural finance revelations about the way people act. He's called it the *Adaptive Market Hypothesis.*

According to the EMH, it is impossible to outperform the market (without taking on more risk), so investors should simply resort to buy-and-hold investing. But we aim to show that this is certainly not true. While we do believe that market movements on a day to day basis are as close to what can truly be described as random, over long periods their movements are far from arbitrary. In fact, a key tenet of our work is to show that markets move in secular trends and that technical analysis can add significant value in reducing risk and improving returns (providing better risk adjusted returns) compared to buy and hold during secular bear market periods, as we are currently witnessing.

USING TA FOR RISK AND TRADE MANAGEMENT

Can you explain your approach to risk and money management?

To reduce risk, we emphasize the importance of maintaining a diversified portfolio – exposure to stocks, bonds, commodities and cash – in proportions that can be varied according to the position in the business cycle. The aim of this approach is to reduce exposure to risky assets when the business cycle is at its riskiest and increase exposure to risk assets when there is enough evidence that the cycle has troughed.

When investing in individual equities and stock markets, populating the equity portion of our portfolio, we use a two tier approach to risk and money management. The first is aimed at minimising losses, whereas the second explores how to maximise returns when winning. To minimize losses, we adhere to the principle of cutting your losers and letting your winners run. To accomplish this, we use percentage trailing stop-losses, with the level of risk taken on each position adjusted using a unique measure of volatility for the stock or market in question; we refer to this measure as the *volatility signature*. The volatility signature of a stock or market is not an optimised number that has historically delivered the best return, but a sensible measure of risk taking into account the historical volatility of a stock (or market), as measured by typical drawdowns in a bull market. By keeping our stops looser than the volatility signature, we have a higher chance of riding a trend to maturity without being stopped out early by 'normal volatility', but at the same time, do not incur massive losses when the trend clearly reverses.

To calculate volatility signatures for all the instruments we are likely to invest in (stocks and markets), we observe the historical pattern of retracements in a well defined trend (the last bull cycle), and use the largest drawdown, up to a maximum of 25%, as a measure of the volatility signature for that market or stock. The basis for this seemingly 'arbitrary number' is down to the rules of money management. Simple money-management mathematics shows that if you lose 5% of your investment, you only need to make 5.26% to break even. If you instead lose 10%, then you need to make 11.1% to reach the high watermark. With a loss of 20%, you now need to make 25% to recover your money; much more difficult, but not entirely impossible. Beyond this, the gain required to break even with growing losses increases exponentially, making it much more difficult to stay in the 'game'. If we curtail our losses within the 20-25% bracket, then we have a much higher chance of staying in the game and recouping losses.

When maximising winners, we aim to answer the simple question: "how much money do we put into each stock or market?" For this we use the concept of a *unit* of investment. No matter how much we like a stock or market, we never buy more than a unit. Since we do not know which of the ideas on our buying list will ultimately turn out to be the best performers, an equal unit allocated to each seems fair. Our unit is determined by our allocation to equities at each stage of the business cycle. When we increase our exposure to equities or we are winning, our unit size automatically increases, when we reduce our exposure to equities or are losing, it automatically reduces. In this way, our unit size remains constant, in proportion to our wealth. This is an *anti-martingale strategy.*

Additionally, we do not need to buy a full unit in one fell swoop, but instead can build up a holding slowly, in incremental steps which can be called *pyramiding.* If we have a new idea, and start to buy, but in fact end up being wrong, then we will cut a small loss. The probability that we can recover from this with our very next idea is really rather high.

Is TA a part of your risk assessment? E.g. do you use support and resistance levels as likely levels to which the market will head?

TA has always formed a core part of our risk assessment at every stage. From the top down, we use simple technical tools and methods to ascertain which stage of the business cycle we are in to adjust our asset allocation appropriately. We use trend following techniques and key intermarket relationships to determine the asset classes most favoured at each stage of the business cycle.

While we remain aware of key support and resistance levels, they do not from a key component of our process. What we do use is the 200-day moving average as a key support and resistance guide. In this sense, not only do we look for the market to break above the 200-day moving average, but we also expect it to find continuous support above this trend to ascertain that it is headed higher. Similarly, to confirm that the market is headed lower, we look for the market to break below the 200-day moving average, and at the same time, find formidable resistance from this trend.

Is it possible to create TA-based risk metrics?

Technical analysis has a large armoury of tools and techniques that can be used to create very effective risk metrics. Very simple indicators such as percentage deviation from long term trends; overbought/oversold indicators such as Relative Strength Index, Williams %R etc; market breadth; volatility indicators, e.g. VIX;

sentiment indicators etc. are all very effective tools that can either be used in isolation or as part of a composite risk metric to gauge how much risk investors are taking before entering a trade. The true strength of these tools and techniques is in providing quantifiable risk metrics, to accurately determine how much risk investors face before putting on a trade or making an investment.

Technical measures of volatility such as Average True Range, Standard Deviation, Chaikin's Volatility can be used for creating position sizing metrics, adjusting position sizes according to the volatility (risk) of the market. Richard Dennis and the turtle trading team were very successful at doing this. They used a very simple volatility based constant percentage risk position sizing algorithm using Average True Range as a measure for the volatility of the market, to determine the amount to risk per trade. We also use a very simple technical measure of risk to determine how closely to trail prices with a trailing stop-loss. We refer to this measure as the *volatility signature*.

How have you optimised your strategies? Is this something you review on a regular basis?

We use very simple technical tools without any need for optimisation; instead, we prefer to use logical parameters for any indicators that we use, to reflect the time frame we are investigating. To give an example, we use a 200-day moving average to track the long-term trend of the market in the context of one business cycle (200 days being one of the most frequently used timeframes for long-term moving average in technical analysis). Additionally, in our stock and market ranking system, we use the same parameters for every market: 25 days for the short-term trend, 50 days for the medium-term trend, 200 days for the long-term trend, and relative strength measured over 75 days. It can be argued that the *volatility signatures* we use when placing stops are based on optimisation, but this is not strictly true, as we do not aim for the best results. Instead, we simply aim for a logical measure, based on historical norms, to separate 'normal volatility' from aberrational one

Traders may find more use for optimisation, but done incorrectly, it is fraught with danger. Adaptive techniques and indicators are another contender to optimisation.

Have you attempted to backtest your strategies?

We have extensively backtested all our strategies, as realistically as we can, across several time frames and differing market environments. While we can make no guarantee about these methods working in the future, we still feel confident when using them, given that they are ground in hard logic and have demonstrated a high probability of working in the past.

We have already shown the backtest results of the 200-day moving average when applied to the US stock market. Now we can talk about the odds of the four year cycle we relate to. It has failed only twice in all the time since Roosevelt was US president and in both cases we got a market crash. One was 1986, which should have been a low; the index in fact rose strongly and even went to late the next year without a problem, before crashing violently in October 1987. The only other time it failed was in 2006, which should have manifested a four year cycle low, but failing this, the markets carried on and crashed again in October 2008. That is two failures out of 19 cycles; which equates to a probability of 90% in our favour. We rarely see odds that good in the investment world; the outcome is not a certainty, but is the way to bet.

We have also referred to the annual seasonal deviation of stock markets, in which we have noted that we can show that only being in the market from late October to May makes about as much profit as being invested full time, but has the advantage of halving the risk. We have tested this phenomenon on 37 markets (the original work was published by authors Sven Bouman and Ben Jacobsen, in a paper written in 2001, *"The Halloween Indicator: Sell in May and Go Away"*), and found that in all cases, share market returns were weaker on average between May and October than the rest of the year, in 36 out of 37 markets, covering both developed and emerging nations; the only country that deviated from this trend was New Zealand.

What are the key performance parameters you look at apart from return?

The key measure we monitor is performance, taking into account drawdowns (Calmar Ratio) – this representing the dollar amount by which investors would be better off, had this not been incurred. In this respect, our strategy is specifically aimed at controlling volatility from the perspective of minimising large drawdowns – as demonstrated by most risk assets over the period 2001-2002 and 2007–2008. Large

146

drawdowns undermine the principal of capital preservation and often require long periods to recoup losses.

How do you deal with false signals?

Our techniques are designed to follow long-term trends, in conjunction with the business cycle, where the trend strength to volatility ratio is high. Accordingly, we use long-term trend following techniques, e.g. 200-day moving average crossover as evidence that long-term moves have been instigated. However, our methods are still susceptible to being whipsawed, but less so owing to the timeframe over which we invest. By investing in a diversified portfolio of uncorrelated assets, even if we are prone to being whipsawed, we can sufficiently reduce the volatility of the overall portfolio.

What is your view on the use of optimised stop-losses?

It is better to set logical parameters than optimised ones. We use a natural measure of volatility which is not optimised but based on historical volatility. It is not optimised as it is not based on the volatility which yielded the best historical performance.

How do you deal with volatility? How does very high volatility affect the efficacy of your preferred strategy?

Volatility is a bugbear in our strategy, as it makes it difficult to discern the direction of the real trend. We aim to reduce volatility by investing in a diversified portfolio of uncorrelated assets at each stage of the business cycle, and invest with a focus on the long-term.

When investing in individual equities and stock markets, in the equity portion of our portfolio, we accept that we have to tolerate a certain amount of volatility as even the best trends do not go up in a straight line. The idea is to identify exactly how much volatility we need to tolerate, unique to every stocks and market that we invest in, to ride out the long-term trend, and at the same time not get caught out by a major trend reversal. Finally, we intentionally curb the amount of volatility we can tolerate to a maximum of 25% for money management reasons, as earlier explained.

COMBINING WITH OTHER NON-TA INFORMATION

What sentiment indicators do you look at?

When gauging investor sentiment, we remain aware of the ratio of bullish versus bearish investment advisors. Two of the most popular surveys which capture this are the *Investors Intelligence* Sentiment Index and the *American Association of Individual Investors (AAII)* survey of its members. We also look at some market indicators that help gauge investor sentiment such as the put/call ratio and the VIX.

Do you often find yourself at odds with the market and/or your fundamentally based colleagues?

We have found that it is normal to find ourselves at odds with fundamentally based colleagues at market extremes, for example in 2007, when the technicals changed quicker than the fundamentals. Additionally, we have found that the concept of a secular bear market has been very hard for a number of fund managers/investors who have a buy-and-hold bias to digest. Prior to the crash, we wrote a number of articles and clearly spelt out in our strategy work that the entire move from 2006-2007 was only a cyclical bull market within the confines of a secular bear market. We also said that the Dow's new highs to 14,000 were, in some sense treacherous highs, meant to lure investors back into the buy- and-hold mentality before crashing them into despair. Many fundamentally based colleagues have disputed this including some very old hands who were around during the last secular bear market (1966-1982).

Do you keep an eye on volume levels and, if so, how do you use them in your decisions?

Given that our methods are based on capturing long-term moves, volume levels do not have as much impact on our strategy as swing traders or short-term investors would testify to; in this respect, price remains the key variable behind our strategy. However, we do monitor volume levels on major indices and markets – either directly or by way of the research we follow. In particular, we look for divergences between price and raw volume or volume indicators such as Joseph Granville's On Balance Volume (OBV) indicator for potential signs of major reversals. However we do not act on them until we see reason to; based on the methods and techniques that form part of our core system.

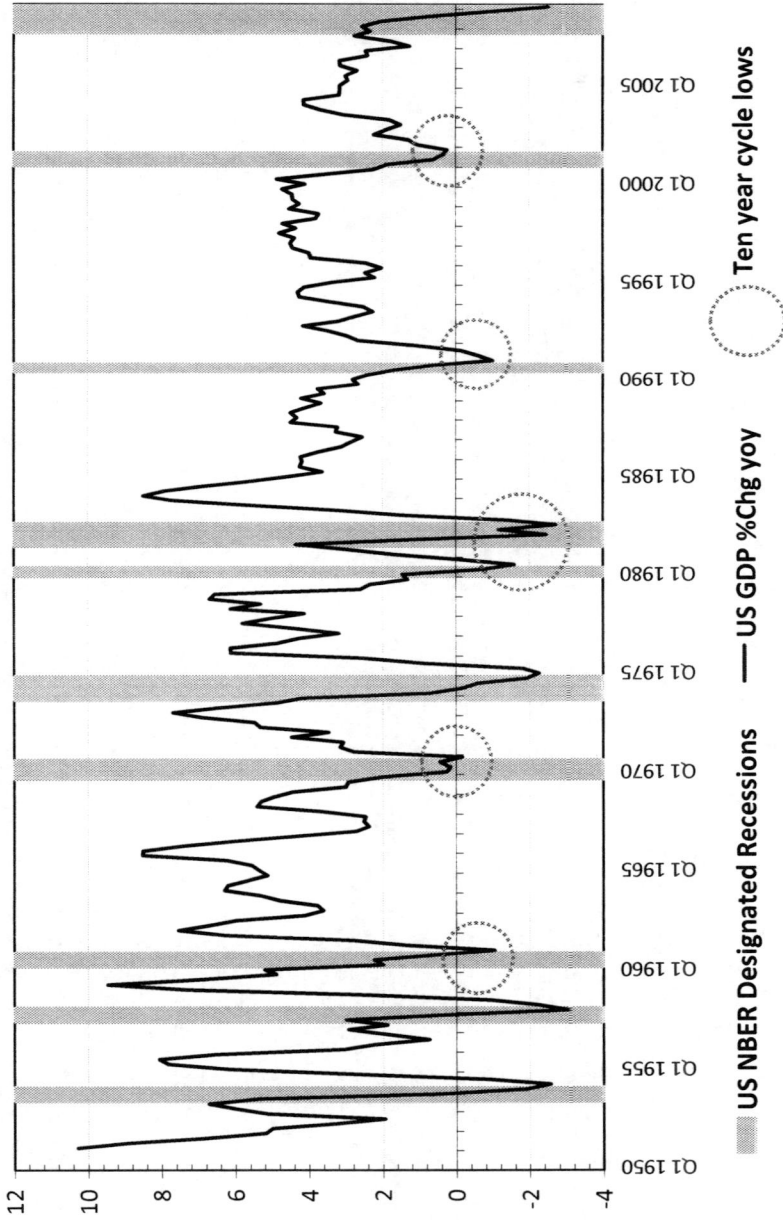

Figure 1: The ten year cycle and recessions in the early part of each decade

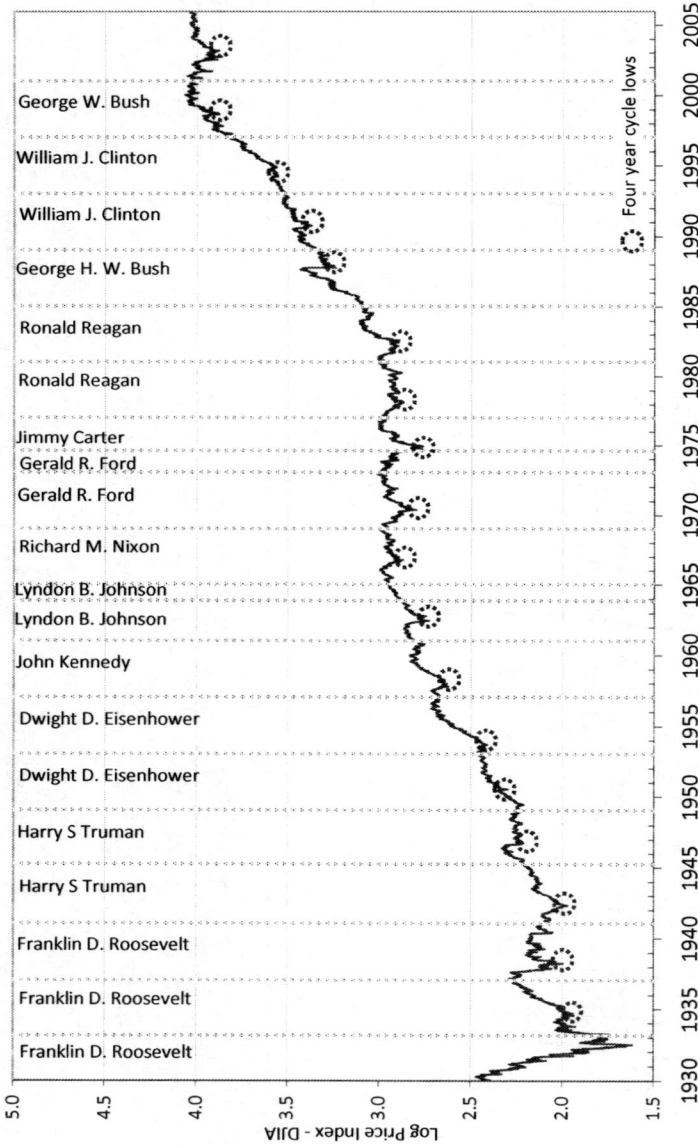

Figure 2: The four year cycle in US stocks (DJIA) overlaid on US presidential inaugurations

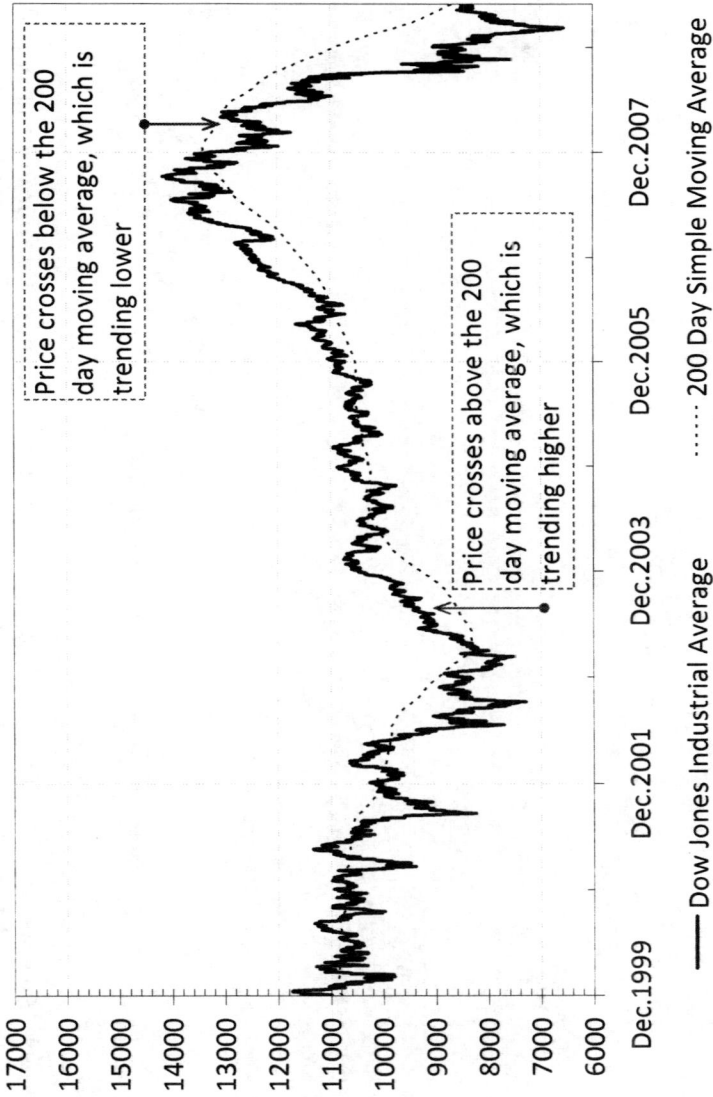

Figure 3: Dow and the 200-day simple moving average (a gauge for the primary trend of the market)

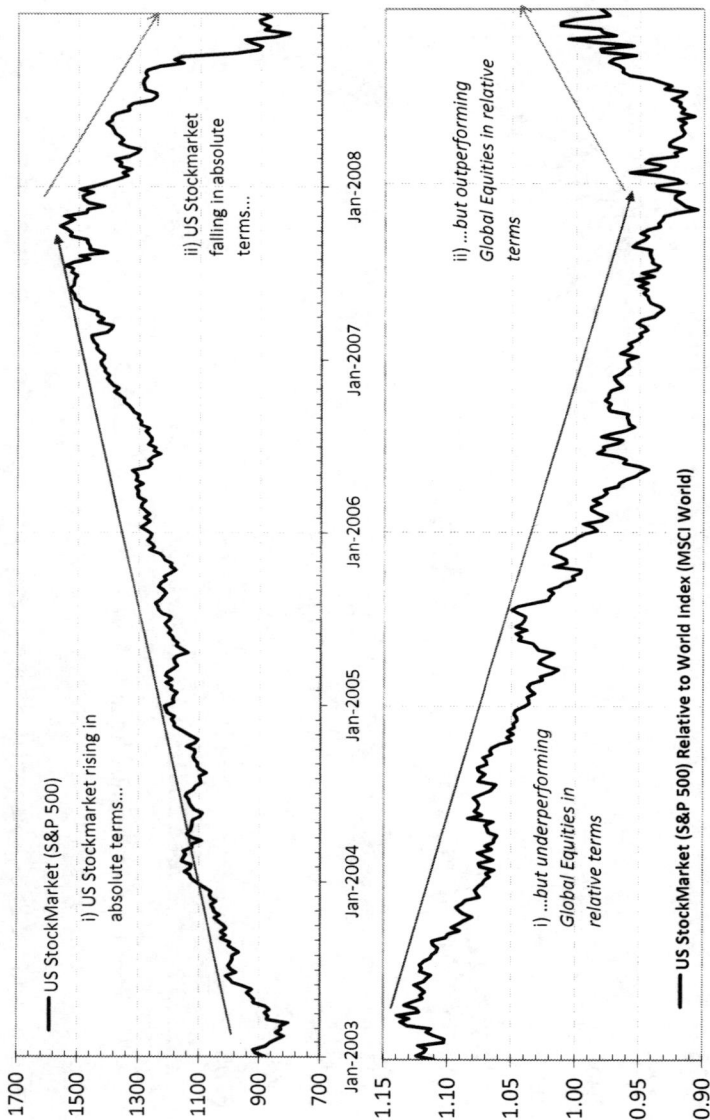

Figure 4: Using relative strength to identify underperformance and outperformance in the S&P500 versus global equities (MSCI World Index)

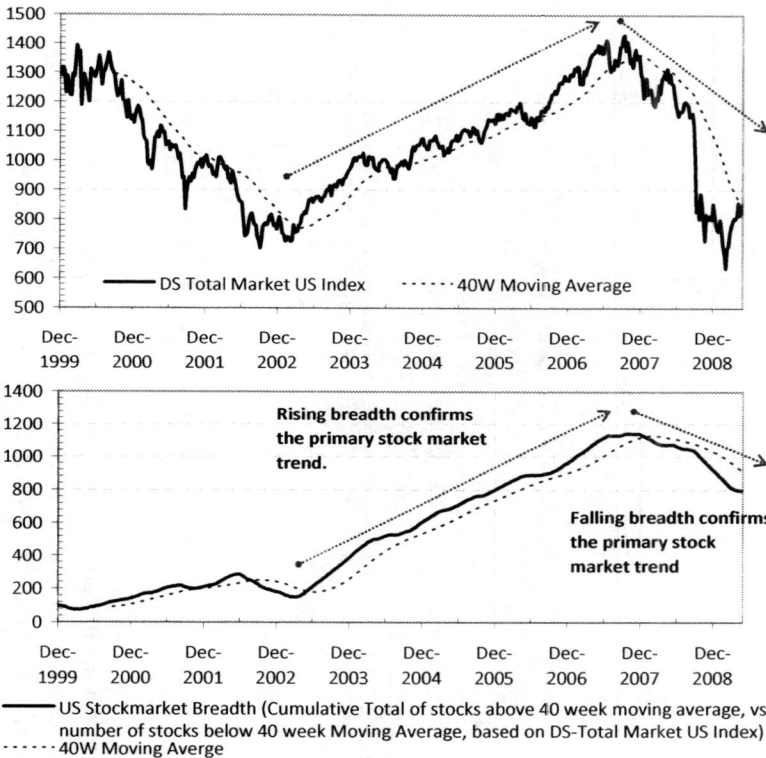

Figure 5: Market breadth confirms primary market direction for the DataStream Total Market US Index

Period & Strategy	Return	Risk		Market Exposure
	Compound Annual Growth Rate %	Annualised Standard Deviation %	Maximum Drawdown %	Time in Market %
Jan 1951 - Dec 2006				
S&P 500	7.87	14.19	46.28	100
S&P 500 timed using 200 day moving average	9.97	10.18	19.11	69
Jan 1966 - Dec 1982				
S&P 500	2.50	15.37	46.18	100
S&P 500 timed using 200 day moving average	8.65	9.41	13.06	55
Jan 1983 - Dec 2006				
S&P 500	10.11	14.61	46.28	100
S&P 500 timed using 200 day moving average	10.00	11.08	19.11	76

Table 1: S&P500 timed with the 200-day SMA crossover rule 1951-2006

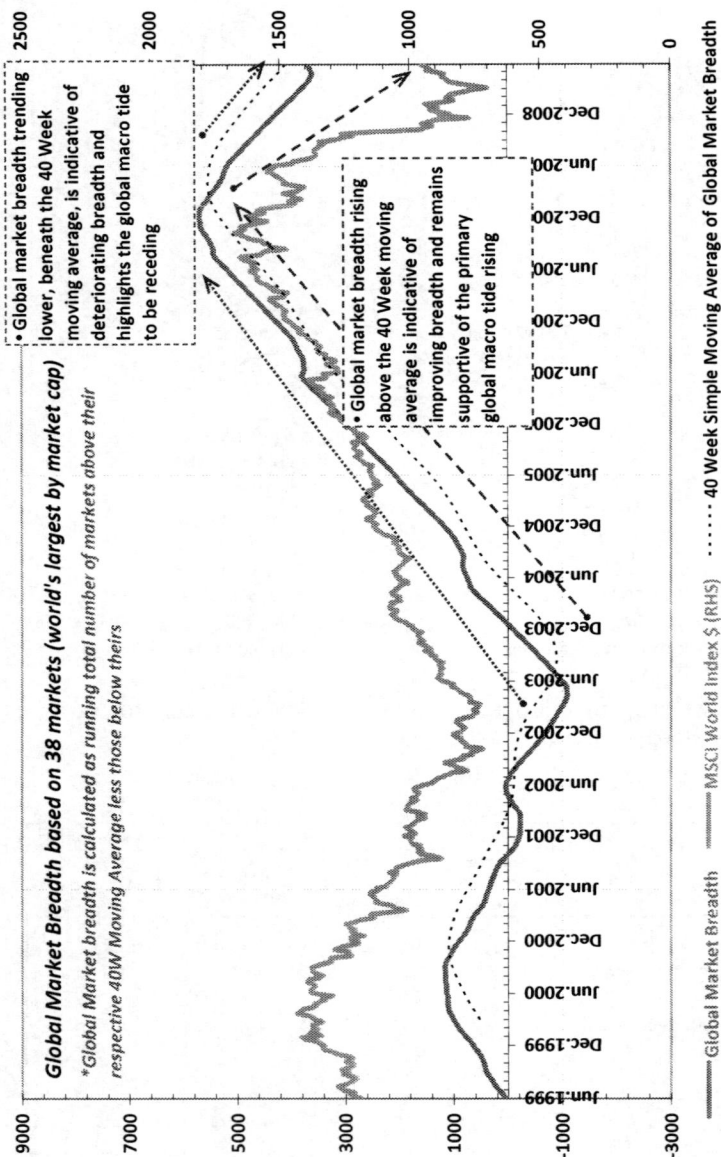

Global Market Breadth based on 38 markets (world's largest by market cap)

Global Market breadth is calculated as running total number of markets above their respective 40W Moving Average less those below theirs

- Global market breadth trending lower, beneath the 40 Week moving average, is indicative of deteriorating breadth and highlights the global macro tide to be receding

- Global market breadth rising above the 40 Week moving average is indicative of improving breadth and remains supportive of the primary global macro tide rising

Global Market Breadth ——— MSCI World Index $ (RHS) .... 40 Week Simple Moving Average of Global Market Breadth

Figure 6: using global market breadth to confirm the direction of the primary macro tide. Global market breadth has been calculated as the total number of markets rising above their respective 40-week moving averages versus the number falling based on 38 international equity markets

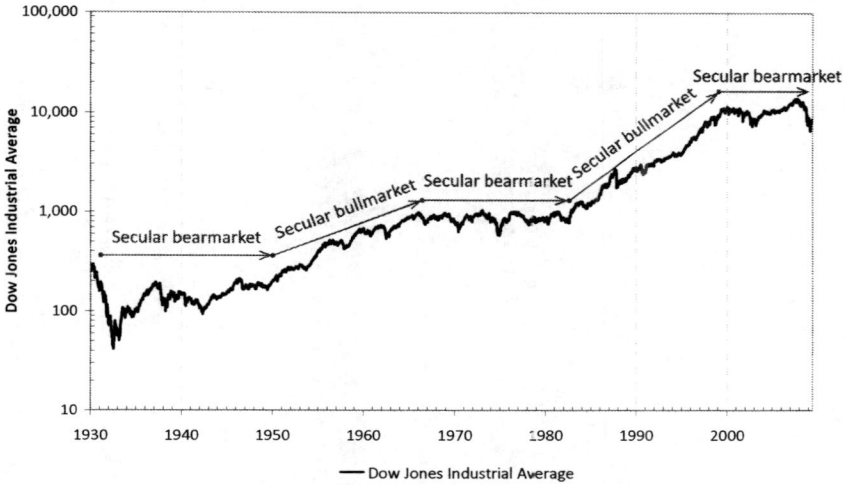

Figure 7: Secular trends, lasting between 16-20 years for the Dow

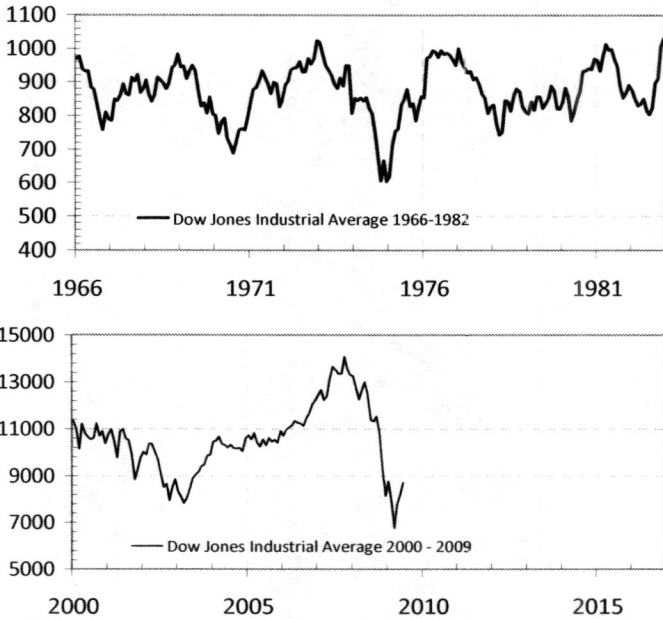

Figure 8: US stocks in a secular bear market akin to 1966-1982

155

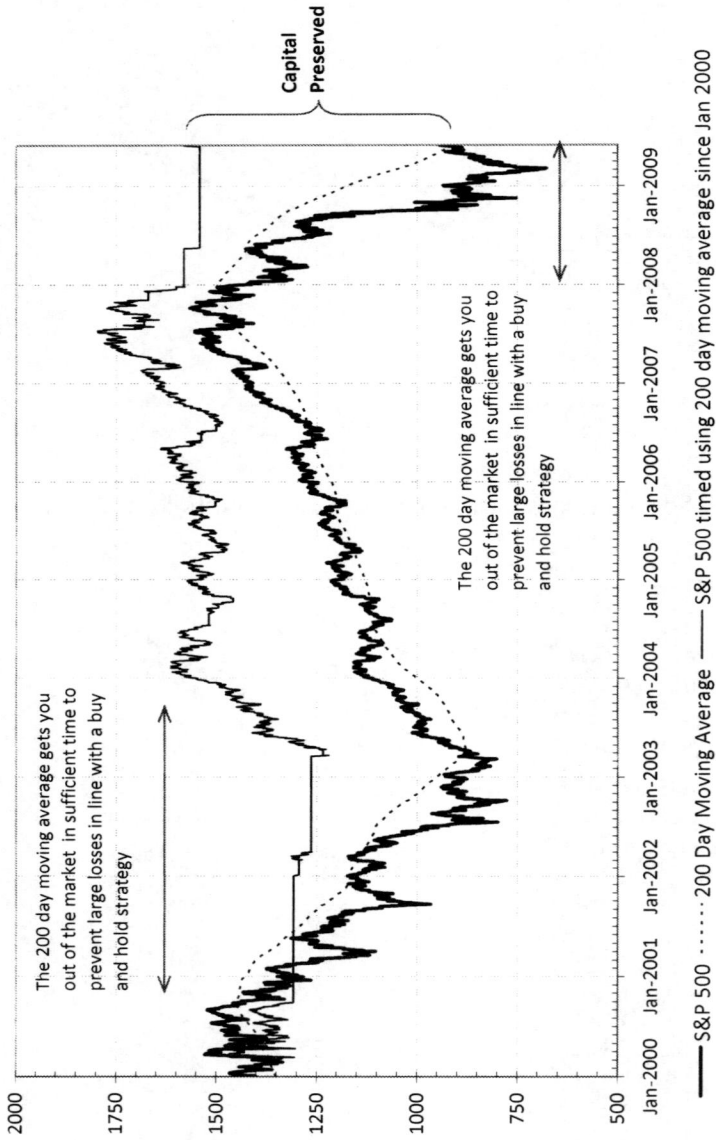

Figure 9: Using the 200-day moving average to preserve capital during secular bear market periods

Capital Preserved

The 200 day moving average gets you out of the market in sufficient time to prevent large losses in line with a buy and hold strategy

The 200 day moving average gets you out of the market in sufficient time to prevent large losses in line with a buy and hold strategy

S&P 500 ······ 200 Day Moving Average ——— S&P 500 timed using 200 day moving average since Jan 2000

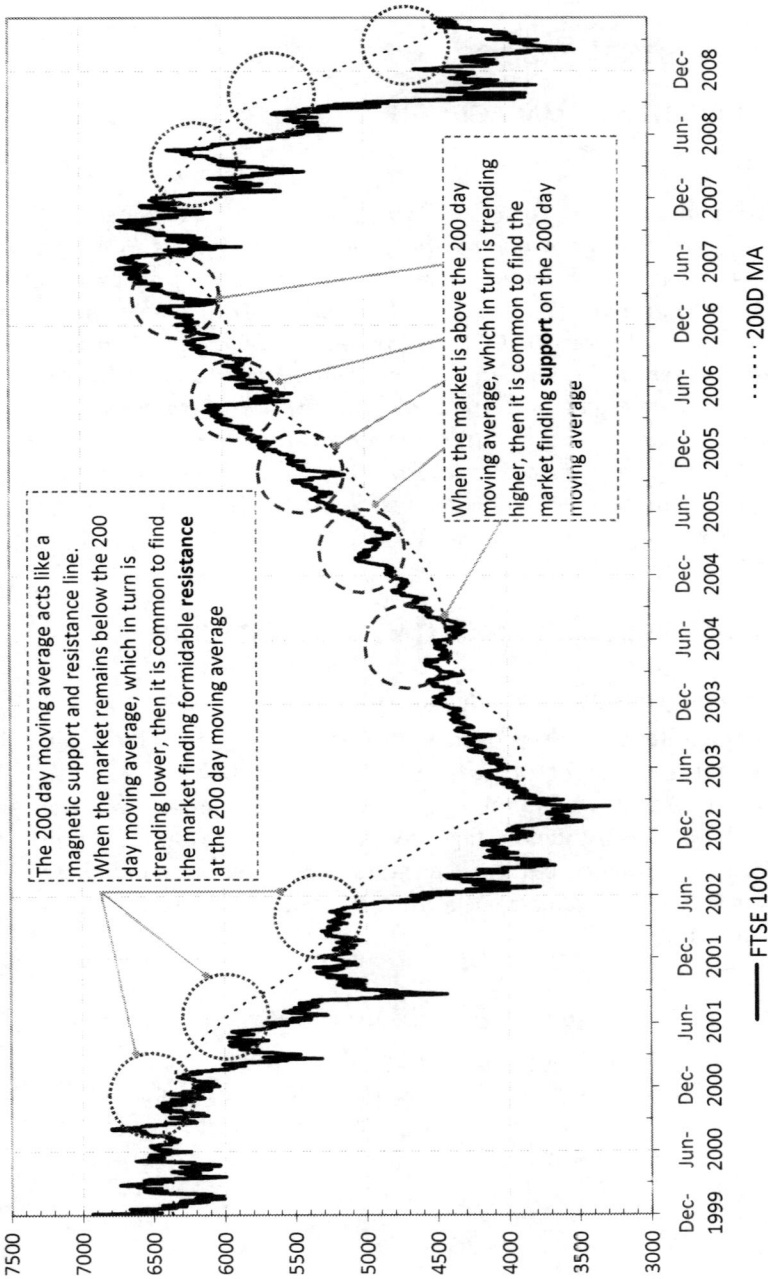

Figure 10: 200-day moving average acting as 'magnetic' support and resistance

The 200 day moving average acts like a magnetic support and resistance line. When the market remains below the 200 day moving average, which in turn is trending lower, then it is common to find the market finding formidable **resistance** at the 200 day moving average

When the market is above the 200 day moving average, which in turn is trending higher, then it is common to find the market finding **support** on the 200 day moving average

——— FTSE 100

······· 200D MA

Chapter 11

JEAN PAUL VAN STRAALEN

MANAGING PARTNER AND PORTFOLIO MANAGER

INIOHOS INVESTMENT MANAGEMENT

Jean Paul van Straalen (CMT, FRM) started his career in 1991 working in the dealing room of the Indonesia Overseas Bank in Amsterdam where he traded short-term interest rate futures and forward rate agreements. In 2000 he joined ABN Amro Asset Management as a senior portfolio risk manager. Jean Paul is now a managing partner at Iniohos Investment Management and Advisory Services in Luxembourg, an independent investment management company that offers global equity management investing for high-net wealth individuals and private and institutional clients. At Iniohos he is co-portfolio manager of their Global Alpha Fund, focusing on large and mid-cap stocks in developed markets.

USING TA FOR TRADE AND INVESTMENT DECISIONS

Can you explain your basic investment style?

It is very quantitative in approach with our models being the main drivers of our investment process. They provide the buy and sell signals which are the input for our portfolio construction. We use these models to identify factors that are most significant in predicting future stock performance and to determine the relative attractiveness of each stock. We then rank them to determine if a specific stock is a potential investment.

What role does TA play in these quantitative models?

We use a TA trend following overlay that screens stocks using momentum, trends, and breakouts of support and/or resistance levels. This is done after we have ranked the stocks quantitatively and used TA to determine which stocks have the best risk and reward profile.

So TA plays an important role in money management for you?

Exactly. We use it to determine when the trade should be exited given specific rules about stop-loss levels. When predefined critical levels are broken, trades will be reversed.

What was your first introduction to using TA?

I started my career in the dealing room of a small merchant bank as a trader in the early nineties. All traders there looked at some kind of TA and it was then that my interest was triggered. The use of TA was not as sophisticated then as it is now, but even then I realised that it is complementary to fundamental and quantitative analysis. It works largely because it is self-fulfilling.

Does your application of TA differ for short, medium and long-term time scales?

Not really. I begin by looking at monthly or quarterly data to see where the main support and resistance levels are. I then scale down to weekly and daily data. For each time scale I use the same indicators such as candlestick charts and the MACD to achieve a more consistent analysis. In that sense, I don't differentiate between time scales.

Do you find that some indicators work better for short-term and long-term analysis?

I find that the Rate of Change (ROC) indicator and Martin Pring's Know Sure Thing (KST) work well. For example, the 12-month ROC is good at generating long-term trend reversal signals. By combining short, medium and long-term data, the KST is good at trend analysis and signalling an impending trend change.

While my main focus is on the trend, I also watch classical chart patterns such as head-and-shoulders for new entry or exit strategies. Tom DeMark's TD Sequential™ also provides potential reversal signals.

For long-term analysis I also look at traditional indicators like the MACD, stochastics and RSI. For the very long-term (5 years plus), the wider secular picture of the stock is obviously important. This includes looking at the four-year cycle (Kitchin wave). Whatever time scale I am looking at, my goal is the same; to try and confirm the current price movement.

You talk about the four-year cycle for stocks. Where are we in the current cycle? What does this say about the outlook for stocks?

There is the Kitchin four-year cycle and the four-year US presidential election cycle. Normally the pre-election year has been good for equity markets, while post-election years have the tendency to be bearish. So given that we have just started a post-election year, this would indicate that the outlook for stocks will remain bearish until the second quarter of 2010, taking into account the assumption of an average decline period of 17 months.

If we look at the Kitchin wave and consider that we made the top in October 2007, then roughly after 24 months we would have a bottom before the uptrend can be resumed. In March this year (2009) we made a 'major bottom' after roughly 17 months from the top in October 2007. Did we see the low of this bear market? By combining the two cycles, maybe this current (2009) bull market rally is not sustainable and we could see in the coming months the last phase of the 4-year cycle. All depends if critical levels will hold otherwise this scenario will be history.

Have you found any evidence that some asset classes are more technically driven than others?

Yes, depending on the breadth and depth of the market, although there is no distinction when we are talking about very liquid markets. Assets that have tick data availability and are widely covered by traders will be more technically driven. In these markets traders are all looking at the same pivot points and support and resistance levels, many of which are published before the start of each trading session. These levels then become key and will trigger trades thereby confirming the technical levels they were based on.

How does your application of TA differ for different asset classes?

We use the same TA technique for all markets, but to compare the various asset classes we apply an intermarket technical analysis approach, (originated by John Murphy), where we look at the bond, stock, currency and commodity markets. For example, the bond market is a leading indicator for the stock market.

Can you give a few examples of intermarket relationships that you think are the most significant?

For the US market, the intermarket relationships are the S&P500, the Goldman Sachs Commodity Index, the 10-year US treasury and the US dollar index. For the European market, I will look at the 10-year Euro Treasury yield, EUR/USD, the Dax or AEX index, and also the Goldman Sachs Commodity Index. For a recovery in equity markets, interest rates should be low. When commodity prices are falling this is also supportive for a rally in equity markets.

Currently in 2009, there is no inflation risk, interest rates are falling and the correction of the US dollar has lead to falling commodity prices. So the significant declines in interest rates and commodity prices have supported the equity indices.

Does the application of TA differ when using it to pick individual stocks as opposed to using it to analyse the index as a whole?

If there is any difference it would be in the application of relative strength analysis to individual stocks. This traditional ratio method quantifies the price strength of a stock versus another stock within the same sector or index.

What about using TA in different market conditions? Are there any conditions under which TA works better or worse than others?

At the present time, market conditions are certainly very different from those of the previous five years or so. I believe that TA does work better in trending markets than in sideways markets if you are a medium to long-term investor.

You have mentioned relative strength analysis. Can you explain what TA has to say about portfolio management and diversification?

Portfolios can be compared with the relative strength ratio against their specific benchmark as long as you have the NAVs (Net Asset Value) or the underlying prices. You can also analyse how the portfolio is diversified in terms of countries, sector or industry group weightings by establishing which sector is trending upwards, downwards, or is consolidating. For example, how is the trend developing between the energy and consumer staples sector?

Charting the relative strength ratio of the various sectors provides you with insights into how diversified your portfolio is. Intermarket analysis is also useful here. For instance, if we are in an inflationary phase, bond prices will fall and sectors that are interest rate sensitive will be the most affected.

INDICATORS AND STRATEGIES

What is your strategy when the charts show a technical pattern such as a head-and-shoulders or a double top?

If I have identified such a pattern I would project the price target from the neckline in the text-book fashion. I will then look at other indicators for confirmation of the reversal pattern before establishing a stop-loss target. For confirmation, I look at volume and divergence with other technical indicators. If there is a sustainable break I will enter a new position with a tight stop-loss.

How do you determine where to place your stop-losses? What are the levels you refer to?

To ensure prudent money (risk) management, stop-loss levels should be identified and determined for each individual trade. One way to determine stop-loss levels is to identify main support or resistance levels, like a longer-term moving average or Fibonacci ratios. The level of the simple or exponential moving average will be your pre-defined level, so if the investment falls below the longer-term moving average, you will exit your position. Other ways to determine stop-losses could be a trendline, a minor bottom or minor tops. For example, a break below or above the trendline can trigger your exit strategy. Pivot points calculated on a daily or weekly basis can also act as pre-defined levels for your trades or investments.

Depending on the size of the investment, we also use the percentage rule in our portfolio. If the investment is losing more than 10% of its value, for example, the stop-loss level of the position is then triggered. Here the pre-defined level can be easily determined based on the percentage for each trade and investment.

You mention Fibonacci ratios. Which ratios do you find most effective or occur most often?

Fibonacci retracements are used to find probable areas where prices will likely stop and reverse back in the direction of the trend. Fibonacci extensions can also be used to identify where a likely price target can be identified. We monitor all Fibonacci ratios but we find the most effective ones are 0.382 (38%), 0.5 (50%), and 0.618 (62%). The 0.214 (21%) and 0.786 (79%) rations are less effective. For extensions, 1.27 (127%) and 1.618 (162%) occur the most.

How do you indentify the beginning and end of a trend?

Identifying market peaks and troughs is one of the most challenging areas of TA. We look at multiple factors including technical, fundamental and economic in order to have a complete picture. For instance, stocks that are early cycle leaders should see an improvement in their relative strength and long-term momentum. I would also look to determine where the market is in its four-year cycle to see if it is likely to be approaching, or coming out of, a peak or trough.

Sentiment is normally very bearish at market bottoms, so extreme levels could signal a potential bottom. Combining all these signals will give you more confidence in identifying troughs and peaks. Currently, I am following Tom DeMark's technical indicators which, in a very systematic way, provide a signal of a potential reversal. Analysing trend following indicators will also provide you with additional signals when a trend commences.

What are the most effective trend following indicators to use?

Price momentum is a leading indicator of a change in price trend direction. Momentum is the difference between today's closing price and the close of N days ago. This is momentum calculated as an absolute difference, but you can also calculate it as a ratio. You just divide one momentum indicator such as the 14-day by another such as the 30-day. These are parameters that I tend to use. This produces a ratio (momentum short/ momentum long) that allows you to compare various assets. Another example of using momentum as a ratio is taking the close of the stock and comparing it to a simple or exponential moving average. This also allows you to compare various securities.

The Rate of Change (ROC) is perhaps the most popular indicator for measuring momentum. This provides buy and sell signals when the ROC line crosses the zero line. Other indicators that can be used include the MACD, RSI and stochastic, but my preference is the ROC.

Does technical analysis have a role when shorting the market?

TA certainly can be used as part of a shorting strategy. Although valuation may still be supportive for an upward price move, signals of a reversal in the market should not be ignored. For example, a downward crossing of the price through the simple moving average would be a typical signal for considering a possible short position. If this is supported by other indicators then one can initiate a trade, but it should be remembered that strict money management is vital. It should also not be forgotten that when markets are trending down, the reverse strategies can be set up for being long in the market.

How do you use moving averages? Which periodicities work best for you and how do you use them to generate trade signals?

My preference is for simple trading or investing rules such as the single crossover method using a simple moving average (SMA) for possible buy and sell signals. As we all know, moving averages only work in a trending market and will do poorly in sideways markets. These crossover strategies can be implemented mechanically, but my preference is to find confirmation with other technicals before trading. The SMA periodicities I use for the daily charts are 10-days and 30-days. For a longer-term perspective the 50-day and 200-day SMAs are the most popular.

If prices reach a major support level, do you wait until it has broken through before buying or selling?

To be sure that the major support level is broken, I wait for confirmation as the break of a support level could be a false signal (a whipsaw). For a buy signal, I wait for the close of the next two trading sessions. The close of the bar or candlestick should be above the major support level. If all other technical indicators confirm the break out, buying or selling will be initiated. Another technique is the use of a specific price percentage target above the major support, e.g. a 2% or 5% break above the support level.

How do you judge if a market is overbought or oversold?

My approach is very traditional in measuring overbought and oversold conditions. I use the RSI, MACD and stochastics again to detect when the market is oversold in a down trending market and overbought in an up trending market. Searching for positive and negative divergence between the price and the indicator can provide an investor with early warning signals.

USING TA FOR RISK AND TRADE MANAGEMENT

Can you explain your approach to risk and money management?

If I get a buy or sell signal from my model, I have to decide how much capital I am willing to risk. The most important step in money management before you enter a trade is to determine and establish a risk/reward target. My risk/reward for short-term trades will be 1:2. With the potential price target set, the next step is to determine the stop-loss price in order to minimize any capital loss. I aim to set a target so that I cannot lose more than 10% on the trade.

What risk measures do you use?

I look at the maximum drawdown and Value-at-Risk (VaR) to get a sense of the risk within the portfolio. Understanding which underlying positions can hurt the performance is also crucial. So besides risk/reward ratios, stop-loss levels should also be in place. For instance, from our quantitative model we derive expected returns of stocks, which we align with their risk profile. So it could be possible that a stock with a lower expected return will enter the portfolio; but this will be a result of its lower risk profile and better risk/reward ratio.

What part does TA play in your risk assessment?

We will ask which direction the market is heading. The classical chart patterns combined with support and resistance levels and Fibonacci techniques will provide us with projection targets for where the market is heading. The combination of these support and resistance levels with other TA indicators (e.g. momentum indicators) will increase the probability of a correct projection.

Another alternative TA technique is point-and-figure charting that provides price target projections based on two different calculations; a horizontal and a vertical count method. When the underlying security or market index is breaking above or below a critical resistance or support level, various methods can be used to make price projections. We will make a trade-off between reward and risk based on these price projection inputs. In our analysis, we will use key support and

165

resistance levels and price projections to analyse where the market is heading.

What results have you obtained from backtesting your strategies?

We have backtested strategies such as moving average crossovers and momentum strategies in various equity markets including Europe, US and Japan. We have asked, which momentum strategy works better, the 1-month reversal or the 3, 6, 9, 12-month? The last backtesting we did was for various momentum strategies; buying the top decile stock of the underlying index and selling the bottom decile stocks based on their momentum ranking. The strategies strongly depend on the time frame that you have selected, but in general, momentum strategies will pay off. Looking at the last two years, selling companies that were out of favour would generate a huge return not only on a 1-month basis, but also over 6 months.

What are the key performance parameters you look at apart from return?

For relative investment strategies we look typically at ex-ante, ex-post tracking error, Sharpe ratio and the Information ratio. But for absolute investment strategies, other risk performance measurements are applicable like VaR in relation to return estimation and maximum drawdown.

What annual return do you generally look for in your trading/investing? How do you adjust this for risk?

For our investment portfolio, we are looking for a return of 3-month Euribor + 2% on an annual basis. In our trading strategies, we are looking for 5-10% return on individual trades given the risk/reward ratio. On a portfolio level, the risk adjusted performance measure that we use is the Sharpe ratio. In this Sharpe ratio formula, the standard deviation of the portfolio return is one of the components to adjust the return for risk besides the portfolio expected return.

We also look at VaR as a risk measure for our investment portfolio. This risk measure should be applied in relation to the return target of the portfolio, and the same applies with the trading strategies. So if the standard deviation of a specific security is too high compared to the expected return target, then no position or trade will be generated.

How do you decide on which position size to take? How much of your capital are you prepared to risk at any one time?

For our investment portfolio, the maximum risk is 10% on an overall level.

What level of drawdown are you prepared to tolerate?

The maximum drawdown can be seen from an individual security level or from a portfolio context. On a security level, we tolerate 10% to 15% maximum drawdown depending on the weight in the portfolio, and for the total portfolio the maximum drawdown is 10%.

Which trade entry strategies do you use?

We will not enter a trade based on one signal. We combine various entry strategies. As well as moving averages, I also use the stochastic. When the fast %K stochastic crosses the fast %D stochastic, or the fast %K stochastic falls below 80 or rises above 30, it will generate trading signals.

How do you use the RSI?

When the RSI indicator is moving from the territory above 70 crossing below the 70 level.

Which trade exit strategies do you use?

Pivot points and breakouts of support levels and resistance levels, depending on whether the strategy is long or short. Exit strategies are essential to any trend following strategy. Aaverage true range (ATR) trailing stops are commonly used with trend following strategies and can be implemented for each asset.

Can you explain what a pivot point is and how you identify them?

A pivot point is a tool mainly used by traders to help determine the best trading strategy for the coming day. But pivot points can be extended for use over a longer-term horizon. Traders will calculate the pivot point at the beginning of each day in order to establish resistance and support levels based on the extremes and close of the previous day. The investor will take, for instance, weekly or monthly data to identify pivot points which will provide them with resistance and support levels of the underlying asset.

The input needed to calculate the pivot point is the previous trading day's high, low and closing price of the underlying asset. The pivot point is simply the weighted average price of these three variables. The resistance and support levels are derived from the pivot point, which is always the starting point of these calculations.

The classic formulas for the pivot, resistance and support points are:

Resistance 3 = High + 2*(Pivot - Low)
Resistance 2 = Pivot + (R1 - S1)
Resistance 1 = 2 * Pivot - Low

Pivot Point = (High + Close + Low)/3

Support 1 = (2 * Pivot)– High
Support 2 = Pivot - (R1 - S1)
Support 3 = Low - 2*(High - Pivot)
The three most important points are the pivot point, Resistance 1 (R1) and Support 1 (S1). The resistance and support levels will be the input for our money management.

How do you decide where to place stops?

When volatility increases, we will lower our stop-loss percentages. These will vary from a 5-10% loss depending on the weight of the stock in the portfolio. By looking at weekly pivot points and Tom DeMark indicators we derive support and resistance levels which tell us where to place stops. The TD Sequential™ indicator will automatically generate a stop-loss level which we will often use as a prime signal.

To set stop-loss levels we also take into account the risk/reward ratio. For short-term trades this should be set at 2:1. The upside potential of the trade is estimated at 14% while the loss is set at a maximum of 7%. For longer-term investments of at least six months, the risk/reward should be at least 3:1 which means a potential profit of at least 40%, with the maximum risk of 10% loss of its value. For trades longer out than this (more than six months), we look at a risk/reward of 3:1 with a 40/50% profit and 10%-15% risk.

168

In order to have clear stop-loss levels, we have to determine and identify the trade's most recent support or resistance level. We just put the stop-loss below that level. Apart from trendlines and Fibonacci levels, the 10 or 20-day simple moving average can act as a support or resistance level from which to set stop-loss levels. For the longer-term, the 120, 200 or 250-day SMAs are used for predefined stop-loss levels.

Depending on the size of the investment, we also use the 'percentage rule' in our portfolio. If the investment is losing more than 10% of its value, the stop-loss level of the investment is then triggered. Here the pre-defined level can be easily determined based on the percentage for each trade.

What is your view on the use of optimised stop-losses?
The issue with these is how they are determined. The risk level needs to be incorporated into any calculation but if you have an algorithm to calculate the stop-loss level, and it saves you money in your backtest, it would make sense to use it. For our longer-term perspective, we have adopted the approach explained in the previous question and so don't rely on systematically generated stop-loss levels.

How do you deal with volatility? How does very high volatility affect the efficacy of your preferred strategy?
Apart from adjusting our stop-loss levels, we shorten our investment horizon during periods of high volatility.

How do you measure changing volatility?
We will usually use the VIX index as an indicator of rising or falling volatility.

COMBINING WITH OTHER NON-TA INFORMATION

What sentiment indicators do you look at?
Sentiment causes short-term, volatile price movements, usually with changes in volume. The Advance/Decline line is one indicator that will quantify market sentiment as this market breadth indicator reflects the action of the general market. With sentiment, we are looking for confirmation of the underlying price. As long as price

action and the Advance/Decline line are moving in the same direction, the trend is likely to continue.

Another sentiment indicator that we look at is the CBOE put/call ratio, which is the volume of equity puts of the S&P500 traded divided by the volume of calls. In these market conditions (2009), a high put/call ratio indicates that pessimism is high in the stockmarket and that investors should not be outright bearish.

Apart from these quantitative measures of volatility, what is the best way to get a general feel for the way the market is thinking?

Besides the technical sentiment indicators, psychological factors can give you a sense of market sentiment. The financial media, such as Bloomberg and CNBC television, are currently covering the recession and saying that the end is not yet in sight. Sentiment is very bearish; the stock market is still in a downward trend and will sell-off on any new bad news. When equity prices start to increase after the release of bad news then maybe it is time to initiate contrarian strategies as this would indicate that the psychological factor is changing. Combining technical sentiment indicators with economic data and psychological factors will give you an overall picture of market sentiment.

You mentioned that volume is important in gauging market sentiment. How do you use volume data?

We monitor the volume levels when we want to enter or exit a trade. Firstly we ask; is volume supporting the underlying price movement? We are looking for various indicators that can confirm a reversal or the continuation of a trend.

For example, when a head-and-shoulders pattern is almost complete we look to see if volume is supporting the pattern. In this example, volume is one of the essential indicators for confirmation because if volume is supporting the reversal pattern, the likelihood of price breaking below the neckline will increase. I like the On Balance Volume (OBV) indicator which can be used if it diverges from price but can also be used to confirm new price highs and lows.

Is the OBV a real-time indicator? What do you think are its main strengths and weaknesses?

We look at volume data of the OBV indicator on a delayed basis; as we focus on medium to longer-term investments this is not a problem.

170

The main strength of the OBV is that it can signal the strength or weakness of the price action. Used with trendline breaks and price divergences, the OBV can trigger effective buy and sell signals.

The weakness of the OBV, like any indicator, is that the signals generated can be false; as such it should always be used in conjunction with other indicators.

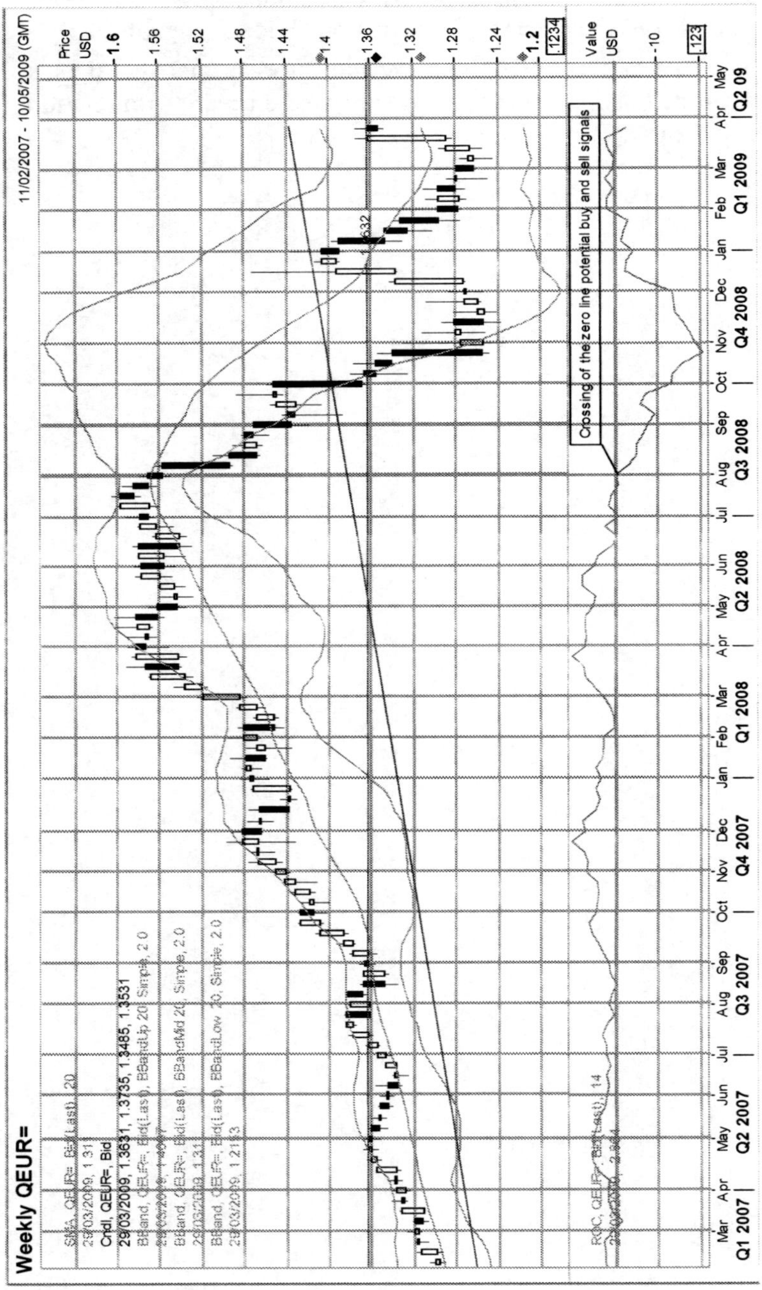

Figure 1 - Rate of Change (ROC) UR/USD   Source: Reuters Metastock

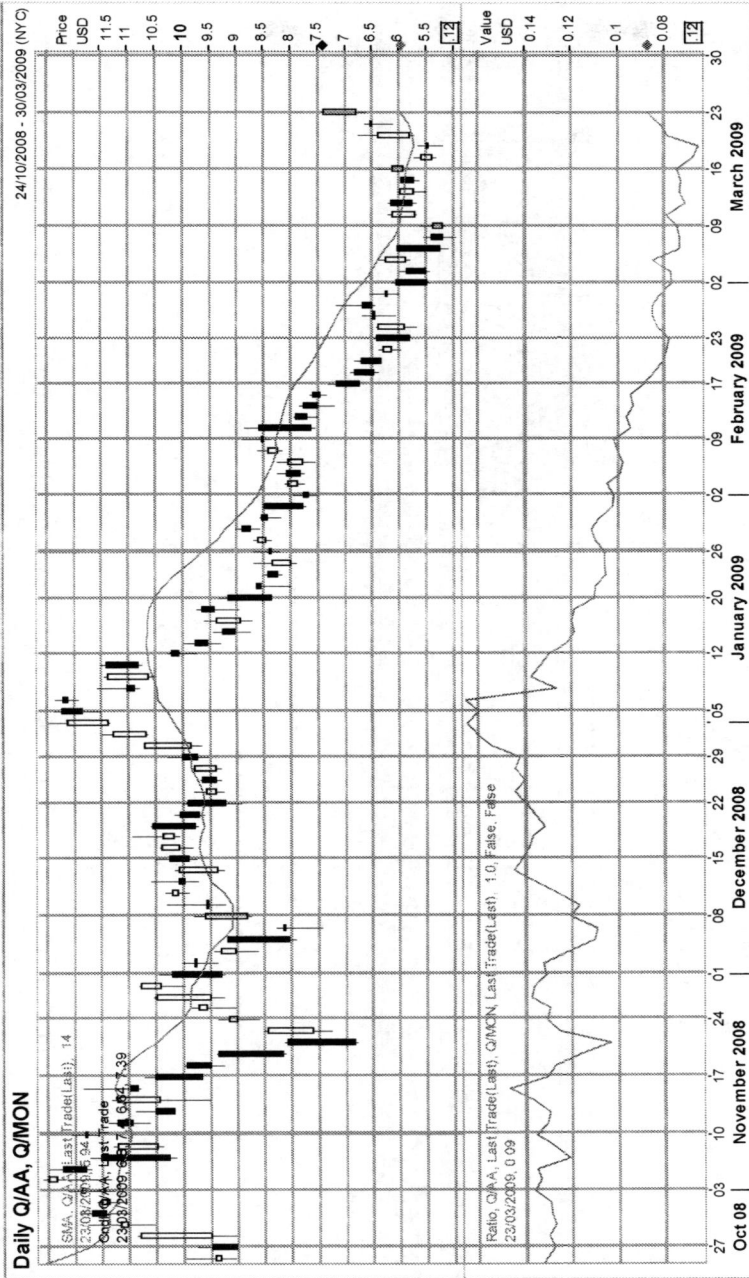

Figure 2 - Relative strength between Alcoa and Monsanto   Source: Reuters Metastock

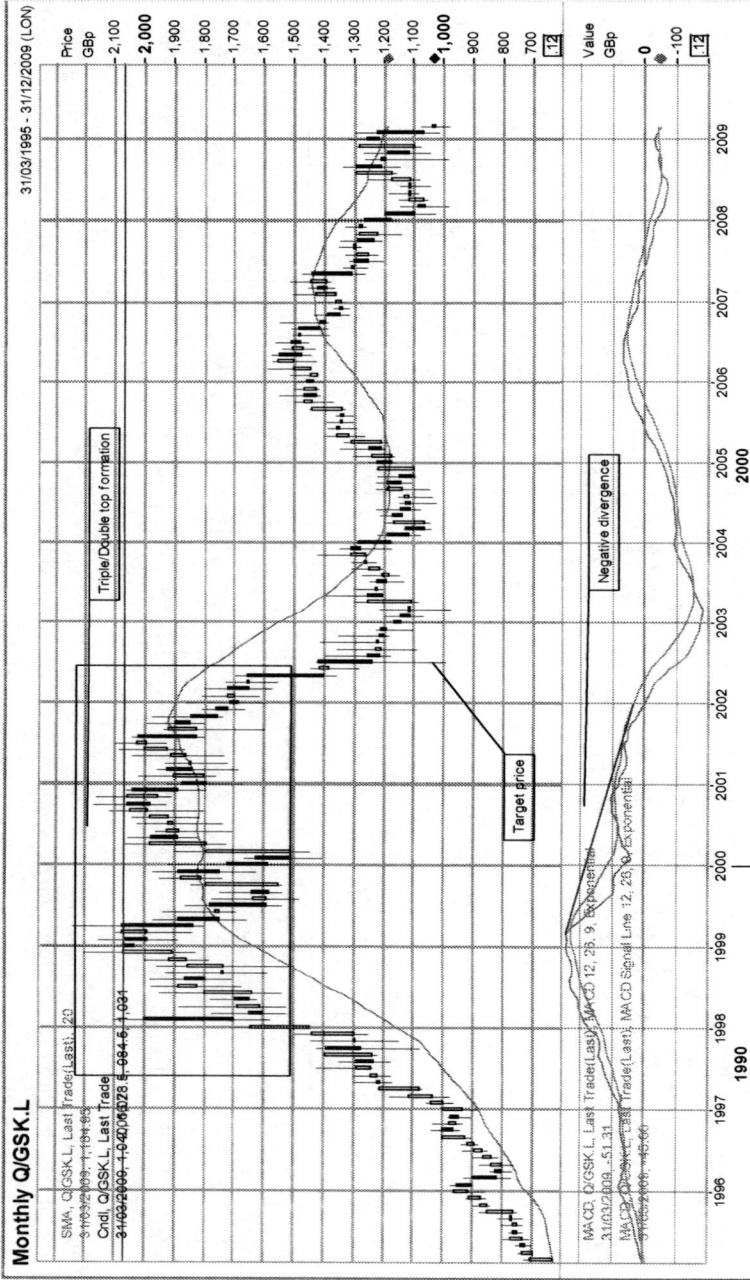

Figure 3 - Double top formation and price target for GlaxoSmithkline   Source: Reuters Metastock

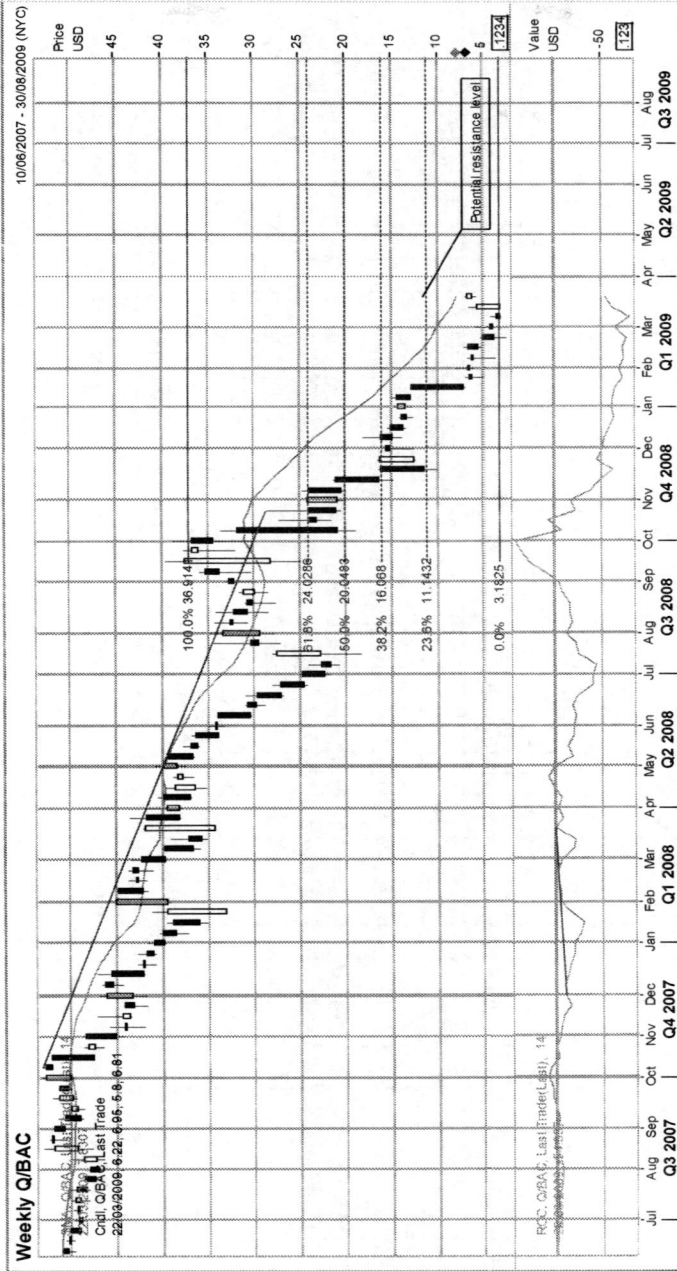

Figure 4 - Fibonacci retracement levels for Bank of America   Source: Reuters Metastock

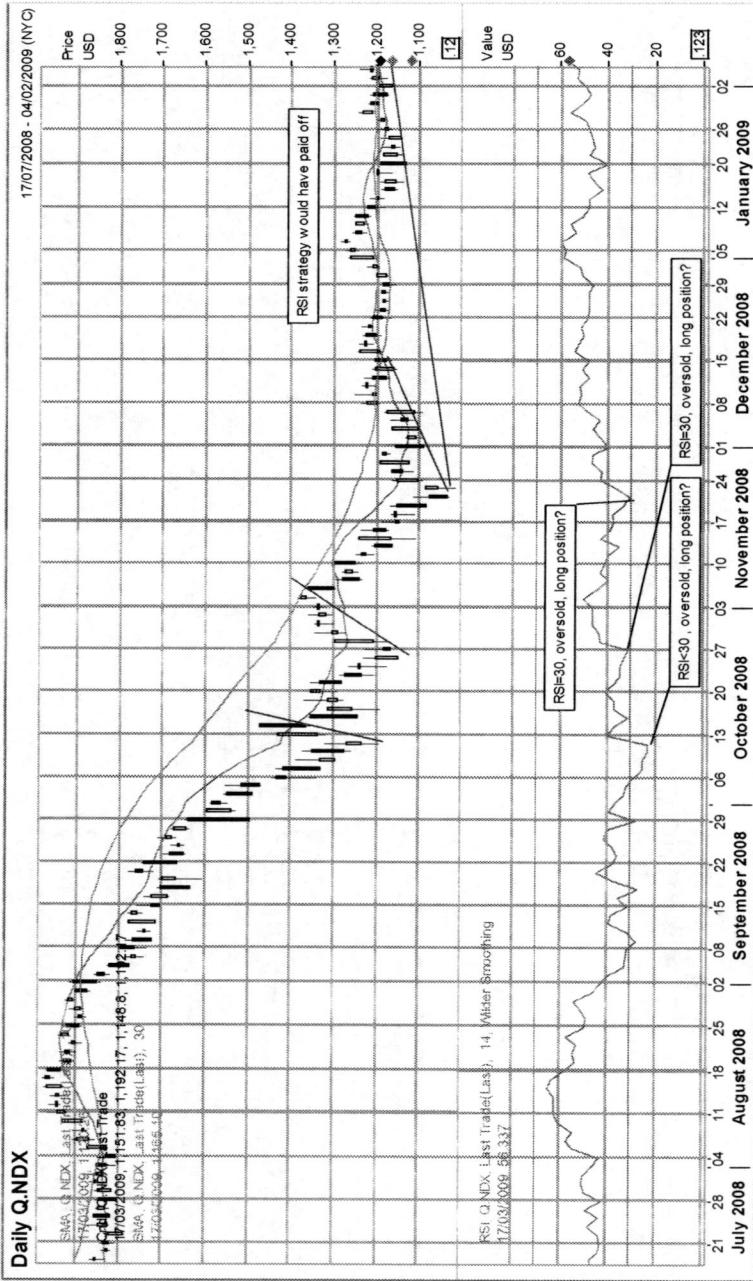

Figure 5 - RSI for the Nasdaq100   Source: Reuters Metastock

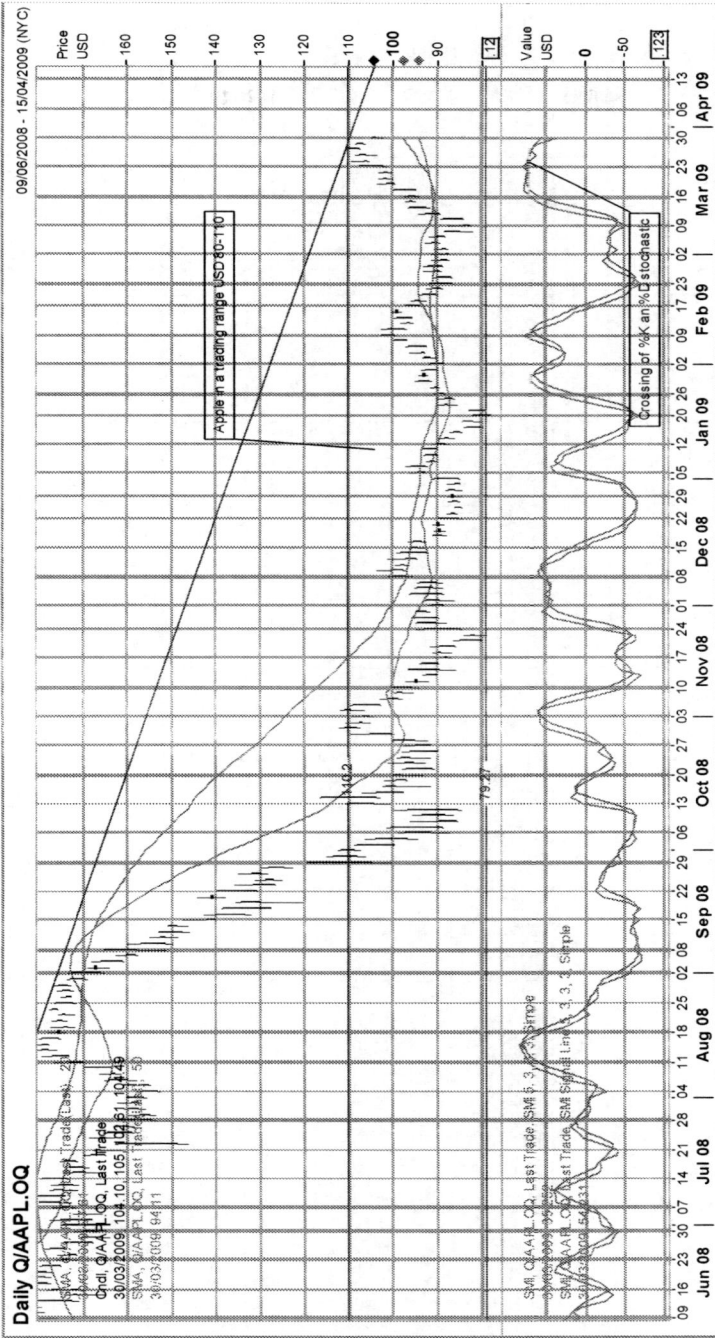

Figure 6 - Stochastic indicator for Apple

Source: Reuters Metastock

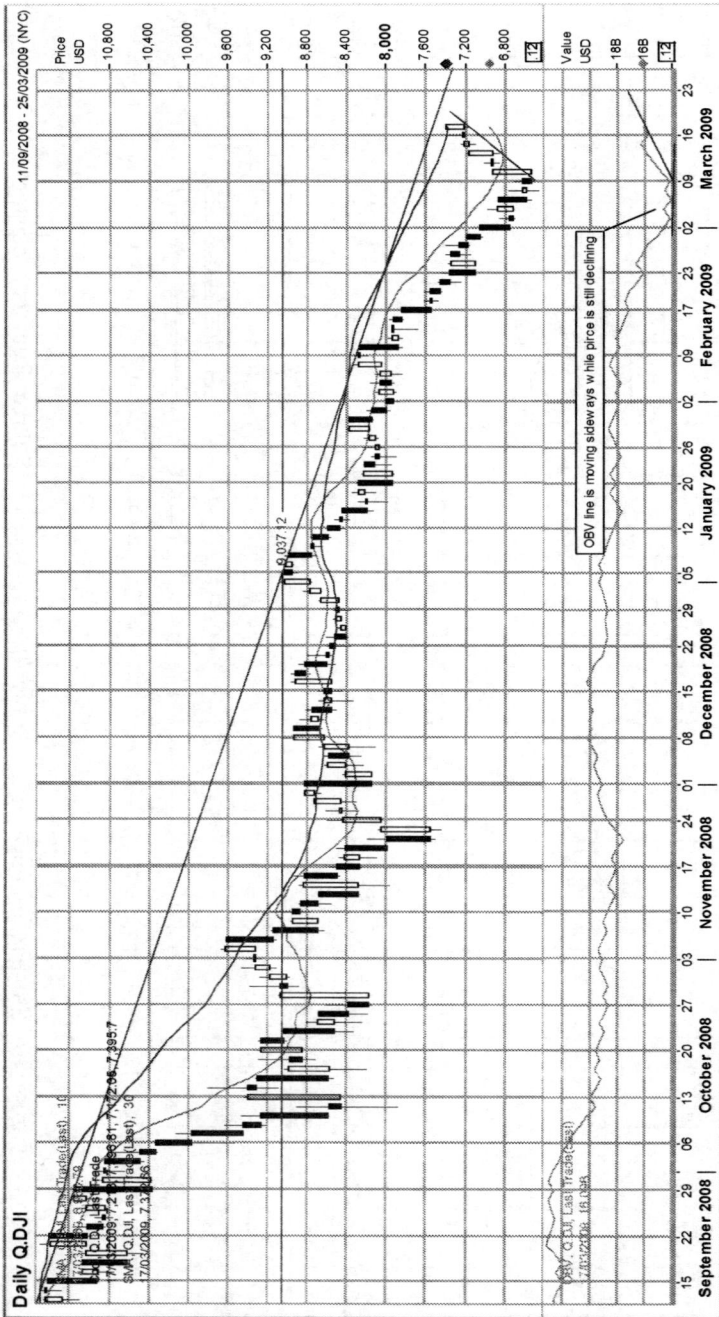

Figure 7 - On Balance Volume (OBV) for the Dow

Source: Reuters Metastock

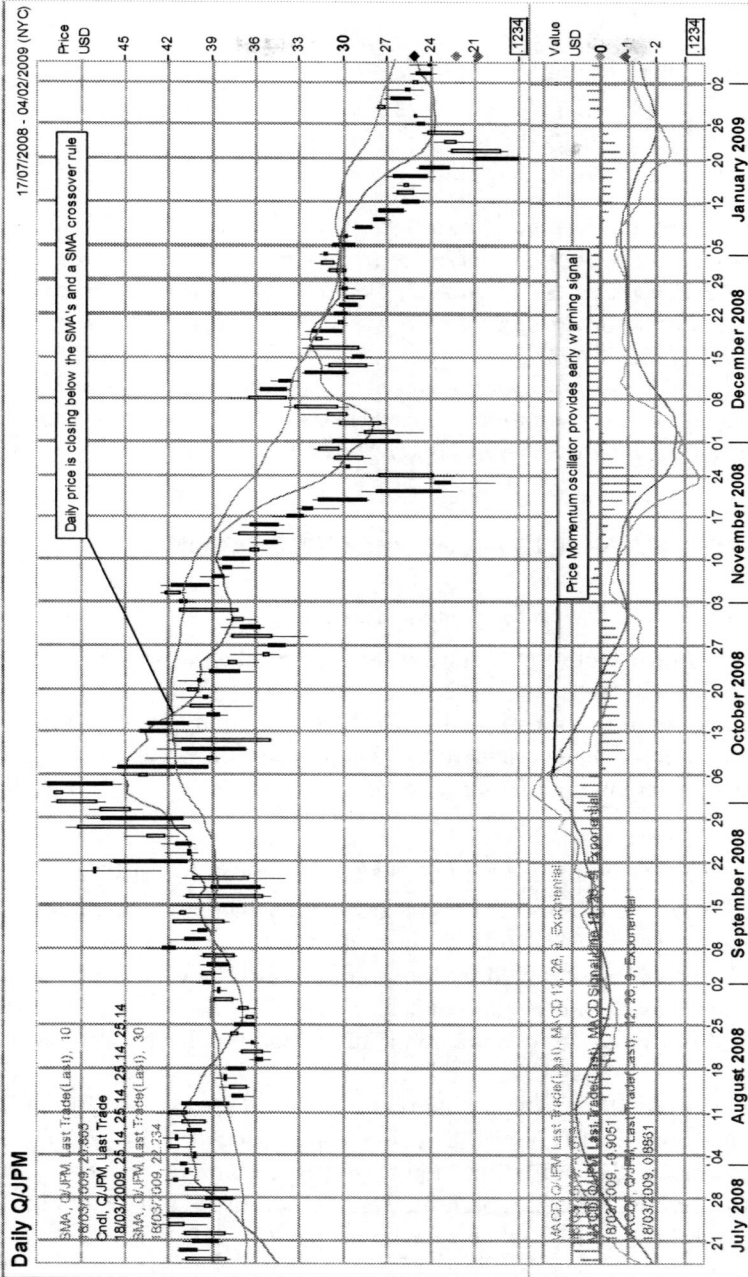

Figure 8 - Moving average crossover and momentum oscillator for JP Morgan   Source: Reuters Metastock

179

Chapter 12

MAXIME VIEMONT

MANAGER SIGMA TEAM

B* CAPITAL, BNP PARIBAS

Maxime Viemont, CFT, joined brokerage house B* Capital, a division of BNP Paribas, in 1999. He went on to set up the firm's technical analysis department and developed QuantiTech™, an investment process based on hybrid trend following strategies. Since 2005 he has been managing the SIGMA team focusing on investment strategies and model-based portfolio management. He works with colleagues Didier Margetyal, who co-manages the European and US QuantiTech strategies, and technical analyst, Lionel Duverger.

USING TA FOR TRADE AND INVESTMENT DECISIONS

Can you explain your basic investment style?

We use a semi-discretionary trend-following strategy, where stock selection is mainly based on price momentum and earning revisions. The management of our positions follows technical analysis principles and related money management rules. This process allows us to select up to 20 stocks depending on market conditions.

Why did you choose to use TA? What made you convinced it works?

Investment is an art, not a science. As such, everyone has to find their own way to succeed. TA is one of these paths. Those who decide to follow it are probably attracted by the richness of the toolbox such as patterns, indicators and cycle studies. Every technician can pick elements out of this toolbox to create the technique that best suits their personality.

Another feature of TA is that it can be applied on almost every kind of asset and on every investment horizon. Advances in trading technology mean that investors tend to become more short-term oriented (the average holding period of a stock on the NYSE is about 9 months today versus more than 6 years in the 50's). This means also

180

that investors react more quickly to immediate price returns. In such an environment, technicians may have better tools than fundamentally-oriented investors as there is no reason for a stock to return to "fair value" (if such a concept really exists) if everyone becomes myopic.

But we are not saying that fundamental analysis is worthless. Some are doing a great job and have a sharp vision of a company strengths and weaknesses. But this method is too time-consuming to allow a large coverage of stocks unless the team is very well staffed. Technicians and quants have a more superficial knowledge of a company so we avoid stocks that we do not understand technically.

Can you explain how and to what degree you use TA in making investment decisions? What technical strategies and indicators work best for the short and long term?

For our technical strategy, we fully rely on technical analysis only for short term trades (i.e. 1 day to 3 months). For our longer term strategies (i.e. 3 months to 2 years), we incorporate up to 50% of fundamentals such as when a trend on a stock is backed by good momentum on EPS. We also adjust our stop losses to the time frame of the strategy: close for short term trades as targets are clearly defined from the start, less stringent for stocks on a long-term uptrend as we do not want to be stopped too early.

As we cannot follow more than 800 stocks with this process, we wanted to develop a quantitative strategy to enlarge the coverage. For the quantitative strategy, some basic technical analysis is used to determine whether we are in a bull or bear market and whether investors are chasing value or growth stocks. After this first step, we only use fundamental criteria to avoid an overlap with the trend-following strategy.

During the recent market turbulence in 2008 has TA performed better or worse than usual? Are there any market conditions under which TA works better or worse than other times?

Our trend-following process showed its resilience in the bear market after sizeable out-performance during the bull years. Of course, we wish we had cut our equity exposure more aggressively, as do most other long-only equity managers.

Do you think TA and quants are closely related?

Technical and quantitative analysis share an essential principle: history tends to repeat itself. Causes may change, but financial markets keep a predictable component as prices depend on investors' behaviour, which in turn, is ruled by their emotions. As human emotions have been the same for centuries, one can suppose that financial markets will develop the same kind of patterns from time to time. That is why technicians and quants will chase these patterns, each group with its own tools, in the hope of finding tradable ones; patterns that will give them an edge over other investors.

Technical analysis gives rules for drawing a pattern, for using an indicator and for finding good entry or exit points. These rules are then generally illustrated with many charts. Technical analysts should not try to show their methodology is right, but just that it cannot be proven wrong. Quantitative analysts test the robustness of their models with statistical methods. As such, quants can never really prove that their models are true or false, just that they may have an explanatory power at a given confidence level.

The historical gap between both methods has been partly filled by the interest of academics in technical analysis over the last decade. Some widely accepted technical rules have been statistically tested* (for a broad study, please refer for example to *The Profitability for Technical Analysis: A review* by Cheol-Ho Park and Scott H. Irwin). The debate around their economical profitability and statistical power is still open to question and will probably remain so, as long as the larger debate about market efficiency continues. At least research on technical analysis has helped to give some credit to the field. However, suffering from a lack of scientific basis, it is still commonly considered with disdain by the asset management industry.

How easy is it to use TA? Do you think training is required?

Technical analysis seems to be an easy-going approach but in reality it is rather hazardous. Indeed, you can easily make a technical strategy just to confirm your positions in a portfolio. In others words, you can see only what you want to see.

INDICATORS AND STRATEGIES

What is your reaction when the charts show a very obvious technical pattern such as a head and shoulders or a double top?

We believe that there is no such thing as a perfectly clear pattern. So whenever we see what is considered an obvious pattern, which is shared by the technical community, we remain cautious. Remember that you must follow many rules to validate a reversal pattern. We prefer patience to anticipation because it's often more profitable and less risky.

What rules do you follow to validate a reversal pattern?

In the case of a bullish reversal pattern like a double bottom I look for one or more of the following: a breakout of a bearish trendline, a change in the volume (low volume on the second bottom then more volume in a bull session than in a bear session), a breakout of the neckline and one or two weekly closes above the new support to validate it.

How do you identify when a trend has commenced and may be nearing its end?

We look for the conjunction of several indicators: sentiment, participation, volume, reversal patterns, divergence on the weekly relative strength index (RSI), and trend breakouts. But a signal is always triggered by price action.

What is the best method for measuring price momentum in the market?

We often look at candlesticks mainly for short term trading. On a daily basis, we follow several indicators such as relative strength, moving averages (20-day, 50-day and 200-day), Fibonacci retracements and targets, gaps, volume, MACD, RSI, ROC and Bollinger Bands. We often watch On Balance Volume (OBV), mainly in distribution/accumulation phases to anticipate the next trend.

For a longer investment horizon, we monitor moving average crossovers, the monthly MACD, major support/resistance levels, volatility, sentiment and participation indicators, and finally Elliott Wave theory. For technical strategies, as already said, we like momentum on EPS to keep stocks for longer in a bull trend.

What candlestick patterns do you use and why?

For short term trading I find that candlestick charts are only useful when combined with other technical indicators. We like reversal patterns such as Dark Clouds, the Engulfing Pattern, Hammers and Shooting Stars.

How can TA be used for sector rotation and asset allocation?

Before selecting stocks, we make an equity sector allocation to choose our preferred sectors. We use the same indicators as for stocks but we like watching relative strength to compare two sectors or one sector to its reference index.

If prices reach a major support level do you wait until it has broken through before buying or selling?

We often wait for two weekly closes before acting in case it breaks through the major support.

If the market is being driven by emotion (such as the post-credit crunch sell-off), is this entirely reflected in the technicals?

We think so. Emotion is reflected in volatility, sentiment indicators, candlesticks or the spread between the price close and the 200-day moving average. The difficulty lies in correctly interpreting them at extremes levels such as those seen in 2008. In fact, we like to watch emotion through our colleagues' behaviour because it gives us precious information, especially for anticipating reversal trends.

How do you judge if a market is overbought or oversold?

We use many indicators such as participation, sentiment, divergence on momentum, and the put/call ratio. For our technical strategy, we always wait for price action before trading.

How do you use momentum and the RSI to gauge overbought and oversold conditions? What parameters do you use for these indicators?

For the RSI we use 8 and 14 days and look for divergence with price. However, price action always takes priority as it is dangerous to follow signals based only on overbought/oversold indicators.

Can you explain how you interpret the put/call ratio and what you look for?

We use the ratio as a contrarian indicator. As such, when it reaches very low levels, we consider that investors are being too greedy. At very high levels, the indicator tends to suggest excessive fear. However, I should stress that we don't give a huge amount of weight to put/call ratio analysis as our backtests show it is not that successful. We just use it as a confirmation of sentiment surveys or the VIX reading.

How inefficient do you believe markets to be? Are some asset markets more inefficient than others?

As active fund managers we cannot be supporters of the random walk theory. News is unpredictable, but it is not the news that drives markets but how investors react to it. For example, markets sometimes rally on bad news or consolidate on presumed good news. This could prove that it is foolish to make market predictions. But it could also mean that sometimes markets exhibit either persistent behaviour (they trend) or countertrend features (they correct) despite the news flow.

From our point of view, emotions are the real driver of a market. As such, stock prices do not follow a Brownian motion as investors hardly go from extreme pessimism to excessive optimism in just a second. That said, making money with active management is not an easy task. After all, most active fund managers under-perform their benchmarks in the long run. This is quite easy to understand as security selection is a negative-sum game. The only way that somebody can overweight a company in his portfolio is if somebody else takes a counter position and underweights this same stock. Only one will be right but both parties had to incur costs in the form of brokerage commissions or software, hardware and research expenses.

We decided to play that game not because we believe that we are smarter than the average investor, but because we believe we have built a more robust process than the average investor. Our process serves as a firewall against some of the cognitive biases into which investors fall.

185

USING TA FOR RISK AND TRADE MANAGEMENT

Can you explain your approach to risk and money management?

We have a clear preference for research which follows the 'keep it simple' principle. We have a limited understanding of state-of-the-art mathematical techniques, so we do not go too far in that direction. Furthermore, it often happens that investors tend to be too confident when they use sophisticated mathematics. Value at Risk (VaR) is a good example of that. Many fund managers asked quants to calculate the expected maximum loss of a portfolio at a 95% or 99% confidence level. Portfolios were then managed or even leveraged accordingly. But last year's extreme levels of volatility proved that these models were flawed because drawdowns well exceeded expectations. So as far as we're concerned, we prefer to look at more basic technical or quantitative research, where we can understand the underlying reasons for their supposed edge.

We have three steps to follow for risk management:

First, we allocate our capital to different strategies according to the investment horizon, coverage and strategy's turnover. In other words, the shorter the strategy, the higher its turnover and the less money we invest in it. So we choose to allocate more money to long-term strategies and at least 50% to quantitative strategies. Then, risk indicators included in our stock selection criteria are part of risk management. Finally, money management is the last step for managing risk. We adopt daily money management with stop losses for technical strategies.

Have you attempted to backtest your strategies?

We have done some backtesting on technical indicators, but to be frank, our technical strategies are more derived from our experience than from the results of backtesting. On the other hand, our quantitative strategy was fully designed via backtesting. For this purpose, we collected fundamental data from more than 10,000 US companies for the period May 1990 to April 2003. We chose to use a very large universe to avoid, as much as possible, survivorship bias by keeping active, as well as defaulted or merged companies. After this optimisation period, we applied the model on an out-of-sample data set covering the period May 2003 to September 2008. As performances seemed robust, we incorporated this quantitative strategy into the US QuantiTech® portfolios in January 2009. We did a similar job on more than 4000 stocks in the Eurozone and launched the quantitative selection model in February 2009. The two lists of 30 stocks that are derived from the programme are followed systematically.

What impact did the turmoil in 2008 have on your returns? What action have you taken to reduce any losses?

We have created a very short-term technical strategy to take advantage of the increase in implied volatility. Moreover, we developed a medium-term technical strategy to pick stocks more easily when there is a rise in false signals on the absolute trend.

What are the key performance parameters you look at?

The performance parameters we choose are very simple: drawdown, payoff ratio, especially for the very short term strategy, volatility, and above all, our consistency in catching outperformance.

How do you decide on which position size to take? How much of your capital are you prepared to risk at any one time?

Each time we buy a stock, we do not exceed more than 2% of our global portfolio. For short-term technical strategies, we place tight stop losses at around 5% and at around 10-15% for our medium-term technical strategies. For quantitative strategies, each position can't exceed 1.7% because of our monthly update

Our drawdown depends on what the market is doing. During bear markets we just want our portfolio to be defensive. For that purpose, we put some stop losses in to adjust our equity exposure when the market is falling.

Which trade exit strategies do you use?

For short and medium-term technical strategies, we have two closing rules: technical target price or triggered stop loss. For the longer-term technical strategies, we wait for a reversal in both price and EPS momentum before selling the position. In fact, this double signal helps us let our profits ride for longer.

COMBINING WITH OTHER NON-TA INFORMATION

What sentiment indicators do you look at? How do you judge what market sentiment is at any one time? What do you use as sentiment indicators away from what the charts are telling you?

When participants' sentiment reaches extreme levels (panic or euphoria), a trend is very close to a reversal. The difficulty is in finding accurate sentiment indicators. Our preferred measures encompass surveys from AAII and Sentix. We also look at the VIX or the put/call ratio. Based on these inputs, we developed a systematic hedging model. The signal from our sentiment based model is usually a bit too early, but we don't mind as the trend-following strategy is, by definition, always a little too late.

Do you keep an eye on volume levels, and if so, how do you use them in your decisions?

Volume is a precious indicator we follow on a daily basis. We use it to understand the liquidity of each stock, and therefore our willingness to trade, but also to estimate the strength of a breakout of a support or resistance level. Finally, we always use it to confirm price action.

Do you often find yourself at odds with the market and/or your fundamentally-based colleagues?

Most colleagues at B*capital are fundamentally oriented. Thus, we frequently disagree on the way to assess the market in general or a particular stock. But we do not try to convert anybody to the world of technical analysis or quantitative analysis. After all, they were also able to outperform the market over the last couple of years. So, the way you act in the market doesn't matter as long as you are comfortable with your process.

Moreover, we know that our approach does not suit every investor. Anyone who decides to invest in our strategies has to forget the 'story selling': why company X has a bright future and a poor valuation or why company Z disappointed and must be sold. We do not fall in love with the stocks we cover since we hardly know them. We can only sell our decision making process to our clients.

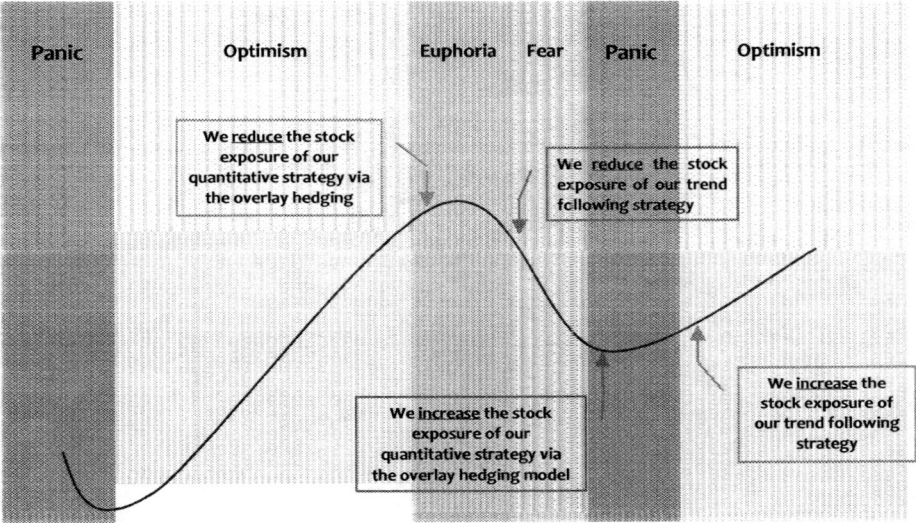

Stock market cycle, emotions and exposure to stocks

PART TWO:
BEHAVIOURAL FINANCE
IN FUND MANAGEMENT

Chapter 13

MICHAEL CLEMENS

SENIOR PORTFOLIO MANAGER

BANKINVEST

Michael Clemens worked as an equities analyst at Sydbank, Carnegie Bank and Handelsbanken in Denmark before becoming a portfolio manager at PFA Pension in 2006. After a spell at ABN Amro, he is now a senior portfolio manager for global equities at BankInvest in Copenhagen. He works in a team of 18 managing around $3 billion in assets, focusing on long-term equities investing benchmarked to the MSCI.

USING TA FOR TRADE AND INVESTMENT DECISIONS

Do you believe that markets are always inefficient?

No, not always. For example, stock markets are much too volatile in comparison to the underlying fundamentals. Robert Schiller discussed this in the early 1980's.

Does BF completely disprove the Efficient Market Hypothesis (EMH)?

If taken literally, yes, but if there is such thing as degrees of efficiency, then not necessarily. Markets are not irrational all of the time, but even though markets are not efficient, history shows that beating the market is still very difficult.

Are markets more inefficient at some times than at others?

Markets are most inefficient when they become complacent which often happens after a long period of above trend economic growth, low inflation, or low interest rates. These are times of representativeness bias and naïve extrapolation as explained by De Bondt and Thaler. Of course, when fear has dominated for some time, the exact same overreaction makes the market inefficient, in the opposite direction.

193

Are some markets more inefficient than others? Can BF be applied more to markets which are considered less efficient, maybe because they are more illiquid?

Theoretically, two characteristics would make some markets more inefficient than others: less liquidity and no 'anchors' of value such as income and dividends. The less liquid the asset or market, the more risk there is of irrational market behaviour, as short selling has no chance of correcting any mistakes. However, even very liquid markets have become irrational as funds flow from less liquid markets in times of panic. A recent example may be flows out of equities into safe investments such as TIPS or Treasuries, when these markets became too expensive compared to long-term fundamentals.

Could a better knowledge of BF have prevented the dot com and credit bubbles?

No, as even the experts are subject to behavioural biases. Institutional biases are also at work, very often against the EMH. Remember that is was also ordinary people who participated in the dot com and housing/credit bubble. You cannot expect them to have a deep knowledge of BF. However, if BF was more widely known among finance practitioners, perhaps the magnitude of both bubbles could have been smaller.

Even though BF provides a convincing explanation for how traders and investors think before making decisions, BF has failed to become a mainstream form of market analysis. Why do you think this is?

There are several reasons for this. Firstly, BF cannot be put into a mathematical formula where it can be modelled. Secondly, our knowledge of BF is still in its relatively early stages, and is up against the powerful and long accepted paradigms of the EMH and CAPM.

Can BF be used to forecast or anticipate price movements?

Yes, with regard to price momentum and overreaction versus mean reversion. These are very powerful BF theories in forecasting price movements.

What is the relationship between technical analysis and BF? Do charts provide the best tangible reference to BF effects?

I do not believe that technical analysis and BF are much related. To my knowledge, while BF is deeply rooted in experimental psychology, technical analysis is more a believer discipline. By this I mean that it is like a religion; either you believe in it or you don't, there is no proof.

But isn't market psychology reflected in the charts, for example in trends, sell-offs and market tops?

Yes. Market psychology is reflected in charts. However, pure TA does not incorporate all the psychology dimensions of behavioural finance. Besides, I do not believe in forecasting based on prices alone; prices have to be 'anchored' to an earnings or asset figure so it becomes a valuation metric instead.

Is it possible to differentiate between intra-day and longer term BF effects? If so, how would you do this?

I don't care about intra-day BF effects, except for the occasional overreaction. While all investment results are a combination of hard work, skills and luck, the latter plays a larger role the shorter the investment horizon.

What BF experiment do you think is most illustrative of market behaviour?

I generally like the representativeness bias type of experiments such as 'Linda the bank teller'.

What questions would you most like answered about behavioural finance and market psychology?

I would like to know more about being able better to identify when 'greed and fear' have gone as far as they can. While some people might believe that knowledge is good for its own sake, I believe that knowledge of BF should help improving returns.

Are there any recent developments in BF that you have found interesting?

I include in BF the field of neuroscience. I think that has been the most interesting development in BF over the past ten years.

Where do you think the latest research in neurofinance will take us? What difference might it make to the field of BF?

I see neurofinance as digging one level deeper than behavioural finance into the chemical and genetic causes of our behaviour. I don't think that neurofinance discoveries will basically change the findings of BF as they really are just two sides of the same coin.

USING BF FOR TRADE AND INVESTMENT DECISIONS

What areas of BF are you interested in and find most useful?

My investment philosophy is long-term investing based on fundamental research. Therefore, I find the theories of long-term Overreaction of great interest. I am a great believer in mean reversion and by using statistical tools, such as confidence intervals, it is possible to find interesting ideas among stocks where the naïve extrapolation caused by Representativeness has gone too far.

Can BF be used to help you place specific trades?

In our firm, we don't trade, we invest. We only buy or sell stocks after careful fundamental analysis, which includes a risk-reward analysis and a total portfolio cost-benefit view in order not to enter into excessive portfolio risks. Hence, a firm entering the portfolio must pass both the test of being attractive on its own merits, and the test of fitting into the portfolio from a risk perspective.

What indicators do you use to quantify market sentiment?

Statistical tools such as confidence intervals help identify when markets are outside their normal range. These tools may be used for both single asset sentiment metrics, such as P/E, and comparative asset sentiment metrics such as the FED model. The real problem is, of course, how to define one's reference period over which to calculate mean and standard deviation.

What are the main obstacles in using BF to aid investment decisions?

I think the biggest problems are discipline and confidence in oneself. All too often, we do not believe or act upon our own research if that deviates much from market consensus. We too often take the stand that we must have missed something since the market obviously disagrees. However, often the market has not done the research you have done, and therefore that knowledge may not be reflected in the market prices.

Is it possible to formulate a trading strategy based on BF?

Many people seem to think so and some people have had success with BF based investing styles. The Fuller and Thaler fund in California is one of the more well known funds dedicated to BF style investing.

Can BF be used to identify market tops and bottoms?

One should not hope or aspire to identifying tops and bottoms. However, one should aspire to identify when we are close to them. My view is that share prices are a function of a random element around fair value (i.e. EMH), and an occasional breakout from this random interval around fair value. Using statistical tools such as confidence intervals helps investors to identify when a move from the historical average is random, and when there is a great chance that it is irrational.

Does BF affect FX and commodity prices to the same degree?

While assets without an income stream (interest or dividends) are, in theory, more prone to bubbles, these are also the assets where detecting bubbles is more difficult because anchors of value are missing. While equities have P/E and dividend yield, and bonds have nominal and real yields, there is no P/E or yield anchor/benchmark for FX or commodities.

Is it possible to properly quantify the impact of behavioural finance? For example, if overreaction exists for a particular share, can this be measured in any way?

Measuring overreaction requires that we define the benchmark of fair value. Since nobody knows exactly the correct fair value, each investor must define his own fair value benchmark against which he measures overreaction. To keep it simple, I use statistical tools, such as standard deviations, which at least give me some indication of overreaction. Assuming that the P/E for the market is 2 standard deviations from its historical mean, that should give me something to think about just as it should if the real interest rate on 10-year TIPS is outside 1 or two standard deviations from its historical mean.

Does BF imply that there is always an under or overreaction to the release of fundamental news?

No; if news is more or less as expected, then BF does not suggest under or overreaction. Furthermore, the least difficult anomalies to exploit are those overreactions to an apparent trend, which is the representativeness bias.

If a market is more liquid, does this imply that the effects of BF on prices are likely to be lesser or greater?

In a market with low liquidity, fewer investors even bother about the market and therefore leave that market more open to biases. Furthermore, low liquidity also means less willingness to short, reducing the possibly of correcting any over-inflated security prices.

BEHAVIOURAL BIASES

Do you use your knowledge of BF to overcome your own biases in investing?

I believe that a few simple check points can reduce one's own BF biases. For example, leaving sufficient margin of safety in the valuation process; trust nobody but yourself and trust your analysis, not your gut feeling; invest for the long run but don't ignore timing, i.e. don't invest when valuation multiples are too high.

To determine when valuation multiples are too high or too low is of course very difficult. I use statistical tools such as confidence intervals and would normally conclude that anything outside +/- 2 standard-deviations is not normal. Hence, stocks where valuation ratios are outside +/- 2 standard deviations are either buy or sell candidates. Stocks within +/- 1 standard deviation are not interesting except for benchmarking purposes. Stocks between 1 and 2 standard-deviations should be on a watch list for potentially deeper research if valuation crosses the 2 STD criteria.

Of the well known behavioural biases, what are the most common among market participants?

It's difficult to say. If one bias is present, typically other biases are present as well. Analysts often display overconfidence and confirmation bias, while investors often display gamblers fallacy and loss aversion. Proprietary traders are subject to more or less all biases, believing they can outsmart the market in the short-term where 'randomness' is much more prevalent than in long-term investing.

What is your attitude to Prospect Theory? Does it still explain much of market behaviour?

The short answer is yes. However, like all theories that try to explain reality, there will be times when theory and reality are not aligned. Since Prospect Theory is a general theory of decision making under uncertainty, the mere presence of uncertainty suggests that anything can happen, but in most cases, people behave as Prospect Theory would suggest.

What behavioural biases do you most look to exploit?

I also look for long-term market overreaction. I believe that fundamentals play a greater role in long-term investing than in short or medium-term investing, which also, in my view, limits the feasibility of certain momentum strategies as portfolio turnover simply gets too high.

You have referred to De Bond and Thaler several times. Can you briefly explain what they say about mean reversion and forecasting price movements?

Generally De Bond and Thaler suggest that stocks which have performed well over the past 4-5 years tend to perform poorly over the coming 4-5 years and vice versa. The main driving behavioural bias is 'representativeness', i.e. the naive extrapolation of past trends. For example, if a company has had a number of good quarters, the market often extrapolates too far into the future, ignoring the power of mean reversion and the economic cycle.

Is market psychology reflected in the charts, for example in trends, sell-offs and market tops?

Yes. Market psychology is reflected in charts. However, pure technical analysis does not incorporate the psychology dimensions of behavioural finance because if it did, it would be behavioural finance and not TA. Besides, I do not believe in forecasting based on prices alone. Prices have to be anchored to an earnings or asset figure so it becomes a valuation metric instead.

You mention your interest in the representativeness bias. Can you explain how you use this and what difference it makes in your investment decisions?

Many analysts suffer from representativeness bias. Hence, when you read research reports, always check the medium and long-term (beyond 3-4 years) assumptions to see if the necessary mean reversion in growth, margins, profitability etc. is taken into account. All too often you see an analyst assuming a margin recovery to peak margins and keeping peak margins going forward. This overstates the value of the company in a DCF model (Discounted Cash Flow). Sometimes you hear an analyst being overly conservative, suggesting that a company with a downturn in returns is doing nothing about it, and hence keep returns below historical averages going forward. If the stock prices have reacted accordingly to these naive extrapolations, then there is the possibility of you making a good investment, or avoiding making a bad one.

Why do you think that assets without a value anchor, i.e. without a recurring source of income like interests or dividends, are more susceptible to biases?

When you look at a government bond, you know you will get the par value of 100 back in X years. You also get an interest income in the meantime. There is simply not much room for disagreements between investors about what the value of this asset is. When you don't know if you will ever get your money back, or if you will not get a recurring income while holding the asset, there is room for speculation about what the asset might be worth. An example was the 3G mobile spectrum auctions in Europe in 2000, which attached exorbitant prices and proceeds to governments bringing many telecom companies near to bankruptcy in the process.

How do you look to exploit the long-term overreaction effect and why do you think markets have such a tendency to overreact?

I try to look at stocks and sectors which have the following characteristics: long-term (3-5 year) underperformance versus the market, cheap valuation and reasonable financial risk. The underperformance and cheap valuation could of course be a so-called 'value trap' (cheap for a reason and should stay cheap because fundamentals will continue to deteriorate), but that is where the analysis steps in. The long-term overreaction occurs because the market naively extrapolates temporary weakness/strength and ignores long-term forces of mean reversion.

Do you think behavioural biases are more prevalent in the short-term or long-term?

I believe that fundamentals dominate in the long run so this means behavioural biases are more prevalent in the short and medium-term. One should, however, also bear in mind that some biases, such as deviations from EMH predictions are 'institutional' in that they are founded in legislation or other types of market imperfections such as transaction costs. Apparent biases caused by such imperfections may take a long time to be corrected.

Do biases always correct themselves?

No, because the market has no memory, only individuals have memory. Each year there are new investors entering the market and these investors (private or professional) are more prone to biases than more experienced market participants who have seen at least one bear market. If by biases you mean bubbles, then they always correct themselves. Often, however, it can take a long time and could even get worse before it gets better. A correcting bubble bias also tends to overcorrect, giving new opportunities for investors.

Are you aware of any behavioural biases in your own investing? If so, what are they and how do you deal with them?

Since our fund is global, benchmark weightings for individual stocks are not important. Hence, herding is not an issue for individual stocks. The most obvious bias is probably the 'disposition effect'. The bias that I actively try to exploit in generating ideas is the long-term overreaction effect.

Is herding necessarily a bad, or irrational, thing to do? If prices are rising doesn't it make sense to buy as well? As such, is herding really a bias?

Herding is not bad in itself. It is herding coupled with overconfidence that is dangerous. When the first losses appear, we mistake it for a short-term correction and believe that the upward trend will continue. When losses continue, Prospect Theory suggests that the disposition effect will lead us to hold on to our losers too long. That is why herding may be irrational.

How would you advise an individual trader or investor to deal with herding?

I would not advise individual investors to trade individual stocks but rather advise them to invest in mutual funds. Only very wealthy individuals should consider trading individual stocks as the consequences of losses are less important. The typical Anglo Saxon asset allocation with more than 50% in equities is a clear case of people not understanding statistics. While in the (very) long run, stocks have done better than bonds, there is no guarantee that this will be the case for the relatively short period (20-25) years in which you are actively saving for retirement.

Was the credit crunch caused simply by a case of overconfidence?

Each period has its fad. In late 2008 and early 2009 it was to be relentlessly bearish. When that has become consensus and lasted for a while, the risk is that enough is enough and the mood changes once more. Overconfidence does not only work on the way up, it also works on the way down. Over-optimism is what hinders us from seeing the downturn until we are in the midst of it.

Chapter 14

MANFRED HÜBNER

HEAD OF BEHAVIOURAL FINANCE

DEKA INVESTMENT

Manfred Hübner, CEFA, began his career as a securities specialist at the Nassauische Sparkasse in Wiesbaden. After several years experience in equity and fixed income research, he became a currency analyst at DZ Bank (formerly DG Bank) in Frankfurt. Manfred joined Deka in 1998 where his responsibilities include fund management and behavioural finance and technical analysis research. He was chairman of the Technical Analysts Association of Germany (VTAD) from 2000-2001 and created and maintains the behavioral finance sentiment indicators at Sentix.

BF THEORY AND INEFFICIENT MARKETS

Do you believe that markets are always inefficient?

We believe that markets can exhibit great inefficiencies from time to time. Behavioural finance states that because emotions play an important role in our decision making, investors make mistakes in their investment decisions. This relates to the way they gain information, and how they use heuristics in their decision making process. However, as long as these individual errors are randomly distributed amongst investors, markets appear efficient. But we see a lot of interaction between investors and due to our nature, we use the behaviour of others as a navigator for ourselves. Individual behaviour therefore has been replaced more and more by group behaviour and market efficiency by inefficiency.

Does behavioural finance completely disprove the Efficient Market Hypothesis (EMH)?

I think so, because supporters of the EMH have an incorrect view of the nature of markets. The idea they have of markets is formed by the field of mathematics or science, so they conclude that if it is not possible to outperform the markets in a predictable manner, then markets have to be efficient.

But the roots of the systematic underperformance of most investors lie within the complexities of human nature. You are better off describing markets as a social entity rather than as a closed-loop control system. Jean-Paul Getty said that if we gave all people at one point in time the same amount of money, we should expect to have huge divergences in the distribution of wealth within a short period of time. That means that it is part of our nature that not all of us are equipped to become economically successful.

However, when it comes to the financial markets, traders and investors don't expect this to apply. The fact that they do is due to over-optimism and greed. That the majority are losing money in the markets is, in my opinion, not evidence of market efficiency but only a sign that an incorrect model of the markets has been applied.

Are markets more inefficient at some times than at others?

The degree of market efficiency varies. You should expect more inefficiency if there is unquestioned, common knowledge in the market and discussions are homogenous. The more investors trade on stereotypes, fads or salient information, the more you should believe in inefficiency.

Are some markets more inefficient than others? Can BF be applied more to markets which are considered less efficient, maybe because they are more illiquid?

Generally, BF anomalies exist wherever humans are acting. In that sense all markets exhibit the same sensitivity for inefficiency. We have found that BF 'rules' lead to better results in markets with a broad participation of investors and where interventions by officials, such as central banks, are not dominant.

Could a better knowledge of BF have prevented the dot com and credit bubbles?

Bubbles are a result of human actions and have a lot to do with regret aversion. Even if a bubble could be identified in time, it would be hard to stop the party before the bubble becomes dangerously inflated and ready to burst. This is because at the crucial point in time such a diagnosis is not the consensus, otherwise it would not be a bubble. It is a market principle that the majority is always wrong when it pays most to be right. That means we should expect bubbles to occur as a part of the game. They will happen as long as humans are acting in the markets.

Even though BF provides a convincing explanation for how traders and investors think before making decisions, it has failed to become a mainstream form of market analysis. Why do you think this is?

BF states that on average, the majority of investors repeatedly make the same mistakes, sometimes in a predictable manner. Despite the fact that you can never say in advance which single investor will make a certain mistake at a certain point in time, you can count on the majority exhibiting the anomalies stated by BF theory.

Investors also overestimate their abilities and underestimate the degree to which their knowledge may be worthless in such a competitive and non-linear business as trading. Finally, a lot of the exogenous shocks that should be the reason for unexpected market movements are instead endogenous effects from investor behaviour.

What is the relationship between technical analysis and BF? Do charts provide the best tangible reference to BF effects?

Technical analysis is very important in our approach because charts reflect the actions of active investors in the market. It is valuable to know the main market direction and to go along with it. But we think sentiment indicators, or what we call behavioural indices, are important as well.

What BF experiment do you think is most illustrative of market behaviour?

It's an experiment many of us have done already for themselves. Consider you are with your partner in an unknown city and you are hungry. You see two, very similar restaurants. There is only one difference: one is full, the other has no guests. You want to make a good impression on your partner. Which restaurant do you choose for lunch? Most people will choose the busy restaurant because it looks like a safer bet for a good lunch. This is an example of the representative heuristic and it explains why humans decide, under uncertainty, to go with the herd and to utilize the information costs other humans have already paid.

What questions would you most like answered about behavioural finance and market psychology?

I would like to know why investors do not learn more from their mistakes, even if they claim to be professionals, and why their customers do not demand more learning from them.

USING BF FOR TRADE AND INVESTMENT DECISIONS

What areas of behavioural finance are you interested in and do you find most useful?

The research of individual behaviour is useful for developing your own trading framework. Group behaviour is of interest if you search for tradable patterns in the market.

Has your knowledge of BF changed the way you trade?

Yes, I have learned about the importance and role of psychology in the markets. An understanding of market psychology helps to identify crowded trades and is useful in managing risks. It helped me to prevent commitment traps, to emphasize the importance of both trends and the right timing of contrarian moves.

Can BF be used to help you place specific trades?

As a result of my BF studies, I am convinced that investors need a framework for their trading. In that sense BF can help on each individual trade. As an example, commitment problems seem related to position size. If you control your exposure in the market then you directly control the probability of potential commitment problems.

What indicators do you use to quantify market sentiment?

I prefer to use the Sentix index which I developed in 2001. Sentix is based on a weekly survey of more than 3000 individuals. From the responses, the index calculates more than 400 indicators on a range of markets and styles. Through Sentix you can gain a more objective perspective on investors' attitudes, risk perceptions and expectations. You can also compare sentiment between groups of investors as well as between markets and investment styles. From that you can see what the current sentiment is, but also what drives investors' sentiment in

terms of investment themes, intermarket relationships and risk
tolerance.

What are the main obstacles in using BF to aid investment decisions?

That it is so hard for investors to change their behaviour although they
know their mistakes.

Is it possible to formulate a trading strategy based on BF?

Yes, there are different promising approaches, both discretionary as
well as quantitative. At Deka we use a discretionary framework based
on technical analysis and sentiment analysis.

*Have you been able to quantify or automate behavioural based
trading?*

Trend following systems are the most common representations of
automated behavioural trading systems and we use them in our
research. Most sentiment analysis is hard to automate because the
problem to solve is non-linear. One example might illustrate that.
Some researchers try to get signals from short-term sentiment
indicators. They apply a simple contrarian rule to sell if sentiment is
bullish, and to buy if sentiment is bearish. If sentiment is extremely
bearish, than these strategies work quite fine, but in the bullish case
they fail regularly.

We found in our research that bullish sentiment is normally not the
end point of a trend; in some cases a sharp rise in bullish sentiment
should be treated as a sentiment impulse that kicks off a bullish trend.
A systematic approach that claims to be robust over all market cycles
has to employ too many variables and exceptions. Such an endeavour
could not lead to a robust and maintainable system.

*What is the relationship between contrarian strategies and BF? What
are the best contrarian indicators in your opinion?*

Investor sentiment fluctuates between greed and fear, hope and regret.
It is like a natural law of markets that the majority has to be wrong
when it is most profitable to be right, at the top or the bottom. But
investors overestimate the need to be a contrarian investor by being
able to pick the top or bottom. Markets do trend most of the time and

it is often very hard for investors to go with the trend and to trade with the flow.

To be a patient trend follower can be a contrarian strategy. Good contrarian opportunities exist for those who recognize that the driving force behind a trend is common knowledge when the thinking of investors has become homogenous. In this type of market, there is not enough thinking taking place. Markets then become unstable and susceptible to reversals.

How can BF help in the risk management of a trading position?

Firstly, as a behaviourist you know the psychology behind losses. From Prospect Theory, developed by Daniel Kahneman and Amos Tversky, we know that losses weigh almost two and a half times more than gains. Pain through losses climb quickly and can lead to an inability to act, or to a hope induced increase in the position. Therefore, it is nearly always the best strategy to cut your losses short before the aversion of loss dominates your mind. Secondly, you should emphasize contrarian thinking and diversification in your research.

Thirdly, you should put price as the sole objective information on top of your decision rules. A valuation approach, for example, means that you should buy cheap assets. Unfortunately this does not imply that every cheap asset immediately goes up. If these assets fall further, your P&L gets damaged but your system still says 'buy'. That means that your system is not correlated to your P&L which could bring you into conflict in following your approach. If you put price first you ensure that the most important rule correlates to your P&L. This maintains your ability to act according to your approach.

Can BF be used to identify market tops and bottoms?

I don't think it is too important to identify market tops or bottoms. It is more important to identify risks in the market. If the trend is up and you are not invested, then you have the risk of buying the market too late because, sooner or later, you may find it hard to defend your pessimistic mood against your self-image. This is known as a capitulation move. So it is always better to panic first if you know that you will panic sooner or later. If the majority of investors are invested heavily in equities and investors get greedy, fed by a media that transmits neat slogans to the masses, then you should reduce your holdings because risks are high. So a behaviourally oriented approach, using sentiment and price information, has a better chance of identifying a top or a bottom in the market than a fundamental approach where most of the input parameters are subjective and therefore prone to be adjusted by sentiment.

What role does BF have in the mispricing of stocks?

Valuation, in the classic fundamental sense, is completely subjective and therefore depends on the perception of reality by investors. Mispricing can only be exhibited against an objective, time-invariant measure.

Has BF helped you spot bubbles and identify when they are likely to burst?

Bubbles exhibit certain characteristics, but it is very hard to identify the exact turning point in time because every major bear market begins with a normal correction. The concept of 'tipping points' may be helpful. A tipping point is characterised by a sudden change in sentiment followed by a completely different view of investors on a specific topic. The change in oil sentiment during 2008 was a good example of such a tipping point.

Does BF imply that there is always an under or overreaction to the release of fundamental news?

No. There are times in the market when investor reactions appear to be very close to perfect efficiency.

If a market is more liquid does this imply that the effects of BF on prices are likely to be lesser or greater?

The more liquid the markets and the greater the number of investors are, the greater the chances for efficient behaviour as well as irrational exuberance and the greater the susceptibility for swings in sentiment.

BEHAVIOURAL BIASES

Do you use your knowledge of BF to overcome your own biases in trading? If so how?

Yes, of course. In the past, I faced difficulties in cutting my losses. I found that this had to do with commitment problems, which had their origin in the size of my positions. As soon as I understood that small position sizes helped me to prevent commitment traps, I was able to cut my losses if my opinion changed. It has developed from a painful experience to a virtually unemotional task.

I also find it difficult to ride my winning trades because I have a tendency to underestimate the joy of winning. As soon as I feel a desire to take profits, I alert myself to be more patient and to reconsider my analysis. I ask myself if my wish to take profits is based on objective results or my desire for small gains. Trading is a game of discipline, patience and humility. You have to work on yourself every day. But you also have to accept your deficiencies.

Of the well known behavioural biases, what are the most common among market participants?

Regret aversion and myopic loss aversion are amongst the most common pitfalls. Regret aversion means that we avoid a decision because it could prove a sub-optimal decision in hindsight. This results in a tendency to decide in compliance with the current norm. Investors may not act on their private information and own thinking because they fear looking stupid in the eyes of the others. Myopic loss aversion means that investors fear to invest in a market because of possible short-term losses. After a severe downtrend, empirical evidence shows that you have better than average chances of a positive yield, but investors may fear further losses because the current conditions look gloomy. They decide not to invest despite the fact that they know it would be in their long-term favour.

Prospect Theory shows that we feel the pain of a loss much more than the joy of a gain, which is one reason for the disposition effect. This bias means that investors use reference points, like their acquisition price, to rate their investments instead of an objective analysis. It is also quite common.

What biases do you most look to exploit?

We look to exploit overconfidence, homogenous thinking, polarization in sentiment, and investor irritation (measured by the Sentix Neutrality Index). Polarization in sentiment means that there is probably not enough divergent thinking taking place. Some neat slogans may shorten investors thinking. For this reason, polarization implies increased risks in the market; if investors are irritated, the Sentix Neutrality Index, which measures the share of investors with a neutral stance in the market, will reach high levels. This is an unwelcome situation for investors because it means a sense of uncertainty exists. Investors will then increase their desire for new information and orientation. As soon as they get this, they start to position the holdings accordingly. Another reason for a high number in the Neutrality Index may be a longer sideways trend in the market accompanying low volatility. As soon as investors get accustomed to a 'boring' market, it is rated as a polarization in neutrality.

How do you decide which biases are operating and their relative magnitude?

It is like a puzzle. We spot indicators in three main areas; price, sentiment, media, flow of funds. We then look for striking features. For example, bullish sentiment has a completely different meaning depending on whether investors are invested or not. If they are invested it could mean the beginning of overconfidence, (if rising prices suggest they were successful), or it may show selective perception (if prices are falling and losses have occurred).

The media can also send a strong message. Imagine a reversal in a bull market where investor sentiment is still bullish. If media participants are in denial and emphasize that there is no reason for a reversal, this could be good confirmation of a new downtrend. If the media is instead concerned that a new downtrend may have started, it points more in the direction of an ordinary consolidation phase rather than a trend change.

Do biases always correct themselves?

As soon as a bias, or a market fashion, is understood and discovered by investors, this behaviour will go out of fashion and it will no longer be the driving force of markets.

Is herding necessarily a bad, or irrational, thing to do? If prices are rising doesn't it make sense to buy as well? As such, is herding really a bias?

You have to distinguish herding from trend following. To go with the trend is a reasonable strategy which is not necessarily done by the herd. Herding means that an investor goes in a certain direction only

211

because others are doing so. To use the information costs others have paid is a bias. In the markets it means doing what the majority of investors are doing. But you never see a lot of investors winning; at least not for a long period of time. It needs a trend to persist for a while before herding kicks in. So a trend follower would have already made some profits before the trade becomes crowded.

How would you advise an individual trader or investor to deal with herding?

Trends are an integral part of market behaviour so to base a strategy on the utilization of trends is a promising strategy. Every major trend ends with some sort of herding. Don't be afraid to be part of a herd as long as you are smart enough to leave the party if your trend following system tells you to sell.

Do you think the impact of the credit crunch will reduce investors' tendency to be overconfident?

The current crisis will inevitably change the institutions, products, and investment fashions in the market, but it will not change the players. Normally a bullish view is more readily accepted because most of us are natural bulls. A more readily accepted bearish view points to a prevailing, pessimistic sentiment in the market. The public always accepts the promoters of the popular sentiment most readily. You should not expect any fad to last forever. As a fashion becomes widely accepted, its most influential time has passed.

Are stock prices necessarily more susceptible to behavioural biases?

Most information in most markets is subjective and therefore susceptible to behavioural biases. I cannot see any major difference between stock markets and other markets.

What technical analysis do you use and how do you use it?

Technical tools may be helpful in our analysis if they are objective and help us identify the psychology of markets, or give us a unique perspective on investor behaviour. We use trend following systems to determine the direction and strength of market trends objectively. We use candlestick charts as a simple but very effective means of visualizing current market psychology. We are also interested in the development of volume and volatility (here we focus on Bollinger Bands) as additional market dimensions.

We are very sceptical about the way some technicians use chart analysis. Because it is a very subjective form of TA, the analyst must be aware not to let his biases about the market prejudice his analysis. Another problem is the use of indicators like the MACD. We only use these in the form of statistically tested strategies to prevent a misjudgement of the indicator's quality due to hindsight.

With regards to the mispricing of stocks, you say that BF effects can be seen in valuation. How does mis-valuation occur here?

We can reduce the impact and the occurrence of biases through an objective framework. The problem with a valuation approach is that if you do not use an objective measure, you will end with a sentiment driven assessment. There is a proven relationship between sentiment and earning estimates of analysts. That means that you can forecast how analysts (on average) will change their earnings estimates if you know how sentiment has changed. It is not the other way around.

How can one tell when investor reactions are close to perfect efficiency?

If you cannot make money on new information, then obviously the market has incorporated the news with perfect efficiency. I define efficiency always in the sense of an investor's ability to make money. A market where I cannot make money is in my view efficient.

Chapter 15

JAN LONGEVAL AND CARL VAN NIEUWERBURGH

INSTITUTIONAL ASSET MANAGEMENT

BANK DEGROOF

Jan Longeval is managing director and head of institutional asset management at Bank Degroof in Brussels. He is also the founder of behavioural strategies at the bank, a team that now consists of five fund managers and three analysts. His colleague, Carl Van Nieuwerburgh, is a senior quantitative analyst and fund manager at the Degroof Fund Management Company.

BF THEORY AND INEFFICIENT MARKETS

Do you believe that markets are always inefficient?

No, markets are pretty efficient most of the time. Behavioural finance's main pitfall is to extrapolate irrationality at the individual level to the level of the crowd. Crowds, however, have their own dynamics. Referring to Vernon Smith or James Surowiecki's *'Wisdom of Crowds'*, under certain conditions, a crowd will be much smarter than its average IQ. These conditions are diversity of opinion, autonomous decision making, access to local information, and an aggregation mechanism (such as the price mechanism of the stock market). When those conditions are met, markets will be very efficient. When one or more of these conditions break down, markets can become quite inefficient.

The dynamics of 'complex adaptive systems' are often missing in the conclusions drawn from BF. Nevertheless, some market inefficiencies, such as the momentum effect, appear to be structural but these kinds of inefficiencies are not numerous. Often, market anomalies come and go.

Does BF completely disprove the Efficient Market Hypothesis (EMH)?

BF completes the Efficient Market Hypothesis rather than replaces it as markets move between different degrees of inefficiency. The EMH does not state that all investors are rational and BF does not state that all investors are raving lunatics. The EMH states that most, but not all, investors are rational. It argues that any irrational behaviour, as it is random, will tend to cancel itself out and that any opportunities arising from this irrationality will be swiftly arbitraged away. BF finds that there can be systematic irrationality at times, and that perfect arbitrage conditions are an illusion. So, to get a holistic picture of market dynamics, you should add the findings of the EMH, BF and complex adaptive systems.

Looking at the three different forms of the EMH, it is clear that BF has even presented evidence going against the weakest form of market efficiency. The weak form assumes that future stock prices cannot be predicted by historical price or volume information. However, price momentum strategies are one of the most recurring anomalies that are exploitable in a number of different markets. As evidence of this anomaly is so widespread, it's fair to say that markets are usually weak form inefficient.

Moreover, long-term price reversals are also contradictory to the weak form of market efficiency. The semi-strong form of market efficiency claims that apart from historical price information, publicly known fundamental information cannot be used to generate outperformance. However, BF is able to demonstrate that sometimes and under certain conditions, the market underreacts or overreacts. The out-performance of low P/E or P/B strategies, for instance, contradicts the semi-strong form of market efficiency. Finally, looking at the strong form of market efficiency which claims that inside information also cannot lead to consistent outperformance, it is clear that select inside information will lead to outperformance, but we don't need BF to know this.

Are markets more inefficient at some times than at others?

This depends on whether the conditions for the 'Wisdom of Crowds' are satisfied or not. If they aren't, the Wisdom of Crowds turns into the Madness of Crowds.

Can BF be applied more to markets which are considered less efficient, maybe because they are more illiquid?

The most liquid markets are the most efficient overall. The more liquid a market is, the more market participants it has, hence the bigger potential diversity of opinion. But even the most liquid markets can be very inefficient at times. At times of large diversity breakdowns, such as the 'New Economy' frenzy, even the most liquid markets will get it wrong. When most investors get overwhelmed by some theme, the few rational investors left standing cannot make the difference. Some anomalies, such as the momentum effect, do not appear to be reduced by higher liquidity. Others, such as the value premium, are reduced by market liquidity. In the US market, the value premium has virtually disappeared and so has the small cap premium.

To illustrate that some behavioural biases might even manifest themselves in the more liquid part of the investment universe, consider that it is much harder to go against the crowd for an investor when a stock gets broad media coverage. Therefore, very liquid stocks at the centre of media attention may even be more susceptible to hypes. When negative news on a stock that an investor holds in his portfolio appears daily in bold headlines in the newspapers, will he eventually not seek confirmation (peer pressure) and sell the stock, even if he thinks the market has overreacted? It is easier to sell the stock in that case, than to go against the crowd and convince others they are wrong. A stock that is less covered by the media, but faces similar circumstances to the large cap stock, will give the investor more autonomy in his decision making.

Could a better knowledge of BF have prevented the dot com and credit bubbles?

Stock market bubbles form and burst according to a typical multi-stage psychological pattern. The dot com bubble could have been prevented had investors been more aware of the psychological biases that lead to bubbles and that are well described by BF. Probably the most harmful bias was the confirmation bias where investors neglected any information that goes against their opinion, preferring to look for, and retain, only information confirming their opinion.

The credit bubble is somewhat different as its origins lay in hazardous behaviour stemming from the greed of a few market participants who must have known that what they were doing would end up in tears some day. At the buyer's end, many investors probably had no idea of the underlying risks. BF's understanding of mean reversion might have helped avoid some of it as it would have called on more prudence and lower leverage. As is so often the case, people get overexcited when things are going well and start overreacting (extrapolating) as a result; but the law of gravity, or mean reversion, always wins in the end.

216

When you draw attention to the high probability of mean reversion kicking in after a long stretch of favourable conditions, you will find many people reluctant to see any reason why the market would mean revert. BF alone would not have been sufficient to time the mean reversion, but it helps to increase your awareness of increasing risk the longer things are good. It also means that you would be more actively seeking information pointing to mean reversion. Many investors were lured into a sense of comfort as they were focusing on low P/E ratios that were based upon unsustainable peak earnings. Using cyclically adjusted P/E ratios would have shown a radically different picture of overvaluation.

Even though BF provides a convincing explanation for how traders and investors think before making decisions, BF has failed to become a mainstream form of market analysis. Why do you think this is?

BF may not have reached mainstream status but it has definitely gained in popularity, especially in the quant community. BF is more mainstream than many people realize because many ingredients of BF are also used in mainstream active equity management, without the majority of investors considering it as a BF element. In certain cases, BF might just have provided the empirical support to a concept that was already quite popular before being empirically supported by BF. For example, practically all equity investors recognize price multiple valuation measures as relevant information, while BF claims value strategies are behavioural by nature. Another example is that large, risky takeovers were probably, on average, already disliked by active equity investors before they were seen in corporate BF as evidence of corporate hubris leading to value destruction.

BF is sometimes seen as fluffy because there are few formulas you can fall back on, as is the case with the CAPM or APT. So, even if there is a keen interest in BF, many people feel lost when trying to apply it. Indeed, how do you model the investor community's emotions and state of mind? There are surveys on sentiment and indirect measures such as momentum and put/call ratios, but a holistic framework for asset pricing is still missing.

Very often, things only become clear in retrospect. Was the 2008 stock market crash an overreaction to bad news or not? Today, at the time of writing, this is impossible to tell. BF teaches that the market can both under and overreact, but how do you know at the time it is taking place? BF would typically advocate a value approach, but also

217

a momentum approach. There's no BF formula that helps you to combine these factors.

How can BF be used to forecast or anticipate price movements?

There is a whole library of BF findings that can be helpful. This ranges from the Winner/Loser Effect to findings on price trends and patterns, momentum, share buy-backs etc. At the same time, BF is not particularly helpful on finding turning points. Overreaction will eventually mean revert, but as of yet, BF has failed to deliver tools to anticipate the tipping point. So as a contrarian investor, you may get destroyed before the market proves you right. BF also helps to anticipate price movements at the aggregate level, but is much less helpful at the level of individual shares.

What is the relationship between technical analysis and BF? Do charts provide the best tangible reference to BF effects?

To the extent that technical analysis captures the psychology of the crowd, it fits well with BF. For instance, trend analysis visualises momentum, and momentum is the result of underreaction. Of most interest is the combination of trend analysis, trading volumes, and sentiment as this makes it possible to feel the pulse and power behind market trends. As such, it helps anticipate turning points. From this angle, BF and technical analysis are quite complementary.

Charts are the handwriting of the investor, volumes his strength, and sentiment his heart. However, there is also tremendous noise in the charts and volume, and it is difficult to filter it all out. TA is also based upon the assumption that history tends to repeat itself and it does, but in different ways. BF can actually help technical analysis to gain credibility as it offers a fundamental explanation of some of the principles technical analysis is based upon.

What BF experiment do you think is most illustrative of market behaviour?

There are so many it's difficult to choose. Among the favourites are studies demonstrating that 80% of stock market movements cannot be explained by fundamental factors, and Vernon Smith's experiments illustrating the wisdom of crowds.

*What questions would you most like answered about behavioural
finance and market psychology?*

A key issue is how to establish normative risk premia: risk aversion
changes over time and is the main unknown in any valuation and
market timing exercise. Most market participants refer to normative
risk premia as constant factors, but they are not. A decent assessment
of where the normative risk premium is at a given point in time
requires a measurement of the state of mind of the investor. Even
though investor sentiment indicators exist, a methodology to convert
this information into normative risk premia is still missing.

I am also interested in having a better understanding of the negative
feedback loops that drive prices far away from fundamental value.
The George Soros 'reflexivity' concept of market dynamics, in which
financial markets not merely discount the future but actually help to
shape it, is probably very close to BF and deserves more attention
from the academic BF community.

BF research should also focus more on the conditions under which
anomalies manifest themselves to different degrees, depending on
stock characteristics and the macro economic environment. Over the
recent past, certain behavioural strategies did not work, and there have
been other periods like that. The statistical significance of the
outperformance using longer time series is still intact though.
However, as markets over time become more efficient, overall alpha
potential will be reduced and it will be of outmost importance to
understand the cycle of market anomalies so that you can add alpha by
playing the anomaly cycle itself.

Ideally, BF would develop a holistic model that incorporates
several of the anomalies it has researched before on an individual
basis, with a conceptually appealing and correct interaction between
all the different factors, as a function of company specifics and the
macroeconomic environment.

*Are there any recent developments in BF that you have found
interesting?*

Over the past couple of years, academic literature has produced
nothing spectacular in the field of BF. Most behavioural biases are
now well known and documented. Thirty years down the road of BF,
it is reasonable to believe that a substantial percentage of market
anomalies have been identified. So, recent research is mainly

improving upon the old findings rather than make exciting new discoveries.

The most exciting developments seem to be taking place in the area of neuroeconomics or neurofinance. BF is rather descriptive and does not explain why investors behave the way they do. Neurofinance goes to the neural roots of decision making and gives a neurological backing to BF's findings.

In the distant future, combining BF, complex adaptive systems and neurofinance should give an in-depth picture of what drives markets. Applied on a large scale we will be able to follow underlying market dynamics in real time. Even though it sounds scary, someday perhaps in 20 years or so, investors and others will have the opportunity to get a neuro profile. Ultimately, market efficiency will reach an extremely high level and markets will become harder to beat than ever.

USING BF FOR TRADE AND INVESTMENT DECISIONS

Has your knowledge of BF changed the way you trade?

Yes, definitely. BF has become the heart of Bank Degroof's active equity strategies since 2000. Before that, stock selection was done in the traditional fashion, i.e. bottom up with company visits, and broker research etc. Today it is essentially quantitative with variables related to market anomalies described by BF. BF has also created a much bigger awareness of behavioural biases we all risk suffering from. BF pushes you to question your opinions and ideas. A mental checklist of behavioural biases is very useful for keeping your investment approach healthy. If you have a strong conviction about a given theme, BF will push you to actively look for information and opinions that go against yours.

The Wisdom of Crowds theory pushes you to ask, and re-ask, whether your idea or opinion is unique enough to beat collective wisdom. We look for ideas that are only slowly picked up by the crowd. The perfect quote on this comes from Jack L. Treynor; *"I see nothing in the arguments of Professor Eugene Fama or the other Efficient Market advocates to suggest that large groups of investors may not make the same error in appraising the kind of abstract ideas that take special expertise to understand and evaluate, and that constantly travel slowly."* BF gives you a more complete understanding of market dynamics, of market efficiency. As such, at least you know what you're up against. Too many investors still invest without a clear view of market dynamics and prefer to concentrate on the micro level. In our view, any micro view is incomplete without the macro view.

What indicators do you use to quantify market sentiment?

The best way to measure sentiment is either through the survey method, which is the most direct, or by looking at price momentum, flow of funds, put/call ratios and so on. Bank Degroof uses surveys of market sentiment by companies such as Ned Davis Research that measure sentiment on a weekly basis. Of course, just following the international media also gives a good idea of where sentiment is.

What are the main obstacles in using BF to aid investment decisions?

In practice, it is difficult to fit a lot of the components of BF into a single investment process in a logically appealing way, and still end up with a diversified portfolio. Many of the market anomalies described by BF are strongest at the tails of the universe and once you start combining factors you may end up in the tail of tails, which is not acceptable from a risk control point of view.

What is the relationship between contrarian strategies and BF? What are the best contrarian indicators in your opinion?

It is perhaps preferable to rephrase this question by asking what the relationship is between contrarian strategies and complex adaptive systems. It is not because BF finds many behavioural biases in the decision making of large groups of investors that it pays to go systematically against the crowd. The crowd is not stupid when certain conditions are satisfied. Being contrarian all of the time is stupid as the crowd will wipe you out.

Successful contrarian investing comes down to going against the crowd when you have a very good reason to believe that the crowd has got it wrong. An in-depth understanding of the crowd's expectations is therefore necessary. Compare these to your own expectations, and if you are able to demonstrate where the expectations of the crowd are wrong, you have a contrarian opportunity. If you find it very difficult to determine what the dominating market expectations are because opinions are very diverse, you are at risk when you go against the market. Basically, it all comes down to the same two core principles: assess whether market

221

conditions are prone to efficiency or not, and check thoroughly why your assessment is better than the crowd's.

Can BF be used to identify market tops and bottoms?

Sentiment indicators are useful at extremes of optimism and pessimism. An excessive optimism reading tends to be followed by a market drop, and excessive pessimism by a market rise. Some behaviouralists criticise the use of sentiment for market timing purposes as sentiment is usually a coincident rather than a leading indicator. That's missing the point; at extremes they become leading. However, extremes in sentiment are only useful for forecasting short-term market reversals. Sentiment in itself is too volatile to serve as a leading indicator of long-term reversals.

What role does BF have in the mispricing of stocks?

BF's originality lies in the fact that it takes finance out of the hands of the mathematicians who liked to assume how people would and should behave. As mathematicians love formulas, they had no issue with plugging in all kinds of convenient assumptions in order to make the formulas work. BF on the contrary, instead of assuming how people would or should behave, starts by observing real behaviour. BF brought the social element back into thinking about finance and therefore, not too surprisingly, found that stocks can get mispriced as prices are the outcome of human interaction in a market context and humans, being humans, can get it wrong.

BF's influence on mispricing is twofold: on the one hand it will correct certain types of mispricing such as value investing; as it gets more popular, investors buy cheap shares and push their prices closer to intrinsic value. On the other hand, momentum investing will probably drive prices to even more mispriced levels until some catalyst kicks in.

Is it possible to properly quantify the impact of behavioural finance? For example, if overreaction exists for a particular share, can this be measured in any way?

This is very difficult because to measure overreaction (or underreaction) you need a good gauge of intrinsic value. Estimating intrinsic value is, by definition, a subjective exercise. You can compare market prices to your own assessment of intrinsic value but only time will tell how good you were at measuring over- or underreaction.

Has BF helped you spot bubbles and help you identify when they are likely to burst?

There is extensive BF research on bubbles and this has been very helpful in spotting them. The Nasdaq bubble was yet another example of bubble formation with overreaction, anchoring, confirmation biases etc all over the place. The difficult part is timing the burst and there BF offers little concrete help. The experimental bubble and burst simulations offer some framework for tipping points, but in real markets the duration of a bubble does not seem to follow any kind of rule.

Does BF imply that there is always an under- or overreaction to the release of fundamental news?

No, not at all. This would imply that investors get it wrong all of the time, which is a mistake. The tests on under- and overreaction find that not all stocks display momentum and reversal. However, it's enough for a minority of stocks to produce strongly superior returns to make the whole strategy profitable.

BEHAVIOURAL BIASES

Do you use your knowledge of BF to overcome your own biases in trading?

Before you can overcome your biases, you have to know what they are first. A good starting point is to take a personality test. A good knowledge of BF and of your own behavioural biases should ideally put you in a constant awareness mode, always on the lookout for your mistakes and the ones committed by others. This requires effort and discipline.

What behavioural biases do you most look to exploit?

Our favourite by far is the overreaction/underreaction cycle, well described by Richard Thaler. Overreaction relates to the inability of humans to look beyond the short run. Once investors get into a certain mood, extrapolation arises naturally. Extrapolation then leads to exaggeration. When the wake-up call from reality sets in, investors first underreact before overreacting in the opposite direction.

Do you think behavioural biases are more prevalent in the short-term or long-term?

Behavioural biases are equally prevalent in the short as in the long run. Time horizon, however, can alter the behavioural bias itself. For instance, momentum is the result of short-term underreaction while in the long run, momentum tends to falter once that underreaction has turned into overreaction.

Is herding necessarily a bad, or irrational, thing to do? If prices are rising doesn't it make sense to buy as well? As such, is herding really a bias?

As momentum remains by far the biggest market anomaly, it makes sense to play it. At some stage, however, the herd will turn and if you're not out of the market by that time, the herd will turn on you. BF experiments have demonstrated extensively that people learn very slowly. They tend to stay in the market for much too long and suffer much of the pain of the downturn. However, a rigorous momentum approach that would push you out of the market once the tides turns can be successful.

How would you advise an individual trader or investor to deal with herding?

To exploit it through a momentum strategy or to respect it if he's a contrarian. Herding can drive market prices miles away from fair value so investors relying mainly upon fundamental value may find themselves pushed out of the market before being proven right.

Some stock relevant information, it could be argued, is by its very nature interpreted subjectively. Does this mean therefore that stock prices are necessarily more susceptible to behavioural biases?

Valuing bonds is easier than valuing equities as it can be done rather objectively. When valuing bonds, you're focusing on the cash flows required to service the debt, while equities are valued on the bias of residual income over and beyond debt servicing. As such, equity valuation requires having a holistic picture of what affects the company's value. This exercise, by its very nature, is extremely subjective which opens the door to behavioural biases.

When you say that the momentum effect appears to be 'structural', what do you mean by this?

We mean that its size (alpha potential) does not appear to diminish over time. The latest work by Dimson, Marsh and Staunton of the London Business School, confirms this. They find there's still a value premium but its size is rather low; a simple momentum strategy however delivered an alpha of 5% and a long/short return of 12% annually for the over the period 1900-2007.

Is it possible to quantify the degree of inefficiency that exists in a particular market at any time?

Yes it is. Here are a few examples:

1. Look for a large deviation of market prices from fundamental values (e.g. comparing current P/Es with normalised measures such as 10-year trailing P/Es, i.e. the Schiller approach)

2. Calculate implicit growth assumptions in market prices and assess whether they are realistic

3. For a measure of the degree of overreaction you could use valuation dispersion: the higher the valuation dispersion, the larger the overreaction has been.

4. Sentiment readings reaching extreme levels

5. Rule dispersion as a measure of diversity of opinion. A 2007 study demonstrated how market crashes are preceded by diversity breakdowns, measured and quantified by rule dispersion.

6. Linguistic/media word search; search the media for the occurrence and frequency of given words which can be used to quantify diversity of opinion

Is it true that all irrationality is arbitraged away? If not, why?

At present, this is not the case because as already highlighted, value and momentum premium still exist. From a behavioural perspective, the value premium relates to overreaction and the momentum premium to underreaction. Over and underreaction are proofs of irrationality. In the future, the degree of efficiency is set to increase as market dynamics and anomalies are better understood. However, this will take a very long time as old ideas die hard and informed traders are constrained by risk aversion and the limits of arbitrage.

There will probably always be periods of extreme financial and/or economic conditions that will increase irrationality at that time. Irrationality, if you define it as prices diverging from fundamental value, can also depend on technical factors such as the forced unwinding of positions by certain market participants.

What are the conditions for the Wisdom of Crowds to be met and for the Madness of Crowds to be met?

James Surowiecki points out four conditions for crowds to be wise:

1. Diversity of opinion (the more diverse the better)

2. Autonomous decision making (to avoid the negative impact on decision making of social interaction)

3. Access to local information (there's added value in local information)

4. An information aggregation mechanism (eg the price mechanism of the stock market)

In a financial markets context, the first condition is the most 'volatile', the 3 other conditions are fulfilled most of the time. Diversity breakdowns do occur and when they do, crowds go mad. Diversity breakdowns are the fuel of any speculative bubble and of any exaggerated downturn.

When you say that value strategies are behavioural by nature, can you explain why this is?

Because the main driver of the value premium is investor overreaction, causing a trend that goes too far. Most value investment styles are contrarian by nature as they play on the mean reversion or the reversal of this overreaction or trend.

How would you define a 'complex adaptive system'?

A complex adaptive system is a dynamic network of many agents, such as market participants, acting in parallel, constantly acting and reacting to what the other agents are doing.

Would you describe herding as irrational behaviour?

Sometimes it is, sometimes it is not. Sometimes, the herd is right: the banking sector since mid-2007 is a good example of the herd being right as contrarians who picked up banking shares too soon were blown out of the water; but herding becomes irrational when the herd is wrong. A smart investor is able to distinguish between the two and will adjust his strategy accordingly. A potentially very successful investment strategy is conscious herding, i.e. playing momentum.

Have you observed any obvious behavioural biases in the FX or commodities markets?

In the FX market, an estimate of the correct fundamental value is more difficult than other asset classes and, as such, it is more difficult to prove irrationality is at hand. In commodity markets the problem is quite similar even though you could use the marginal production cost as an estimate of fundamental value. If that is taken as the reference, it is reasonable to state that overreaction is at work as commodity prices have often deviated far from this measure of fundamental value. One obvious bias that is present in all markets is the momentum effect.

Chapter 16

COLIN MCLEAN

MANAGING DIRECTOR

SVM ASSET MANAGEMENT

Colin McLean is Founder and Managing Director of SVM Asset Management in Edinburgh, a firm specialising in UK and European equities investment as well as global fund of funds. At SVM he leads the management of their long/short equity funds, investing on behalf of both retail and institutional clients. Prior to establishing SVM he was CEO of Templeton International's European operations.

BF THEORY AND INEFFICIENT MARKETS

Could a better knowledge of BF have prevented the dot com and credit bubbles?

Credit bubbles seem to reflect a gaming behaviour against ineffective regulation. Certainly a better understanding by regulators of this might have reduced the potential to circumvent the aim of regulation. For dot com and other market bubbles, there is evidence that faulty learning models can encourage this behaviour in individuals, quite separate from a crowd effect. As markets rise, individuals can trade more and can associate that trading with profit. I think that is hard to stop other than for individuals and investment firms generating the right type of feedback and trading analysis.

Even though BF provides a convincing explanation for how traders and investors think before making decisions, BF has failed to become a mainstream form of market analysis. Why do you think this is?

I think that behavioural finance is still under development. Great strides were made with the work of Daniel Kahneman and Amos Tversky, but BF now needs to incorporate more recent critiques of that work and develop areas like neurofinance and emotional finance.

228

It takes a long time for a new theory to enter an exam syllabus for professionals, and this is just beginning to happen now.

What is the relationship between technical analysis and BF? Do charts provide the best tangible reference to BF effects?

I believe that BF does point to price patterns and has close links with parts of technical analysis. Technical analysis gained a lot of credibility in 2007 and 2008 during the banking crisis and sharp fall in global stocks.

Charts do provide a good reference to some BF effects, and I believe the most credible academic research on BF has been by people such as Professor Terence Odean (University of California, Berkeley), by analysing actual trading records. While academic analysis of technical patterns has not been helpful to date, I think further, better practical studies should start to support the linkage between technical analysis and BF effects.

How do you think behavioural effects are apparent in price charts? Can you give an example?

I think the unwillingness of investors to take losses is often shown in sharp share price falls accompanied by higher volumes (capitulation), sometimes also followed by a brief recovery or sideways trading. For example, British Telecom (BT) which is standing well below the price at which it floated 25 years ago, has shown this type of behaviour over the past two years, as have many banks. Almost every BT holder will have lost money and will now have little certainty on dividends either. Fear of losses means greater risk is now being run.

Can you explain why you find the work of Terence Odean particularly useful?

Much research on behavioural finance has been conducted by psychologists and may not reflect how professionals behave in the real world with meaningful incentives. I find some of that work a little abstract as it tries to divorce decision making from the more typical workplace environment. That is why I like the research of Terence Odean because he started by focusing on analysing actual trading records. Overall, his approach is very empirical and real-life. In `Learning to be Overconfident` he has shown how rising profits in a bull market can encourage overtrading, with success being wrongly attributed to trading activity. Many view this bubble-type herd behaviour as a collective phenomenon, where Odean's research points to it being more within an individual's control. I think he is right in concluding that most people trade too much and do not learn from mistakes.

What BF experiment do you think is most illustrative of market behaviour?

The endowment effect is a strong one. The Kahneman and Tversky studies show an unwillingness to give up what we already own, which does ring true with the way many investors view their portfolios. I think it explains a lot of inertia in the market and in stock prices, combined with momentum as investors gradually look more critically at their existing holdings.

What questions would you most like answered about behavioural finance and market psychology?

I think that further study should be able to help professionals structure their data collection to minimise confirmation bias. Better presentation of information day-by-day to a manager could also help minimise errors in perception and analysis. I would like to see BF deliver practical results on how information is best gathered and processed day-by-day.

Are there any recent developments in BF that you find interesting?

The role of unconscious processing is important. I particularly like some of the research of Gerd Gigerenzer (Max Planck Institute) that challenges some of the prevailing wisdom in BF. He has done some good work on what heuristics are helpful, and on the usefulness of some apparent biases. We may come to find, in terms of eliminating biases, how to recognise when biases might be useful.

USING BF FOR TRADE AND INVESTMENT DECISIONS

Has your knowledge of BF changed the way you invest?

I have tried to incorporate some of the BF findings particularly in trying to identify excess trading and the impact of overconfidence.

More rigorous evaluation of decisions in trading history would be helpful.

Can BF be used to help you place specific trades?

BF is rarely the only factor I consider in placing a trade, but it can support an understanding of why analysts might be missing something fundamental in a company that we have identified through accounting analysis.

What are the behavioural biases that exist in accounting analysis?

Companies often use framing to present results in a positive context early on. Individuals often anchor on an initial view, which may highlight success first, drawing out adjusted earnings rather than those of the accounting standard. Hector Sants of the FSA picked up this theme in a talk he gave in March 2009. Determining fundamentally that a company is not growing or generating cash, or possibly might be using share buy backs or acquisitions, might be evident from the numbers in the company report which is often where the basic earnings appear. But many investors and investment analysts may have stopped at the more positive report on adjusted numbers given early on. That positive spin, often with language very biased towards the positive even in a company's bad year, can make it difficult to assimilate bad news later on, so strong is the Anchoring Effect.

What indicators do you use to quantify market sentiment?

I use a range of indicators including volatility, momentum and liquidity. For individual stocks I look at moving averages and the RSI.

Which moving average periodicities do you prefer to use?

I would probably say the 50-day is the one I used most. I have generally found this to be the most useful; and it may reflect some aspect of human behaviour with a 50-day memory smoothing out the impact of performance reporting periods each month. What matters is the relationship with the longer-term, 200-day moving average. It is worth knowing whether a trade, supported by fundamental analysis, is going with or against momentum, or if there is no clear trend to worry about.

231

How do you use moving averages and the RSI?

I do think that an overbought level (RSI at 70%) is usually an indication that there will be a better buying opportunity within an upward trend. Similarly, opening short positions at an oversold level (RSI 30%) adds risk, so I avoid them. When fundamental analysis indicates we should be short of a stock, it may still be worth being patient for a week or so to find the right timing. That is, I am less interested than a foreign exchange trader might be in buying oversold stocks or selling ones that are overbought. I generally use it as an aid to timing when a fundamental decision has already been made, just to minimise the risk of entering a trade at a short-term, extreme point.

I do think that stocks moving up through their shorter-term moving average, as it moves up through the longer-term one (Golden Cross), is a useful pointer to continuation of a trend and further gains. The opposite, the Dead Cross, would be a useful pointer to shorts, if fundamentals also supported it. This sometimes happens with an over-owned and overrated stock, giving a good short opportunity.

What are the main obstacles in using BF to aid investment decisions?

Against a background of relatively low market liquidity, sentiment can drive prices very sharply and persistently away from realistic values. Formulating the right timeframe and position sizing is the main challenge.

Is it possible to formulate a trading strategy based on BF?

I do not believe a trading strategy can be based entirely on BF, but it does point to reducing unnecessary trading, structuring position sizes to recognise overconfidence, and incorporating base rates. We have not been able to automate trading but have formulated some rules in terms of not adding to long positions that are overbought, and not adding to short positions at the point where they are oversold.

What do you mean by the base rate?

By base rate, I mean the underlying prevalence – the average incidence and pattern. If stocks within a sector correlate 80%, it is more useful to build a strategy around that than it is to make switches between the stocks. An analyst has to be very good to make it worth switching or running a pair trade. If analysts are 60% right, they should generally not be trying to beat base rates that exceed that level.

232

How can BF help in risk management of a trading position or investment?

I think BF can encourage some simple heuristics to overrule emotion or overconfidence at times when position sizes should be changed.

Can BF be used to identify market tops and bottoms?

I have not found a way of identifying market tops and bottoms, although technical analysis can help in timing and that does, I believe, reflect BF.

What role does BF have in the mis-pricing of stocks?

I think that companies can present information in a way that encourages faulty analysis, while anchoring discourages analysts from fundamental re-appraisal. This can mean that periods of relative strength can run for three or four years under a new management or new strategy. Conversely, analysts appear slow to recognise company failure or dramatic deterioration. I believe anchoring is a factor in this; but halo effects also encourage confusion between good companies and good investments.

Can this mispricing be quantified in any way? For example, if overreaction exists for a particular asset, can this be measured in any way?

I think it is difficult to quantify the impact, although a sharp share price fall on bad news creates two key psychological levels: share price before and after which act as anchors for some period before one is clearly discarded.

Has BF helped you spot bubbles and identify when they are likely to burst?

I still find it hard to identify bubbles using BF. Research points more to this being a failure of individual learning models and behaviour rather than some crowd or communal activity. The problem is that bubbles can take some time to burst, and you could be in danger of being a year or two early. I believe fundamental news can be analysed correctly, and it is important to assess the impact of short positions on any reaction.

BEHAVIOURAL BIASES

Do you use your knowledge of BF to overcome your own biases in trading and investing?

I think that reducing trading frequency and managing more consistent (even) position sizes can help to address overconfidence. In some areas the base rate is strong and hard to beat by fundamental analysis. For example, if stocks within a sector correlate 70% or more, it will be hard to justify switches within the same sector. Systematically reassessing decisions and abandoned trades is also instructive.

Of the well known behavioural biases what are the most common among market participants?

I think that confirmation bias and overconfidence are the most common with the former being the most systematic source of errors in investment. The endowment effect, whereby sale of shares is slow as a company's outlook deteriorates, is also helpful for short positions. I also believe that information searching is as important because actual analysis and confirmation bias can blind an analyst to contrary evidence, shutting down the search process too soon. It is unlikely that their analysis will be correct after that.

Do you think behavioural biases are more prevalent in the short-term or long-term?

I think behavioural biases are more prevalent in the short-term. Fundamental information such as company results and dividend cuts do finally bring reality checks and true values to companies.

Do biases always correct themselves?

I think that biases do largely correct themselves, although timescales can be long and less helpful for investment decisions.

Are you aware of any behavioural biases in your own investing? If so, what are they and how do you deal with them?

I think that dealing with regret on trades, or those trades not entered, is a difficult issue. Having some simple heuristics such as reducing overall exposure, by say one-third, if an adverse pattern emerges rather than waiting to identify what specifically has gone wrong, can be useful. Having rules on changing position sizes or moving at stages from one into another will help overcome the impact of market timing and potential regret.

I tend to implement positions either one-third or 50% at a time, but sometimes a decision is deferred because of the fear of regret. This regret may be over the timing of implementation, rather than the actual action needed. By trading one-third, I generally am less concerned if my timing proves to have been wrong. I think the balance is a matter for each individual's personality, but balancing action versus regret, and a fundamental decision versus timing of implementation, is important and best handled by simple rules.

I think when trading risks have increased, or portfolio results have been unexpectedly poor - and this can be analysed as reflecting a particular sector, theme or market pattern - there can be a tendency for professionals to delay decision making until they can decide on the individual stock changes. Making a prompter decision on reducing overall exposure to a theme, by say, one-third, is more useful at that stage than discriminating between stocks. Allowing an individual position size to grow to a disproportionate level in the portfolio is an indication of overconfidence, although it is harder to trim a holding when it is performing well.

Switching between stocks within a sector may also indicate overconfidence in analysis. Some sector constituents correlate very closely: the correlation between BP and Royal Dutch Shell over the past 18 months is 88%.

Is herding necessarily a bad or irrational thing to do? If prices are rising doesn't it make sense to buy as well? As such, is herding really a bias?

I think that momentum can often indicate a steady recognition of underlying change and may not be a bad thing; price momentum often follows underlying earnings momentum, for example. Some traders use momentum effects in reverse and I think herding is a pejorative term that is not helpful in discriminating between what works and what doesn't.

How would you advise an individual trader or investor to deal with herding?

Looking at the consensus in research is helpful, but it is also important to examine competitor portfolios. Sometimes the herding represents a wish by investors rather than a strategy that is actually reflected in portfolios. Often what is reported as a consensus trade is still not the stance of the majority of portfolios.

Even though most investors are aware of behavioural biases, to what extent do you think investors actually act to exploit them?

I think investors unconsciously pick up and often exploit the behavioural biases in the market. Traders can develop a good sense of the short-term implications of behavioural patterns. However, acting to avoid one's own behavioural biases takes work and a discipline that I suspect few have adopted.

What bias do you think the market as a whole tends to exhibit the most?

I am not sure that the market has an overall bias, but I certainly think that the high level of stock turnover recently, such as short holding periods although market volumes are also low, indicates a lack of conviction in fundamental value. It does show that many traders in the market are more comfortable with momentum trading and clear market direction, which works well in clear bull and bear markets, but conditions have been more challenging in the first half of 2009.

Do you think that biases differ between different asset classes?

My own experience is with equity markets and I find it harder to comment on others such as FX. Commodity markets do seem to correlate well with equities and behave more like them now.

Chapter 17

VOLKER HERGERT

SENIOR EQUITY STRATEGIST

LGT CAPITAL MANAGEMENT

&

OLIVER GUNTER

SENIOR EQUITY STRATEGIST

LGT CAPITAL MANAGEMENT

Volker Hergert and Oliver Gunter both began their careers working as equity analysts with LGT Bank in Liechtenstein and Frankfurt. They then became co-head of research and head of strategy respectively with Bankgesellschaft Berlin. They now work with the investment management (equities) division of LGT Capital in Switzerland.

BF THEORY AND INEFFICIENT MARKETS

Do you believe that markets are always inefficient?

We do not generally like the notion of market efficiency. We prefer to differentiate between functional and dysfunctional markets. A market is functional if prices reflect market participants' expectations for the future, irrespective of whether these expectations prove to be realistic with perfect hindsight. It is dysfunctional if prices are mainly driven by factors like liquidity.

When people talk about efficient markets, they usually mean that markets correctly reflect all available information. This assumes that information is given objectively and can be evaluated in an objectively correct way. Systems Theory (or 'complex adaptive systems') has shown that this simple notion of information is not helpful. Firstly, information is contingent upon the observing system, i.e. an observed event has different informational content for different observers.

Secondly, due to the economy's and the market's complexity, self-reference and resulting uncertainty, there is no uniquely correct way to evaluate such information. How market participants select and interpret information depends on their frames of reference. With this in mind, markets are neither efficient nor inefficient.

Can you explain in a bit more detail what you mean by Systems Theory?

Systems Theory refers to the study of autonomous, self-organising entities as pioneered by Humberto Maturana and Heinz von Foerster. One of the key properties of such systems is that they do not react to an external input in a linear or cause/effect kind of way. Rather, their reaction to external stimulus is determined by their internal structure. This structure in turn is constantly being adapted by the system's internal operations, leading to 'circular' or self-referential processes. Examples of such systems are a living cell, a human brain, an individual company, and the economy as a whole.

Does BF completely disprove the Efficient Market Hypothesis (EMH)?

BF has a hard time disproving the EMH because the EMH is quite resistant to empirical evidence and common sense. BF has failed to make use of advances in systems theory to undermine this foundation, so is in a weak position because it does not offer a solid counter-theory; it is more a collection of empirical observations. In our view, BF itself is not the endpoint of scientific progress. Rather, it is paving the way for an emerging new paradigm which is likely to focus on evolutionary processes.

What do you mean by 'evolutionary processes'?

We are talking about the emergent (i.e. higher-level) order that results from the interaction of a multitude of investors. This differs from the subject of neurofinance which, in our view, takes a step back by looking at the individual brain. While this may be important to understand the behaviour of an individual, it does not help to understand the rules that govern the interaction of many individuals.

Can you give a few examples of evolutionary theories?

Examples of evolutionary theories include Kurt Dopfer's Evolutionary Economics, Thorsten Hens' Evolutionary Finance, or Andrew Lo's Adaptive Market Hypothesis.

Could a better knowledge of BF have prevented the dot com and credit bubbles?

It depends who has the knowledge. Investors (at least the smart money) have always known about BF even before academics came up with the idea. Still, there have always been bubbles. However, it would be a good thing if regulators and central bankers were more cognisant of limitations to their idealistic model world. A solid understanding of BF and other concepts (e.g. George Soros' Theory of Reflexivity or Austrian Economics) would help. And yes, in principle, it is possible for determined and wise policymakers to prevent the worst extremes of bubbles and their fallout.

Even though BF provides a convincing explanation for how traders and investors think before making decisions, BF has failed to become a mainstream form of market analysis. Why do you think this is?

BF does not offer 'recipes' on how to make money or how to structure a portfolio. Any strategy that promises above average returns will tend to be copied and arbitraged to the point where there is no return left. BF is more a collection of rules of what not to do. The market is competitive, self-observing and adaptive. However, scientific theories can provide investors with general guidelines to help them ask the right questions, to differentiate between sensible and not-so-sensible approaches, and to avoid outright mistakes.

Also, don't forget that BF has been created as an empirical research project to point out weaknesses or anomalies in the established theoretical construct of rational investors and efficient markets. It is not a project to find new ways of making money in the markets. Whenever BF does suggest any trading strategies, you find that these do not differ materially from many approaches already employed by practitioners.

How can BF be used to forecast or anticipate price movements?

Nobody can forecast price movements. However, there are some general patterns that have been pointed out by BF such as short-term overreactions, medium-term momentum persistence, and long-term mean reversion. This is all well-known to experienced investors, so we won't dwell on this further.

Making use of evolutionary concepts (as mentioned earlier) that go beyond BF opens up interesting possibilities to detect shifts in future return distributions. Basically, trends are driven by the gradual adoption of new visions by investors. As a trend proceeds over time, the market's expectation structure is changing. There are clearly defined phases in this evolutionary process that offer distinct risk/return profiles. In plain words, there are good times to be invested in a trend and there are bad times. We have developed instruments to identify the different phases of a trend (rejection, polarisation and synchronisation with respect to the driving theme) and to make exactly this judgment.

What is the relationship between technical analysis and BF? Do charts provide the best tangible reference to BF effects?

Price charts do not tell the whole story. They do not, in most cases, show what is happening to the underlying market psychology, or put in very simple words, they show that a trend exists but not why it exists (and therefore we do not find early signals for imminent trend breaks in price charts). So, what else can be done? The changing structure of investors' expectations is the fundamental driver of any price trend, so it would make sense to directly analyse this structure. For example, the progression from rejection of a new theme (phase 1), to polarisation of opinions (phase 2), and finally to synchronisation (phase 3) can be analysed using 'reverse valuation'.

This instrument shows the evolution of implied expectations over time and is a valuable illustration of the changing structure of market expectations. For example, we often observe that in phase 2, the market is not willing to extrapolate recent fundamental improvements into the longer-term future. Hence, implied valuations trail realised return on equity (ROE). We call this phenomenon the 'normalisation gap'. In phase 3 this gap between what is realised and what is expected is closed. Markets now extrapolate recently recorded fundamentals into the future which is a sign of a 'synchronisation bias', and an early indicator for a trend break.

How do you conduct reverse valuation analysis? How do you measure this quantitatively?

We have constructed a simple tool (a kind of reversed DCF model) that calculates the future trend level of return on equity and earnings per share (EPS) implied by given share prices, for individual companies, sectors and markets. Comparing these implied levels to historic averages, historic extremes and to themes about potential future changes gives us an idea what the market is pricing in. In our terminology, this helps to determine the phase a trend is in.

Is it possible to differentiate between intra-day and longer-term BF effects? If so, how would you do this?

One of the behavioural patterns we mentioned above is short-term overreaction to new information. However, it is not easy to detect because you have no time to analyse it properly. We prefer to observe the gradual change in investors' perceptions as it becomes manifest in medium-term momentum persistence, i.e. trends.

Why do you think the market tends to overreact to market news?

The market does not generally tend to overreact to news. Sometimes it seems to overreact, but there are times when it underreacts, and times when it appears to have no such biases. There are a few basic mechanisms at work here:

- When investors lose faith in established frameworks, they are no longer able to 'normalise' current data. Accordingly, most recent data is accorded too much weight. This happens in the later stages of any bear market, including the most recent one.

- When investors embrace 'new era' arguments, they base their actions on expectations about very long-term structural changes. In these instances, they tend to underreact to evidence to the contrary. This happens in the later stages of all major bull markets, including the New Economy and BRICs, energy, and commodities manias.

- Overreaction or underreaction is also a function of the structure of trading strategies. For example, if the variety of trading strategies declines and a few strategies become dominant, they will impact on market volatility. This happened recently with crowded quantitative strategies. Noteworthy for their impact on market volatility and reaction to news are algorithmic trading strategies, and the proliferation of leveraged structured products, such as ETFs.

Do you have an example where overreaction is corrected in the short-term and could have been exploited?

When FCX announced on December 3rd, 2008 a suspension of the dividend and large production cuts, the stock plunged. The main reason for the bad result was falling metal prices. Now, these price falls had been old news. The impact on the company's results and capacity decisions was not surprising. In addition, at that time, the market had already priced in even more drastic and sustained profit declines. So, the drop was an overreaction, discounting a well known fact twice. The stock in fact marked the final bear market low two days later (around the level reached after the initial price drop), and proceeded to outperform the market significantly from then on. There were many such cases in the final bear market stage, and we clearly identified and exploited those opportunities at that time.

What BF experiment do you think is most illustrative of market behaviour?

There is no experiment known to us that would adequately represent the most fundamental characteristic of financial markets, i.e. high-stakes decision making under conditions of radical uncertainty and intense public communication. The best laboratory is the market itself.

What questions would you most like answered about behavioural finance and market psychology?

We wonder whether BF will ever make it from laboratory experiments on individual behaviour to a new capital market theory that explains the interaction of market participants. We have tried to create this missing link in shaping our own interpretation of BF and take this as a base for explaining what is going on in the marketplace.

With this in mind, we have created different tools to analyse changes in market expectations to get early indications of imminent trend breaks. However, we lack any significant backtest of our finding periods long ago. It would be fascinating to find out whether these tools would also have worked centuries ago. For the time being we are just content that they seem to work today.

Are there any recent developments in BF that you have found interesting?

We think the most interesting development in academic research is the growing interest in evolutionary concepts. BF is ultimately going to be absorbed by such evolutionary theories.

USING BF FOR TRADE AND INVESTMENT DECISIONS

What areas of behavioural finance are you interested in and do you find most useful?

The most useful aspect is what BF calls 'herding'. A deeper understanding of the key variables driving this herding process is valuable for practical investment management.

Has your knowledge of BF changed the way you invest?

More than BF, our personal way of thinking and investing was shaped by systems theory. Starting out as financial analysts, we soon realised that even the best analysts systematically fail when it comes to predictions. So we started to ask, why is this? The answer is radical uncertainty. This naturally leads to the question of how analysts and investors form expectations when we cannot know anything about the future. The answer is given by systems theory. This led to the development of our concept of 'observe the observers'. We do not form opinions on uncertain fundamentals (first-order observation), but observe how other observers deal with fundamental uncertainty (higher-order observation). So our primary analytical focus is the market-internal expectation structure.

What are the main obstacles in using BF to aid investment decisions?

In its textbook form, BF does not offer recipes for security selection or portfolio construction. You should just take BF as a starting point for interpretation and develop your own concepts.

What indicators do you use to quantify market sentiment?

We use all standard sentiment indicators such as various risk appetite indicators, flow data, surveys on investment positions, or sentiment surveys. In addition, we put a lot of qualitative work into 'meta communication analysis' i.e. the analysis of how analysts and investors are arguing. We are interested in recognising the themes that are driving communication and signs for rejection, polarisation or synchronisation with respect to these themes. There are recurring patterns in communication, and in the formation of expectations, that help to correctly identify the phase a trend is in. Talk is cheap, though, and arguably the best sentiment indicator is reverse valuation analysis, i.e. the quantitative analysis of which expectations are actually priced into markets.

Which flow data do you use? How valuable do you find this data?

We look at things like flows into mutual funds, insider buying, and institutional flows. Taken alone, this data is of limited value but combined with the other instruments, it is quite helpful.

What is the relationship between contrarian strategies and BF? What are the best contrarian indicators in your opinion?

BF offers a strong justification for contrarian strategies. The best contrarian indicators are what we call signs for 'phase 3 synchronisation'. The most powerful synchronisation signs include reverse valuation, indicating that a theme has been fully priced and large-scale shifts in asset allocations by investors, due to psychological or institutional reasons can only happen on clear, objective and decisive evidence. Examples would be the shift by US pension funds into New Economy sectors in early 2000 or the shift into commodities in early 2008.

Have you been able to quantify or automate behavioural based trading?

Most quantitative trading strategies are consistent with BF. This is because BF and quants are doing the same thing. They are searching for anomalies or inefficiencies using the same type of quantitative backtesting technology. These models suffer from the same weakness, though. They are based on historical price behaviour. Such behaviour (correlations, for example) can and will change violently from time to time without prior notice.

For our own method of 'observe the observer', we have defined factors that differ substantially from traditional quant factors: we talk about themes and their attraction potential, about the structure of market expectations, about trend phases and trend structure. While we obviously use data, we have not fully automated our process. We are convinced that with this approach, we get a better assessment of shifts in future return distributions.

Why is 'phase 3 synchronisation' so called?

The evolution of investors' expectations always starts with a theme that creates new uncertainties. Initially, the majority of investors will reject or even fail to notice the new theme. If the theme persists, expectations will begin to become polarised. In the end, the market might end up embracing the new theme, pricing it as a near-certainty. If this happens, the market's expectation structure has become synchronised. Of course, not everybody will believe in the theme. Some will reject it while others will opportunistically run the trend. However, in terms of market impact, the 'doubters' have become a minority with negligible impact on prices. Note that synchronisation is a major market inefficiency.

How can BF help in the risk management of a trading position?

Investment risk is shifting, due not to objective changes in fundamentals, but as a result of how the market constructs and prices these fundamentals. Specifically, from a risk management point of view, it is time to reduce a position whenever there are signs of phase 3 synchronisation, no matter how convincing the fundamental story appears to be, and vice versa.

Can BF be used to identify market tops and bottoms?

Yes, definitely. A phase 3 synchronisation leads to a transition although this is not necessarily a turning point; sometimes it is just a pause before the trend resumes its old direction. However, under certain conditions, a transition is highly likely to be the start of a new trend in the opposite direction. Such conditions include the severity of the mispricing at extreme points, and the degree that such mispricing leads to distortions in the real economy. If the latter factor is significant, a countermove is highly probable.

What role does BF have in the mispricing of stocks?

Systematic mispricing of stocks results from the synchronisation of individual expectations (herding in BF terminology). This synchronisation is brought about by self-referential communication processes and can in fact lead to synchronised expectations that (with perfect hindsight) are revealed as being exaggerated.

Is it possible to properly quantify the impact of behavioural finance? For example, if overreaction exists for a particular share, can this be measured in any way?

We have to get rid of the notion that there is an objectively correct fair value and psychologically driven deviations from this value. Prices are always the result of constructions of reality by the market, so there is no efficient ideal against which deviations could be measured.

So, overreaction cannot be measured. However, it can be defined so that it can be used in trading strategies. We define it as follows: when a stock reacts strongly to news (say, an earnings statement) that very clearly had already been discounted in prices, then markets price the same fact twice. This is an overreaction that is likely to be corrected in the short-term and can be exploited profitably (if it is not too late to react once you have finished the analysis).

Has BF helped you spot bubbles and help you identify when they are likely to burst?

We think it is a bit unfortunate that BF tends to be reduced to extreme situations like bubbles, implying that investors most of the time deal rationally with less extreme situations. Communication driven construction of reality by the market is going on all the time, along with the related structuring of expectations. If you understand this basic everyday process, you no longer see bubbles as an anomaly, but just as a particular phase. But yes, BF has helped us to identify bubbles when they were inflating. It is not possible to forecast in advance when they will burst, but our BF concept provides us with observation points to see in time when they do burst.

Does BF imply that there is always an under-reaction or overreaction to the release of fundamental news?

No. Most of the time markets react in normal ways to news releases. A normal reaction occurs when markets can easily integrate news into existing explanatory frameworks. Underreactions occur towards the end of large trends, when contrary information tends to be ignored. Overreactions occur in the later stages of large trends, as well, as the synchronisation of expectations is driving outsized reactions to trend confirming information.

BEHAVIOURAL BIASES

Do you use your knowledge of BF to overcome your own biases in investing?

We try at least to avoid the typical psychological traps that academic BF research has revealed. Take for instance that famous short movie of two teams playing basketball. One team being completely dressed in white, the other one completely dressed in black. They play very quickly on a small ground and just try to have as many ball contacts as possible. The observer's task is to count the contacts the white team has made with the purely white ball. No easy task, but some observers really manage to give the correct answer afterwards. The interesting aspect of this experiment, however, is that nobody notices the black gorilla that mingles with the basketball teams and gently beckons to the camera. This is because the task obliges you to fully concentrate on white; a nice example for selective perception.

We, as BF oriented portfolio managers, take this little story as a strong reminder of how easy it is to be deceived by selective perceptions. Imagine, for example, how seductive it is to only notice positive news on stocks you are invested in and to neglect the bad ones. This is because this is the normal psychological mechanism to justify your former decision of investing in this particular stock.

Of the well known behavioural biases, what are the most common among market participants?

The most common bias is the least known one: the tendency of convictions to be attracted by a dominant theme. As a result of this, the market in the late phase of a trend develops a systematic bias that we call a 'synchronisation bias'. This is the most important of them all. Most of the well known individual biases lead to individual mistakes, but do not impact prices in a systematic way. However, it is important for each investor to be aware of such potential decision traps.

There are numerous biases cited in the literature, many of which act against each other. How do you decide which biases are operating when, and on their relative magnitude?

We focus on how the market's communication impacts the structure of investors' expectations. During the course of a trend, systematic biases are changing. In the early trend phase, a new vision meets perceptions that are shaped by historic, backwards-looking frames of reference. Thus, the market tends to underreact to the new potential. This bias might be called 'stickiness' (of established frames), and the result is value. In the final phase of a trend, investors' expectations are re-synchronised. This process of expectation adaptation produces momentum, and the result is a systematic mispricing we call synchronisation bias.

Do you think behavioural biases are more prevalent in the short-term or long-term?

For our investment process, the more relevant question is whether you perform better with short-term trading or long-term investing. For us it is easier to observe the factors driving a longer-term trend rather than identifying short-term overreactions and reacting to them just in time. Trends last longer and have higher amplitude the more complex the driving theme is. For the S&P500, four principal investment decisions in the last ten years would have been completely sufficient.

Do biases always correct themselves?

For biases that impact market prices in a systematic way, the answer is yes, or else it would not be a bias. These are the biases that we are interested in. On the other hand, psychological biases lead to individual mistakes, but do not necessarily impact prices systematically. Therefore, they do not correct themselves, except through the fact that individuals with the strongest propensity to make mistakes are likely to drop out of the markets pretty fast.

Are you aware of any behavioural biases in your own investing? If so, what are they and how do you deal with them?

Everybody is subject to biases all the time. Hence, it is important to design investment processes so as to minimise the negative impact of biases. Many BF pundits claim that pure quantitative strategies are objective and therefore not subject to biases. We think this reasoning is dangerous. The quant just replaces some biases with others such as belief in a model.

In our own process, we apply a number of safeguards. For example, everybody holds explicit or implicit core beliefs. It is important to make these beliefs explicit in order to be able to challenge them. We know exactly what our core beliefs are. Another important issue is being systematic and disciplined. Having a clear process and sticking to this process is probably the single most important contributor to good performance in the long-term. Being systematic does not mean you have to apply a quantitative process. It simply means you have to be very clear about your analytical process; what type of information you look for and how you evaluate this information.

A third factor is intellectual exchange. If you work alone, there is a risk that you lose it sooner or later. At the other end of the extreme, there is vast empirical evidence that groups (e.g. investment committees) are very bad at decision making. We think the best solution to this dilemma is to make your own decisions, but to have a circle of soul mates who share the same investment language. This can be a formal or informal network or a small team of colleagues. Importantly, the primary role of the others is not to confirm your own view, but to look for biases and inconsistencies in your thinking and to challenge it. They have to ask questions such as, which information is your view based on? Why did you select this information? (to confirm a pre-held view?) Do you neglect conflicting information? Is your selection and evaluation of this information consistent with your investment process?

Is herding necessarily a bad, or irrational, thing to do? If prices are rising doesn't it make sense to buy as well?

There is a difference between herding and herding. Bad herding results from being infected with a crowd view. You get sucked into a trend at the worst possible moment. Good herding results from recognising herding in the market (observe the observer), and can lead to the decision to follow the trend, or if herding has become extreme, to bet against the trend.

Is the result of herding always a bubble?

No. Herding, in the sense of phase 3 synchronisation, always leads to inefficiencies that can be exploited. However, a bubble is an extreme case of this process that requires special conditions.

Do you think the market's propensity for overconfidence will change, given the credit crunch and 2008 stock market decline?

Overconfidence is a typical human behaviour and does not depend on market conditions. Over-optimism and overconfidence stem from the illusion of control and knowledge. People just tend to believe that the accuracy of their expectations increases with more information. Academic BF research has shown us that this is a misconception.

Obviously, being bearish on the economy and the market has become more fashionable in the wake of this crisis. But this is not the first economic crisis and people seem to have learnt nothing from the last centuries. So our best guess is that they will justify their failure by arguing they did not have enough information. They will correct this mistake by collecting more information in the future, thus feeling better prepared for the next event, and then fail again.

Some stock information, it could be argued, is by its very nature interpreted subjectively such as change of management, corporate meetings, new products etc. Does this mean therefore that stock prices are necessarily more susceptible to behavioural biases?

In our view, it is the very nature of every asset market that prices are driven by soft factors such as those you mention for the equity market. But do bonds, currencies, commodities, real estate or other asset classes really work in a different way? If there were a quantitative algorithm that could explain what is going on it would have been found. If we want to understand markets we should stop trying to understand them as a subject of natural science. Instead, we should accept that they belong to the social sciences, and thus are characterised by radical uncertainty and biases, whatever the traded good is.

INDEX